Disability and Contemporary Performance

Disability and Contemporary Performance explores the relationship between contemporary performance practice and disability, and investigates the ways in which disabled performers challenge, change and work with existing stereotypes through their work. Encompassing the fields of performance, cultural and disability studies, Petra Kuppers draws on the insights developed by theorists such as Foucault, Merleau-Ponty and Deleuze to question the assumptions of tragedy and loss that are traditionally associated with the disabled person and to suggest new understandings of disability and identity politics. She draws on numerous examples of individual performers and groups from the UK, North America and Europe who constantly challenge stereotypes through the media of live and installation art, theater, dance and photography, including Mat Fraser, Jo Spence, CandoCo and L'Oiseau Mouche, and opens up new and lively perspectives on contemporary performance practice, identity politics and cultural conceptions of disability.

Petra Kuppers is Assistant Professor of Performance Studies at Bryant College. She is Artistic Director of the Olimpias Performance Research Projects and she has written extensively in the fields of cultural, performance and disability studies.

Disability and Contemporary Performance

Bodies on Edge

Petra Kuppers

Routledge
Taylor & Francis Group

NEW YORK AND LONDON

First published 2003
by Routledge
2 Park Square, Milton Park, Abingdon, Oxon, OX14 4RN

Simultaneously published in the UK
by Routledge
270 Madison Ave, New York, NY 10016

Reprinted 2005

Transferred to Digital Printing 2008

Routledge is an imprint of the Taylor & Francis Group, an informa business

© 2004 Petra Kuppers

Typeset in Goudy by
Keystroke, Jacaranda Lodge, Wolverhampton

Library of Congress Cataloging in Publication Data
Kuppers, Petra.
    Disability and contemporary performance : bodies on edge /
Petra Kuppers.
        p. cm.
    Includes bibliographical references.
    (hardback: alk. paper)
    1. Sociology of disability. 2. People with disabilities and the performing
arts. 3. Artists with disabilities. 4. Arts and society. 5. Arts – Political
aspects. 6. Social problems in art. I. Title.
    HV1568 .K87 2004   2003010108

British Library Cataloguing in Publication Data
A catalogue record for this book is available from the British Library

ISBN 10: 0-415-30238-2 (hbk)
ISBN 10: 0-415-30239-0 (pbk)
ISBN 13: 978-0-415-30238-8 (hbk)
ISBN 13: 978-0-415-30239-5 (pbk)

Contents

Figures

Acknowledgements

Many people have helped this book's journey. It has been a most pleasurable journey, allowing me to marvel at the ingenuity, the creativity and the richness of politically challenging and exciting art, and to immerse myself in the different but related pleasures of critical thinking.

I would like to thank Rosie Waters, Talia Rodgers and Diane Parker at Routledge for commissioning and publishing this book. Penny Florence at Falmouth College of Art has been a challenging and nourishing reader of many of the initial ideas which developed into these chapters here, and the feminist research group she led was my most important academic home. The late Anna Marie Taylor at the University of Wales, Swansea, made a lot of the thinking in this book possible by supporting my community art practice, and I want to remember her for her vision and her commitment to arts for social change.

A fellowship at the Contemporary Arts Department at Manchester Metropolitan University allowed me to develop my thoughts, and I want to thank my colleagues there. I also would like to thank Liz Goodman and Franc Chamberlain, who urged me to edit a special double edition of *The Contemporary Theater Review* on performance and disability. It was during this time that I met many of the artists and theorists whose work is discussed in these pages.

I continue to thrive in the intellectual support of the Pembroke Center for Teaching and Research on Women at Brown University, and I want to thank director Elizabeth Weed, and seminar leaders Mary Ann Doane and Anne Fausto-Sterling for allowing me to participate as a Visiting Scholar, as well as the community of scholars who welcomed me there.

The actual labor of assembling this book has been made possible by the collegial atmosphere at my home institution, Bryant College, and I want to express my thanks to the members of the English and Cultural Studies Department, as well as to others on this interdisciplinary campus who have been friends and discussion partners. Many, many students have been my helpers in developing these thoughts, and I want to mention in particular the group of undergraduates with whom I embarked on the 2002 Medical Vision/Medical Performances course at Bryant College, as well as the PhD students whose work set me thinking in ever new directions, in particular Anna Fenemore and Maria Walsh.

The British disability arts, dance and interarts communities were my home for ten years, and many people there have shaped my own coming out as a disabled woman, and my understanding of art politics. I particularly want to thank my friends Sophia Lycouris, Ju Gosling, Caglar Kimyoncu and the team of the Disability Film Festival in London, and many of the artists discussed in these pages.

My other communities include the US disability studies crowd, where I want to thank in particular Rosemarie Garland Thomson, Brenda Brueggeman, David Mitchell and Sharon Snyder; and the members of Performance Studies International, whose fascinating conferences have allowed me at various times to assemble people I really wanted to get to know better (and write about).

I have been lucky to find wonderful readers and discussion partners: many thanks to Carrie Sandahl, Harley Erdman, Adam Benjamin, Kanta Kochhar-Lindgren, Elizabeth Walden, Rebecca Schneider, Susan Broadhurst, Dee Reynolds, Peter Taylor, Greg Downey, as well as some generous anonymous readers out there.

Some of the material discussed here has been accessed with research support from the Laban Guild in the form of a Lisa Ullman Scholarship, two disabled scholar grants from the Society for Disability Studies, a conference grant from the Centre for Performance Research, a Gertrude Lippincott Award from the Society of Dance History Scholars, and a summer research grant from Bryant College. A number of arts grants have provided me with the means to explore the praxis of the theories at the heart of this study, and to widen my horizon as an artist/scholar: a production grant from the Digital Summer Festival in Manchester, UK, a Chisenhale Performance Research Award, a Mind Millennium Award and a grant from the National Endowment for the Science, Technology and the Arts.

Nothing would get done without the purring things on my desk, and the dog below it. And last, and most importantly, all my thanks to my rock and my first reader: Thanks, Bob.

A shorter version of Chapter 3 has appeared in *Contemporary Theatre Review*, 11: 3+4 (2001); a shorter version of Chapter 5 in *Trauma and Cinema: Cross-Cultural Explorations*, ed. E. Ann Kaplan and Ban Wang (Hong Kong University Press, 2003), and a different version of the epilog in *Theatre Topics*, 10: 2 (2000). I am grateful to the editors and publishers for kind permission to use this material in its revised form.

Figure acknowledgements

1 Jo Spence (in collaboration with Tim Sheard) *Exiled*, from *Narratives of Dis-ease* (reproduced by courtesy of the Jo Spence Archive, Terry Dennett)

2 Mat Fraser as Sealo, photograph by Ashley (reproduced by courtesy of the artist)

3 Publicity card for 'Sealboy: Freak', design Dan Jones (reproduced by courtesy of the artist)

4 André Brouillet (1887), *Une Leçon Clinique à la Salpêtrière*, showing Charcot demonstrating on Blanche Wittmann (reproduced by courtesy of the National Library of Medicine)

5 Elisabeth Löffler in *Einblicke* (video-still by courtesy of Daniel Aschwanden)

6 Bill Shannon, publicity still (reproduced by courtesy of the artist)

7 David Toole in *Outside In* (reproduced by courtesy of MJW Productions)

8 Compagnie de L'Oiseau-Mouche, *Le Labyrinthe*, photograph by Bruno Dewaele, publicity postcard

9 Martina Nitz, in *Sensation of Motion in Time*, photograph by Christa Zauner (reproduced by courtesy of the artist)

10 *Body Distance Between the Minds*, Gerda König and Marc Stuhlmann, photograph by Jo Kirchherr (reproduced by courtesy of the artist)

11 Celeste Dandeker and Margaret Williams, director of *Outside In* (reproduced by courtesy of MJW Productions)

12 Contact 17/GoAccess publicity postcard (reproduced by courtesy of the artist)

13 *Navigating the Body* (web-capture) Susan Harman

14 *Traces*, video-still, photographer Margaret Sharrow (reproduced by courtesy of The Olimpias)

Every effort has been made to seek permission to reproduce copyright material before the book went to press. If any proper acknowledgement has not been made, we would invite copyright holders to inform us of the oversight.

Performance and disability

An introduction

The terms at the heart of this study, performance and disability, hold multiple, contested and partisan histories. Their meeting points in disability performance – performances by disabled artists – create unexpected encounters, fleeting moments, puzzles and unanswerable questions – above all, as I will show in these pages, these meetings are characterized by a flow of energy, and a way of being alive, that negates fixity. Fixes on the nature of disability, and on images associated with it, can become unstable.

There are many genealogies and origin-myths that surround both performance art and performance studies,[1] but as a starting point for my exploration I direct your attention to Baudelaire's Paris, analyzed and read by Walter Benjamin. It is in these passages that Benjamin develops his account of the flaneur, a performer of and in the uncertainties of modernity.[2] There are many aspects of the flaneur that have become stalwarts of critical theory's engagements with Benjamin, but I want to look at one minor figure in the city: a small citation in the Baudelaire book, a brief glimpse of an absurd practice that queers the whole of the arcade. One of the flaneurs of gay Paris is the person walking a turtle:

> Around 1840 it was briefly fashionable to take turtles for a walk in the arcades. The flaneurs liked to have the turtles set the pace for them. If they had their way, progress would have been obliged to accommodate itself to this pace.
> (Benjamin 1976: 54)

This strange turtle walker carries a range of meanings, many of which resonate with my project in this book, and with the meanings of disability as a social discourse. The turtle walker as a public figure brings something private, from the hot-house of the terrarium, into the great open marketplace of modernity. Carefully controlled environments with regulated temperatures are transgressed, and the zoo runs into the street. Private bodies and public stories meet in the performance. Difference leaves its allocated spaces and mixes in the street. Taunts and injuries are the risks that are embraced in order to assert one's individuality, to claim one's space on the pavement.[3] Many of the artists in this book use performance as a means to break out of allocated spaces, and they often utilize public spaces outside the theater in order to challenge ever more effectively the concept of allocation and categorization.[4]

The turtle walker inflects the narrative of the city: the idea of the turtle in the city echoes for me the stories of the trickster; the incongruous figure of creative chaos, whose tail or fingers get burned and who shapes the world with a comical and creative touch. Like the trickster, often out of place or tone, the turtle's slow pace subverts the city's rhythm by its presence. Benjamin's descriptions and analysis of culture and its workings is never devoid of humor and irony, and the disabled artists[5] who in this book take to the streets, the web, the ice-rink, the stage, gallery and screen know much of this survival humor of the minor key, 'Galgenhumor' – gallows humor. Crip jokes can be harsh and discordant, but are also often elegant and charming. A light touch can subvert the rigidities of fixed situations and sedimented certainties about the places for disabled and non-disabled people. Like the turtle walker, the disabled artists' strategies discussed in these pages show an awareness of the effects of actions that are 'en passant', minor, that do not necessarily grab the center stage but that tweak at conventions. Ways of telling become important: nuances inflect familiar stories, allow new perspectives on different forms of embodiment to emerge. The performance is the reiteration of the seemingly familiar in a bracketed, framed format; a conscious placement of one's body into the visible, tangible scene of a show. Similar to the slow walk of the turtle walker disrupting the flow of the city, creating a different rhythm, the performances I investigate in this study often insert their difference as a matter of formal elements, rather than new, or 'positive' images. They question ways of doing, ways of knowing, as time slows or space expands. 'Authenticity' is not the object of these performances: the emphasis is on the new created in the encounter, not on a presentation of an essential self, or a fullness of disclosure.[6] Dwight Conquergood develops an understanding of performance as dialogic, as an activity whose aim is openness: performance aims to 'bring together different voices, world views, value systems, and beliefs so that they can have a conversation with one another' (1985: 9). The turtle walker fashions a new persona out of the strange elements modernity has brought to the city, and ventures out into the familiar/un-familiar world. The turtle traverses an environment not built for short, stubby legs, its agency is in question, and yet it converses with the alien environment with every step it takes – no other option is open to it. In uneasy alignment, dialogues of being in space develop. Within the larger game-plan of city life, turtle walking in the city is a minor, tactical insertion into a systemic whole.[7]

The turtle is also a figure of modernity in relation to colonial histories, hidden narratives of displacement and relocation, hybridity and travel. The city of the turtle walker knows the places where the Others are: 'here be dragons', the old description of unchartered places, has been displaced, and instead of white spots on paper maps, the impenetrable and different Other inhabits close quarters of the no-longer familiar cityscape. Performance makes a new cityscape. It both erects and celebrates new knowledges, orders them for public consumption, makes them accessible in ways that mere language cannot (yet). The new city is not quite tangible, it is emergent in the live-ness of time progressing. The city street is in advance of the textbook. Knowledge has arrived into powerstructures when it translates itself from its living form into public discourse. And in turn, knowledge feeds back into new forms of aliveness and seeing life. Disabled performers are often aware of the knowledges that have been erected around them: tragic, poor, helpless, heroic, struggling, etc. In the laboratory of the performance situation, these knowledges can be re-examined, and questioned again and again. Just as the turtle signals a certain penetration of money and lifestyle into the cityscene of Paris, the disabled performer in contemporary art signals a historical moment where a culture is examining its bodies, sorts and counts its differences, allocates new quarters, and reinvents itself. Performance is a place where cultural un-certainties can find expression – the unknown is framed by the conventions of the stage or the gazing scenario. The hybrid performances collected in this book challenge again and again the complacency of the frame, setting safe knowledges and embodied experience against one another. Like the turtle walker, who has created a kinetic relation to (in Benjamin's writing, invariably) *his* new pet in the act of walking, a culture ready to examine its 'outsiders' can find itself aligning itself into new relations with them, relations that might not so easily be categorized as 'oppressor' and 'oppressed'. The flaneur, the turtle walker: these are figures that are signs of their times. As they are trying to impose their leisurely speed and optic regime on the city around them, the city as the modern city comes into being, and in turn provides and modifies spaces for flanerie. Agency disperses, as the will to shape reinforces and reinscribes itself in the performances of the everyday, in the daily habits and passions of citizens. The disabled performer likewise is a sign of her times: a point in modernity when extraordinary bodies have a currency as lifestyle accessories, when any shock or alienation value is eroded by the ubiquity of difference that is consumed and repackaged. Traditional framings that keep life and art apart assert themselves in different form in this post-modern world: as art enters life, its power to hold meaning diminishes, and transmutates in forms that elude concepts such as agency, strategy, political impact and social responsibility.

The performances of identity at play in this book are also performing culture: setting out scripts for what can be performed, what is meaningful, what can be read, always ready to react to the twists of contemporary cultural forms and their resistances to the political. And like the stubborn turtle walkers, the disabled performances described here insist on their moment: their fleshliness in a specific space and time, their having been there. Here, performance is a marker of existence in a fleeting world. This sympathetic magic of performance is at work in the hopeful and melancholy project that binds my analyses to Benjamin's mocking tone. With the analysis of disabled performances in this book, I am using the critical tools of my time, tools provided by philosophers suspicious of the alignments between knowledges, to work openings into the tight fabric of a world that drapes itself in certainty.

Disabilities

Conventionally, an introduction includes definitions of the core terms under investigation, but offering these would already undermine my purpose: this book is about an undoing of certainties, a questioning of categories, about unknowability and difference. With this, my study seeks to acknowledge and subvert the structural position of 'disability' as a marker. The history of the representation of disability and illness can be seen to be structured by attempts to contain the Other, to isolate it, present it as outside 'normal' society and bodies, and thus to exorcise its threatening, disruptive potential. In this book, those traditionally cast as the Other are the originators of voices, performances, images and scenes. I will argue that the disabled artists in these pages understand the pervasiveness and persuasiveness of medical knowledge and social differentiation based on medically and culturally controlled difference, and I will show how they turn to subversion. Their strategies as analyzed here embrace not containment, but infection: they dissolve the stability of categories, and posit openness and change, instead. I intend to show how the aesthetic vehicles used by these artists to engage social fears and containment procedures echo this interest: they explode traditional art's boundaries, challenging the notion of genre, creating uneasy hybrids of art and the everyday. Time and space, living body and sedimented knowledge, semiotics and phenomenology start to leak into one another, start to overwrite one another, and begin to move.

With this, the artists represented in this study acknowledge *and subvert* the mechanism Sander Gilman discusses as the connection between social fantasies of control and aesthetics:

> Our examination of the image of the sufferer provides us with rigid structures for our definition of the boundaries of the disease, boundaries that are reified by the very limits inherent to the work of art – the frame of the painting, the finite limits of the stage, the covers of the book, the perspective of the photograph, or the narrative form of the novel. In placing such images within culturally accepted categories of representation, with 'art', we present them as a social reality, bounded by a parallel fantasy of the validity of 'art' to present a controlled image of the world.
>
> (Gilman, 1988: 2)

Like turtle walkers, contemporary art has often tried to subvert the frame – an agenda at the heart of modernist art practice – but in the performers under consideration here, this formal gesture is joined by the awareness that the content of disability representation is intimately joined with the conventions of 'disease images'. Thus, in an extension of Gilman's argument, the employment of hybrid and turtle art – art that challenges social readings of the 'proper' in relation to high art, pop culture, the web, the streetscene – can extend the hybrid's vibratory destabilization to the psychically invested certainties of social knowledge about appropriate bodies.

But what is this term 'disability' with its uneasy alignment with concepts such as illness, disease, congenital difference, poverty, and with the readings of degeneracy, tragedy, loss, victimhood?

Disability is a deeply contested term used to describe individuals (or a people?) that are in a position of difference from a center.[8] Already, even this vague description is problematic: how the center is defined, how center and periphery interact, what fantasies they hold of one another, is different in different contexts. Crucially, the act of ascribing 'disability' to a person is not value-free: effects include stereotyping, harassment, paternalism or hate, as well as benefits, accommodations, etc. The act of naming someone 'disabled' can also undercut any answering back: one of the definitions of disability is focused on a lack of agency[9] – just as women have been constructed as 'less rational' or black people as 'more animal-like', disability can preclude communication as its conception structures what kind of social involvement *is not* proper.

Disability as a social category is not the same as race or gender, but it shares important aspects with these ways of knowing difference. All three terms relate to differences that are constructed as binaries and as biological, and that come to carry heavy weights of excess meaning: like race and gender, disability structures people into separate categories.[10] Meanings and metaphors are attached to this binary structure of disabled/non-disabled (i.e. 'normal'), similar to male/female, or white/non-white. Feminist theorists such as Judith Butler and Elizabeth Grosz opened up the issue that this allocation of meaning was not something done to an unproblematically present body which enters meaning whole and innocent: bodies themselves are only available to us through meaning, the notion of fabric, matter, or materiality itself is meaningful only because it is discursive.[11] We only know our bodies through the knowledges available to us:

> It is not simply that the body is represented in a variety of ways according to historical, social or cultural exigencies while it remains basically the same; these factors actively produce the body as a body of a 'determinate type.'
>
> (Grosz, 1994: x)

Performativity has become the name by which the social/biological meaning exchange can be focused: the body comes to be seen as an arrangement of meanings that is produced by social knowledges, by a system that aligns bodies and meanings in a grid of 'biopower' (Foucault, 1978). Biopower is created by two interlocking systems which focus on knowledge gathering. First, surveilling science disciplines create data about 'normal' bodies (through garnering statistics and creating catalogues about mortality rates, sexual practices, illness incidence, psychological development, etc.). Second, individuals 'discipline' themselves or give attention to being 'normal' in the everyday, that is, they engage in self-surveillance. Together, the two mechanisms, at the micro- and macro-level, articulate an embodied *and* scientific vision of what it means to be a member of this specific, historic society. The effect is 'a society of normalization' (Foucault,

1980: 107). Each living moment of this individual body as it knows itself and moves itself, re-produces, 'performs', re-inscribes this system by living this moment as a gendered, racialized, disabled/non-disabled entity. There is no 'outside' to this system, but moments of openness and difference can be found within it as part of its living, changing nature: knowledge is always in flux and process. 'Performativity' as a term points to the embodied, living quality of knowledge, and its continuous production of truth.

These allocations and penetrations of meaning, problematic as they prove to be in each individual situation, impinge on individual lives. To a disabled person, certain medical plans or private insurances are denied. A person might be discriminated against in the job market, or housing associations might be able to legally turn her down. Outside the institutions, other people might assume knowledge about the disabled person: knowledge of heroic cripples, twisted madmen, whiny losers, idiots savant, fed by popular cultural depictions of disability as the Other to the 'norm'.[12] The presence of the disabled person is problematic in many social situations: it threatens a shift in the status quo, a momentary visibility of one's own body or self as potentially different, as one is faced by that which is 'disruptive' (this mechanism is explored in more depth by Lennard Davis, 1995: 128/9, also 1997). The binarisation of disabled/'normal' recoups this threatening difference, smoothes it into the fabric of meaning. But every encounter with the Other, every performance and citation of the order, makes Foucault's 'biopower' system momentarily visible and inserts the sliver of difference into the safe spaces of 'normality'.

In relation to disability, the main themes that are aligned with specific differences are tragedy, loss, and dependency. Like people stereotyped by the structural meanings of gender and race, disabled people use cultural interventions in order to subvert and query these meanings, and disability culture emerges as a counterculture. The chapters of this book chart some of the forms that these disruptions of conventionalized meanings take. One problem with the allo-cation of 'disability' to a person is the cloudiness and uncertainty that surrounds the term. At most points in the recent history of Western civilization, the term 'woman' was relatively unproblematic: a deep consensus ruled this definition, pushing complicated cases to the margins, even though the definition has been challenged as less than natural many times, and continues to be a focus of analysis today.[13]

In relation to this, the term 'black' shows a more diffuse hold on specific forms of biology, complicated by the term's historic changes, from 'nigger' to 'black' to 'African American', 'Caribbean', etc., from specific subcultures defined by diasporic experiences, myths of 'homeland' or religious affiliation. Like 'woman', 'gay', or 'black', the term 'disabled' holds a history of both oppression and pride: after a long historic period of predominant negativity,[14] disabled people have re-claimed their differences as a source of communality and cohesion in the face of oppression. Civil rights groups and forms of culture have founded themselves on the difference policed by the term.[15]

But what about the term 'disabled' as a social descriptor? Does this term define a common core for a social group? Rosemarie Garland Thomson offers 'extra-ordinary' versus 'normate' bodies as a way of capturing the dynamic between disabled and non-disabled. These terms provide a good starting place, in particular since 'normate' is less transparently 'value-free' than the statistical term 'normal': 'normate' speaks of categories, of practices to keep people in place. But the opposition of terms can only be provisional: too many different forms of embodiment are captured by the various alignments between the term and individuals. Wheelchair users, people with chronic pain conditions, mental health system survivors, people of different stature, people with sensory impairments, people who experience cerebral palsy, people with 'disfigurements', people with cystic fibrosis, cancer fighters and survivors, people with learning difficulties: each and every one of these 'medical' descriptions are contested. All have been umbrellared under the term 'disability' – and in turn, disabled communities have questioned the inclusion of some of these people, including people with mental health issues or learning disabilities, or 'illnesses' such as cancer, in their ranks. Writing in disability studies often reflects an awareness of these issues of naming and categorization: 'disability is not a universal category but a strategic name marking diverse differences' (Wilson and Lewiecki-Wilson, 2001: 10).[16]

My own way of coming out as a disabled person, that is, accepting my medically diagnosed and phenomenologically felt difference as a cultural and political identity category, was complex. I have a congenital pain-related impairment that did not receive medical diagnosis until I was in my late teens. I am an on–off wheelchair and crutch user. When I became a chair user, I didn't know that I would move as a bipedal again, and, as I am writing this, I don't know which forms of locomotion and accommodations I am going to use in the future. My condition isn't fixed. Various aspects of this personal experience of disability on the edge of private experience, public diagnosis and political identity echo with the complexities of 'disability' as a language marker:[17] many aspects of embodiment are private, and exclusive. Sharing the reality of pain with one another, finding a language for it, is highly problematic, something that the medical regime is finally recognizing. Struggling to find and place pain allowed many disabled performers to develop a complex relation to language and bodily fantasy. The fact that somatic experiences, fantasies, linguistic categories and social meanings all interact in creating not only a person's place within social frameworks and in language, but also in that person's experience of selfhood is recognized by Grosz, as she surveys Freud, neurophysiologist Paul Schilder (1950) and Merleau-Ponty for theories of gendered subject formation:

> The body cannot be simply and unequivocally identified with the sensations provided by a purely anatomical body. The body image is as much a function of the subject's psychology and sociohistorical context as its anatomy.
>
> (Grosz, 1994: 79)

Different experiences run together in the malleable, changeable act of 'being a self'. Disability sits uneasily on the limits of different readings, in particular in its value-scheme: if the social meaning of disability is negativity and tragedy, but one's own body is the shifting place from which and with which one knows the world, how can one twist social meaning and personal experience together, or keep them apart? There is no 'pure' body, no 'pure' self, no 'pure' social world, and a theory of touching and texture which acknowledges the positionality and interweaving of knowledges is called for.[18] In the readings of performances in this book, this intertwined hybrid knowledge becomes the object of the performances' desires. Ailbhe Smyth writes:

> Continuous plurality, non-sequential simultaneity. There is no story of my body, only the daily, momentary mediations between experience, senses, memory, desire, understanding – meditations between my body and beyond.
>
> (Smyth, 1998: 19)

Plurality, simultaneity, multiple stories, sensory contact and desire machines: these are guiding metaphors for my readings of performances. Uncertainties and non-fits between knowledges find their way into this book, as do touchings and moments, energy and materiality, in ever shifting kaleidoscopes.

My own disability experience shifts with time. At the same time, many aspects of the social reality of lived disability are not willing or easy to shift and change – one's 'diagnosis' identifies and labels one for a significant amount of time, and accommodations and services are usually awarded on the understanding that need is stable. For many, being disabled means being fixed: in time, in a condition, by specific symptoms. A medical history can become an albatross, carried around and in the way of new relationships, job applications, treatment regimes, etc. Breaking the certainties constructed around a subject's unity in time is an important political agenda for many disabled people. The chaffing of supposed certainties with other ways of coming to know one's being in time and space is a not uncommon experience of people who acquire disabilities later in life, or experience cancer, AIDS or other conditions that change the storyline of one's body. Eve Kosofsky Sedgwick talks about her breast cancer experience as 'an adventure in applied deconstruction', where she experiences the 'instability of supposed oppositions that structure the experience of the "self"' (1994: 12). Time, cause and effect, past and future, are some of the certainties that are questioned.

Performance is time-based: it takes time, rehearses time, restructures time, overlays time, creates multiple presences and absences. In the performances discussed in this book some of the adventurous ways that bodies are set in motion include intervening into the time-frames offered by statistical probability, or into the certainties of cause and effect. And in the every-day of social role-play, many disabled people I know 'perform' their disability to the medical regime if they require certain accommodations, pain killers, disabled parking plates, etc. Knowing that one's body isn't 'natural' or 'fixed' means that the act of taking on disability as a social phenomenon can be an act(ivity), a role, a story, that needs rehearsing, a story that isn't available transparently, but that needs mediation. The power of language, the skill to describe symptoms meaningfully to the specific doctor/patient encounter, the skill to portray effects of interventions and medication to social workers or fellow citizens: these are all performance behaviors disabled people who have long histories in the medical theater and the social stage engage in consciously and unconsciously. Performance in the sense of creating a meaningful intervention in the flow of time and space is taking place in many social encounters focusing on disability: telling a story of one's life, marrying the everyday to the extraordinary, is as much a performance as ordering symptoms for a doctor to see, or a social worker to assess. In this sense, construction and deconstruction, and the meeting and mediation of private and public body effects are always already part of the disability experience. The performances at the heart of *Disability and Contemporary Performance* take these powers of storytelling, space-making, truth-saying, time-shaping, and make the frames of everyday experiences, private experiences and public knowledges visible.

Structure

This book offers six chapters and an epilog which all use conjunctions of art work and theoretical writings to shift the images and emotions set in motion by the term 'disability'. The first two chapters deal with histories and pre-existing stories that create the ground for contemporary disability performances on stage, on the screen, or within other art contexts. The history of disabled performers is mainly hidden, and not on the center stage of conventional theater. Even though disability has a strong currency in the history of drama (the blind Oedipus, the physical difference of Richard III or the limping Laura in Tennessee Williams' *The Glass Menagerie*, the countless lost souls of melodrama with their 'afflictions', Lady Macbeth's and Ophelia's descent into madness, etc.), disabled people themselves rarely get to play those parts.[19] Just as the actuality of disability is crowded off-stage,[20] disability as metaphor is central to many histories of cultural creativity (Mitchell and Snyder, 2000).

In Chapter 1, I examine the intersections between reading mechanisms, existing meanings that can be tapped into for a performance, and the encounter between the 'real' of disability and the texts of art. I examine the notion of the 'blind spot' and read Foucault's analysis of the Panoptikon in order to see clearer the intervention of disability in the economies of meaning. The main art work under discussion is a photo, a performance trace, an invitation to a reading encounter, issued by Jo Spence, a British photographer and cancer fighter. Chapter 2 presents important moments in the history of disabled people's visibility on stages: the stage of the freakshow, and the medical theater. These histories will be introduced obliquely: through a lens of contemporary performance art citing these heritages.[21] As examples of performers who create work that consciously addresses these pasts stand Mat Fraser, a British performer who created *Sealboy: Freak*, a show dealing with similarities and differences between historical freakshows and the contemporary 'freak' scene, and Greg Walloch, a US solo performer whose work has addressed medical theater situations.

The next two chapters investigate traditional avant-garde performance practices for their potential to the disabled performer. Body performance has a rich history, but not all strategies developed by non-normative artists interested in identity politics can easily be adapted by disabled performers. Amelia Jones writes about artists engaging the abstract, non-body-centered, 'phallic' conventions of art history and criticism

> by exaggerating performing the sexual, gender, ethnic, or other particularities of this body/self, the feminist or otherwise nonnormative body artist even more aggressively explores the myths of disinterestedness and universality that authorize these conventional modes of evaluation.
>
> (Jones, 1998: 5)

Disabled performers indeed need to recapture their bodies and re-mobilize their meanings in new forms of performance encounters; but the exaggeration associated with Brechtian alienation techniques, 'piling on the images', doesn't work well if the image associated with disability is a flight from the self, a desire to be other. Chapter 3 will investigate these connections between 'being' and 'performing', moving towards an understanding of performativity that allows disabled artists to insert a sliver of difference between their bodies and the audience's readings. The artists whose work will provide examples for these strategies in action include the Austrian group *Bilderwerfer*, US 'Crutchmaster' Bill Shannon, and the UK's CandoCo dance company and their creation of *Outside In*, a dancevideo.

In Chapter 4, I will put the use of body art in Artaudian frameworks of sensual assault, intensity, and presence in conjuncture with the disabled body. How can the disabled body perform a difference that does not evaporate in the intensity of a self/other dialectic? If the disabled body is merely shock, no desire towards its potentiality for difference can be generated. The artists explored in this chapter move delicately between shocking intensity and forms of seduction that allow the potential for engagement. Examples will include work by Compagnie de L'Oiseau Mouche, a French performance group; Societas Raffaello Sanzio from Italy; a performance directed by Japanese director Erika Matsunami in Germany; Cologne's Gerda König from the performance group DIN A 13; and the UK's Aaron Williamson.

The final two chapters are concerned with the unanchoring of knowledges surrounding living bodies. Media technologies are deeply involved in creating genre encounters, setting up expectations and preparing the ground for knowability. The two chapters investigate how film narrative and cyber-aesthetics can be used and played with to present alternative modes of access to disabled embodiment.

Chapter 5 offers a reading of trauma as a concept on the edges of the linguistic and the physical. An extended reading of one work, a filmdance created by Darshan Singh Bhuller with Celeste Dandeker, offers perspectives on genre-mixing, on a body caught between histories, and a figure laughing at the act of reading. The chapter aims to present the challenges disability holds up to the smoothing functions of narrative.

I offer readings of a different way of touching the unknown in Chapter 6: here it is an emphasis on the phenomenology of a touch/vision, developed out of readings of Merleau-Ponty. I use his work to create new perspectives on disabled embodiment in cyberspace. The post-modern, image-rich world of the Internet is the location for virtual performances: fractured but still bodily encounters between performers and spectators. Websites developed by the German performance group Contact 17 and by Canadian webmistress Susan Harman are the art works I discuss in order to tease out these hopeful readings on their trajectory towards difference.

The book ends with an epilog section, 'Toward the unknown body', and with glimpses of community art where political actions transpose the theories developed in these pages. I am chronicling a community art project developed with mental health system users, and present how the notion of 'perceptual challenges' allowed us to move beyond theories of visibility to a wider embodied field. As we were working over a period of years, unknowability and liminal visibility became more important than either 'positive images' of people with mental health diagnoses, or the absolute refusal of sharing ourselves in a social environment. The resulting experiment brought together a range of actors, participants, videographers, and social workers in a new encounter with disability.

In all of my readings in these chapters, my desire aims towards a form of un-knowing that unfixes certainty about otherness, but that still remains able to act as a dialogue ground with our social and cultural reality. Social change and respect for difference are at the heart of this study, not normalization or a smoothing out of differences into a uniform world. As I will show, disability performance can begin to enact the clashing of stereotypes and knowledge, certainty and openness, at the moment that a breath moves us.

Chapter 1

Practices of reading difference

In the US TV series OZ (1997–2002), about life in a high security prison in the US, Augustus Hill is the narrator who introduces us to characters, comments on story lines and expounds moral dilemmas. Augustus is a young black man who has a spinal injury and is a wheelchair user. Within the universe of this prison drama, his disability is used as an enabling device for Augustus: he can see events from a different perspective, make links, and act as a chorus for the viewers. Within the narrative economy of the series, Augustus's wheelchair acts as a prison for his body – allowing his mind to be freer than the minds of his fellow inmates. Augustus's disability in the prison is a narrative choice: Harold Perrineau, the actor playing Augustus, is non-disabled, and Tom Fontana, one of the executive directors and writer of the OZ series, made a narrationally driven choice to include Augustus in his cast of characters – a choice that can be read as being determined by the meanings of disability in our culture. Fontana explained that he wanted a narrator, a 'Greek chorus', and he wanted that person to represent a minority and be in a wheelchair.[1] He wanted 'somebody who suffered even more than any of these guys . . . (his) understanding of the universe would be more acute'.[2] This statement reveals a pervasive attitude towards disability as a metaphor and shorthand: it sums up and presents in an economic way a deep form of 'difference' – a difference that creates a distance from the 'universe' of 'normal people'. To open up this world of deep and profound difference, all a non-disabled performer has to do is get handy with a wheelchair.

Performers can perform disability, and this performance has currency, tradition and weight in the social sphere of popular culture: film actors playing disabled characters have carried off a number of Oscars, making it seem that acting disabled is the highest achievement possible. There is plenty of scope for actors interested in taking on this challenge: both our popular and our high art heritage provide many instances of disabled characters, from Richard III to Quasimodo, from the X-Men to Captain Ahab. What we see much less is disabled people as artists and originators of artistic social texts and practices. In this chapter, I want to move from non-disabled certainties about disability to disabled perspectives on these certainties. Starting out from the Augustus character, where a non-disabled person plays out contemporary complexities surrounding disability in a popular cultural text, I will chart a course to one of a series of photographs made by the British photographer Jo Spence titled *Narratives of Dis-ease*, where a disabled woman uses photography to play with temporality.

Using the location of a prison as a starting point, this strategy allows me to weave together some of the core strands of my discussion: visuality and resistance, center and periphery, blind spots and silence, categories of otherness, common-sense knowledge, popular cultural narratives, and art interventions.

Cultural studies scholars argue that every system has a point from which the system's organization is invisible, naturalized, 'normal': any social organization looks complex and incomprehensible from the outsider perspective (imagine a Martian ethnographer visiting Wimbledon, the British tennis event), but smoothes into a background structure once one is inside, part of the system. In *Discipline and Punish*, Michel Foucault emphasizes this inarticulate center in his reading of the Panopticon, where spatial configuration and social structure are interwoven, becoming the source of knowledges about others and self. He discusses the specular indistinctness, the blind spot at the center of the Panopticon, a prison system of total surveillance in which the one who sees is not seen, is invisible to the system. In the panopticon, a central point where the guard sits has visual access to all cells which are clustered around it. The prisoners are on display, and Foucault uses the language of the stage to show how the space of the prison structures social roles. From a heaving mass of the dungeon, the prisoners become individual performers in a social theater: '[The cells] are like so many cages, so many small theaters, in which each actor is alone, perfectly individualized and constantly visible' (Foucault, 1979: 200). The theater metaphor is extended: like an actor in front of a darkened auditorium, the prison-inmates cannot see whether or not the guard is currently watching them from the command post. This structure allows for the self-surveillance of the inmates: since they cannot see when they are being watched, they internalize the oppressive, surveying gaze: 'Hence the major effect of the panopticon: to induce in the inmate a state of conscious and permanent visibility that assures the automatic functioning of power' (201). Foucault posits this is an example of the historical technologies that created modern subjectivity in the encounter between the visible, individualized subject and the invisible, impersonal institution. The working of the powerfield that binds everybody together is invisible: it is eclipsed by the blind spot that becomes that which is 'natural', 'normal'. To every subject of the system, the location of the system within her own conceptual framework is invisible, and not directly open to intervention.

Foucault's formulation of the modern subject sees its formation as historically determined by specific technologies and practices. In Foucauldian theory, the subject isn't hardwired to a life of lack and loss, but is structured into systems through historically specific arrangements of knowledge and discourse. The subject can be seen to be in a complex engagement with agency: the subject acquires a position within the system through acts of repetition, through performance, through practices. Knowledge becomes sedimented into bodies by repetitions, by everyday actions, by learning 'how to behave'. And through this emphasis on the living, everyday nature of knowledge and discourse, 'things-held-to-be-true' as acts of repetition, difference finds entryways into the system. Every act of repetition is minutely different from the previous act. Every citation of the law distances the law from its 'original'. Foucauldian difference is more powerful than a binary Other/self position in that it has the ability to change the system, rather than affirm it by strengthening its boundaries. There are no fixed positions, but instead power, in itself neutral, flows and aggregates, creating recognizable, but not ontologically grounded, zones of center and periphery. The system isn't built on a subject's need for self-affirmation, but on groups and powerstructures. These powerstructures are mobile units, and can shift. If difference accumulates, a qualitative shift can occur. The system lives, and mutates. The technology of prisons changes, although the underlying structure of internalized surveillance is reinforced through an overwhelming number of practices that structure the Western social world: from fashion and discourses of beauty to medical practices that 'normalize' people, from classical Hollywood narrative and its coding of the relationship between the visual and the emotional, from colonial scientific practices that read character and intelligence from skin-color and head-shape, to contemporary law enforcement practices such as visual scanners and e-mail surveillance.

The system lives, and therefore changes over time as infinitesimal differences accrue. Resistance to the system is problematic, though: like the Panopticon, it is a self-sustaining system that invades behavior and knowledge structures, and there is no way out. At the same time, the blind-spot of the Panopticon rests in its inability to monitor itself, to be conscious of the many tiny everyday changes that encrust its practices, and that put pressure on its mechanisms.

In cultural studies analyses, a lot of attention is paid to the kinds of resistances that do occur, and to how these resistances align themselves with the larger system, are incorporated and become part of that which is fought against: a periphery practice is investigated, and put into a structural relationship with the center. A study concerned with disability representation needs to acknowledge the structural issues of center and periphery. Disability as a discourse is secondary – it is the invisible, normalized, 'blind' spot of the dominant, 'able' – note how, in the formulation 'blind spot' the negativity of disability as a concept of language becomes apparent. Given this secondary nature of disability as a conceptual cat-egory, and the impossibility of stepping outside *and* embracing the identity marked by 'disability', it becomes important to chart resistances, show incremental moves towards change, celebrate the historical march through the system's institutions, and art's place within that.

At the same time, for a disabled person, disability is not secondary. A disabled person's own 'normality' can be in conflict with the norm of discursive formation. 'Disabled' is the phenomenologically normal experience, but one that is coded as 'periphery' rather than 'center', as 'abnormal' rather than 'normal', from the outside by the ascription of the term and social status of 'disabled'.[3] Thus, a disabled person experiences her form of embodiment both as primary and secondary at the same time, as she is structured into the certainties and languages of the system (a form of double consciousness-embodiment that is familiar from post-colonial studies). A gap opens up – one's own blind spot becomes visible as it conflicts or oscillates with the vision from the center. Here, disability is experiential – a lived experience which resists linguistic structuring. The experiential nature of this knowledge stands in a complex relationship to discursive knowledge formations.

This chapter will move from different readings of Augustus in OZ to a proliferating, baroque unfolding of different reading mechanisms offering themselves to me when contemplating the Spence photograph. The motor for these multiplying readings lies in Foucault's panopticon, as I align it with the social gaze on disability, accepted, incorporated, and reiterated by disabled people living under its survey. Every time the diagnostic or medical gaze captures the disabled person, every time the social gaze distances her lived experience and substitutes it with a script of 'proper' narratives, every time institutions structure the ways that disabled people think of themselves and of their relations to others, the panopticon of social life reiterates itself. The structure relies on visibility and interpretation, and is rigid in its allocation of secondary status to disability. At the same time, though, the structure is vulnerable to encrustation and tectonic shift, as its power axes become overburdened with reading scenarios. Too many desires, stories and slight differences in interpretation stress the certainties that try to keep prisoner and prison guard apart. In the prison of OZ, guards fraternize with inmates. Transgressions abound, and the oppressive systematicity of the prison system is commented on by the story-arc and by the characters. But the wider system that allocates secondary status to disabled characters, to black people, to non-heterosexual people, to women, to people from non-bourgeois social classes, and to drug-users remains firmly in place, as OZ's characters play out their stereotypes. Against this, I will use Spence's performance photograph to think about more structural, formal interventions and transgressions. In the wider social system of disease and disability referenced by the Spence image, I will read for seduction machines, for pathways, minor stories, and openings that destabilize her image as 'victim', as subject of a medical gaze, and as the abject other to non-disabled living.

The Prison of OZ

OZ uses visuality and surveillance as metaphors for contemporary life, and comments on it through story lines and formal elements. The episodes consciously comment on the set-up of highly visible surveillance mechanisms, with high-tech desks for prison wards blinking in the backgrounds. Technologies of media surveillance are complemented with equally elaborate behavioral practices within the prison population: signs, rituals, modes of communication are both constructed by and constructed against the system. Within this elaborate rat cage, Augustus's position as the high-tech, special-effects magic-realism character mediates the different systems of domination and entrapment enacted in OZ. And outside OZ's narrative universe, the viewer is caught within the ritualistic enactment of weekly

TV schedules and within the metaphorical framing of US race relations and their endless production of victims, perpetrators and prisoners.

Into this terrain of surveillance and the law enters disability as a marker of difference, into a position of transcendence, surveilling in turn the narrative scene. An early episode of OZ explains that Augustus Hill was a drug user, that he shot a policeman dead in the course of a raid which surprised him in bed with his wife, and that a number of armed officers chase him naked over the rooftops. After apprehending him, one police officer, learning of his colleague's death, throws Augustus off the roof.

This episode shows the importance of readings for disability signification. In the course of this brief narrative segment, Augustus's disability figures in a number of ways. First, it is used as a device that singles him out among the prison population and bestows upon him the position of storyteller of the show. During his soliloquies to camera, Augustus and his wheelchair are often rotating in free space in a glass box, a reconstruction of a prison cell in glass rather than steel and concrete – a narrational no-where land, away from the constantly surveilled reality of the prison, and into the surveiling gaze of the TV audience, instead.

The signification of disability starts to shift gears in the scene where Augustus is thrown off the roof: disability here becomes the just reward for a slothful, violent life, an act of revenge. At the same time, his nakedness on the roofs shows his vulnerability, and the slight, delicate vulnerability of his frame stands in deep contrast to the armed and suited policemen – who are white to Augustus's black. Vulnerability, victimhood, are further aspects of the signification of disability in popular culture.

In the discussion of sexuality and love, further significations of disability are activated: cultural taboos around the act of 'lovemaking' and the physical specificity of disability encounter the curiosity, the staring of the non-disabled at the disabled other. The episode actually shows Augustus's wife helping him to place himself on the bed of the conjugal visiting room (but not the sexual act itself – the viewer's voyeurism is not rewarded). In the scenes surrounding Augustus's pre- and post-disability lovemaking the racial connotations of Augustus's skin color come most to the fore: the 'black stud' stereotype is at work in his persona.

Disability works within OZ's narrative by making Augustus a more thoughtful lover, one more attuned to the emotional aspects of sex – a narrative that works well with stereotypes of disabled people as 'feminized' or sensitive and (often in the case of blindness) ESP-talented.

In all scenes focusing on Augustus in his chair, gazes are foregrounded. In one episode where Augustus is discussing his sex life, the camera cuts back again and again to his friend's eyes, staring at Augustus through the metal prison bars. In his scenes as storyteller, rotating lynch-pin of the prison, special effects surround his smiling face and the dreadlocks framing it – the metal and glass world of the prison, the rotating wheel of the chair. The physical impossibility of his suspension gives extra weight to his character. He reads the prison and its moral world, and we read him and his disability as a sign of privilege, of access to 'deeper knowledge', as the opposite to 'action' (that is how Tom Fontana envisaged the scenes with Augustus in the spinning box: 'a breathing space for the audience after the action', DVD commentary, 2002). It is from this position apart, yet enclosed, that Augustus can see what others can't: he can see beyond the blind spots set up by immediacy and the pecking order. Away from the center, the workings of the prison, its social order and its narratives become apparent to him. He can see people's actions in a larger frame, comment on them with fore- and hindsight or announce events as inevitable given the prison's dynamic.

Already we see how readings multiply, creating a dense web of inter- and intratextual references that intersect in my reading practice in the image of the wheelchair user. Beginning to read OZ through this lens shows the importance of pre-existing knowledges, discourses, as well as pre-existing emotional values to any act of representing disability – on screen, on the stage, in a photo, in words.

Disability as a concept asks for a thorough and careful analysis of reading practices, the investigation of different blind spots, different ways of making meaning, and an analysis and awareness of the power structures inherent in any acts of performativity, performance and mediation. In the discussion that follows, disability comes to figure not only as a player within an image field, where certain meanings accrue to it, but as a placeholder for forms of difference that do not lend themselves to easy opposition. In Jo Spence's photography, culture's exiled other, its pain and its difference, comes into view.

Jo Spence: Performing death

The other trace of a performance I want to discuss in this chapter is Jo Spence's photo sequence *Narratives of Dis-ease* (1990), with my main focus on the second photo in the series, called *Exiled*. I am using this photo by reading it as an intersection between semantic meaning and the embodied reader, focusing on the phenomenology of reading. Phenomenology is a series of philosophical practices that find their founding moment in the observation of enworldedness.[4] Phenomenology holds that knowledge of the world is constituted *in* the world: not as a separate mental entity observing the realm of the bodily, but instead in direct interaction and deeply involved in the flesh and the world. And in turn, the world is substance, united in the same field of presence as my own embodied being. In this world, objects do not come to me and my senses as categorized 'things' that find their place in a mental storage system, but I encounter them as densities, and as others. In reacting to them, I interact with them, and act in an intersubjective world. Phenomenological approaches to reading practices focus on the openness of the text to the reader, and on the labor necessary to create a temporary whole in the act of reading. Roman Ingarden introduces lacunae, or 'Unbestimmtheitsstellen', 'spots of indeterminancy' to discuss this intertwining of reader and text. The creation of the text is never finished, but open.[5] This interactivity is part of the appeal of reading. Filling in the lacunae, making the text part of one's own world, is the performance of acts of concretization: a dispersal of creativity away

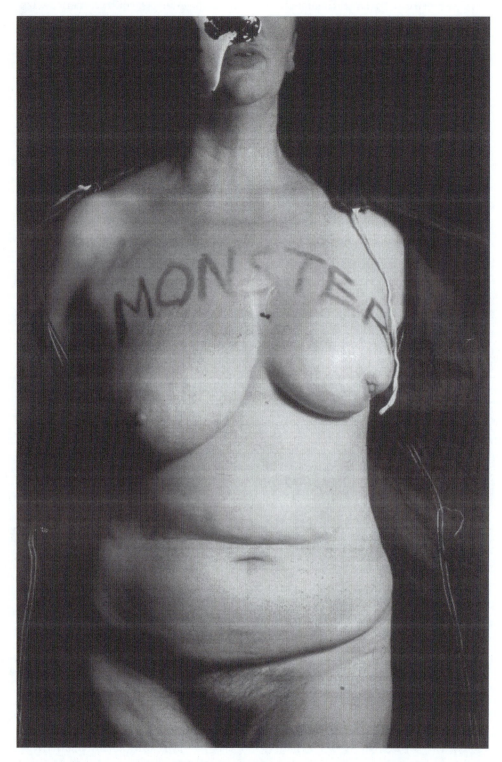

Figure 1 Jo Spence (in collaboration with Tim Sheard): *Exiled*, from *Narratives of Dis-ease*. (Reproduced by courtesy of the Jo Spence Archive, Terry Dennett)

from an author to a reader/author field. In effect, this way of focusing on reading practices leads to similar results as poststructuralist reading theories, which posit a radical openness of the text itself: signifiers always signifying in excess of the signified, setting up a chain of supplementary meaning that destabilizes any hold on language. Phenomenological reading theories, however, set up this always incomplete act as a source of life: instead of the death (of the author), the world of intersubjectivity is full of moving life. I love the photograph of Jo Spence, in the sense that Roland Barthes meant when he described the act of reading as an act of love, defined by the intertwining of text and reader, led by passions and desires (e.g. 1977). I have high hopes when reading it, am emotionally invested, and touched by its smooth surface, and the privacy of the flesh that exposes itself to me freely. After being familiar with it as a core image in many feminist textbooks, I finally encountered a more auratic version of it in a museum in Edinburgh: not as a small format paperback book reproduction, but as an object with weight and size, in a museum's white corridor high up above the city. But both in its more monumental version on a wall, and in its context of feminist writings, *Exiled* sets up traces of another presence – a presence in some ways now gone from this world (Jo Spence has died), but alive in its effects on me. It is this physical vocabulary of reading that captures my reasons for selecting this particular photograph. It is the physical involvement of sensual appeal, kinetic pleasure and affect that draws me to live and filmed performance and other representations of the disabled body. I find that my sensual and bodily reactions show me the way to a corporeal engagement with representation and theory suitable to my position in the world. With this I hope to step further on the unknowable way that Elizabeth Grosz is pointing towards:

> To [give an account which provides materials directly useful to women's self-representation] would involve knowing in advance, preempting, the developments in women's self-understandings which are now in the process of being formulated regarding what the best terms are for representing women as intellectual, social, moral, and sexual agents. It would involve producing new discourses and knowledges, new modes of art and new forms of representational practice outside of the patriarchal frameworks which have thus far ensured the impossibility of women's autonomous self-representations, thus being temporally outside or beyond itself. No one yet knows what the conditions are for developing knowledges, representations, models, programmes which provide women with nonpatriarchal terms for representing themselves and the world from women's interests and points of view.
>
> (Grosz, 1994: 188)

These new knowledges, or awarenesses of knowledge's workings might lead us towards giving a place in the world to the other – not a place as other, kept away by the power of the binary, but within the same horizon of living.

Depicted in the photo is the torso, lower half of the face and upper half of the thighs of a woman wearing a half-mask, with the word 'monster' written across her neckline, and framed by a green surgical gown. A range of different 'meaning-carriers' are at work in this multivalent photo. Written language and visual signifiers position the central body in various poses of abstractions: from the general 'person' to the specific 'female', from the medical photo to the art historical nude,[6] from the general 'natural' to the othering connotations of age, size, health, class and agency.[7] A hierarchy and polyphony of meaning is open to the reader: the specific flesh of a specific person, the flesh of femininity, the matter of age, the sign of excess, the absence of health, the object of a structuring gaze.

The problems of defining the meaning-making medial environment are enacted by Jo Spence's photo: the discourses of medicine and its surveillance-codes meet the genre of the art-photograph, the 'natural' body meets the 'performative', theatrical body. The body in its materiality and extension meets the two-dimension photographic representation. Tracy Warr, in a discussion of 1970's body art, points to the power of the body in communication:

> Every body is implicated in the sufferings or pleasures of other bodies. It can-not be an objective observer. 'To say that one never suffers alone, is not a simple cliché. The laws of identification and of communication between images of the body make one's suffering and pain everybody's affair' (Schilder, 1950: 149). In the presence of another human sentience much has to be acknowledged. The body forces the inescapable realization of an essential intersubjectivity.
>
> (Warr, 1996: 4)

The representation of the body, though, can work to hold the power of the body to communicate in abeyance: any frame to the encounter can deflect the impact – just like twenty-first century body artists cutting their skin and forcing blood can feel like a tired gesture to a by now solidified historical canon of this form of practice. This mute witnessing of the body in body art can seem politically empty – its challenge is too easily contained. The spectator can flee the implications of the suffering human body by making the witnessed event into a spectacle.[8] But different from many performance artists, Spence's 'altered body' is non-theatrical – the cuts are not made in the name of art. The boundaries of theatricality still stand untouched by cutting or piercing, momentary incursions into the stability of the 'normal' body that, given time, will heal. Disability art is radically different from much body art – choice, and the issue of an individual's agency, even the boundaries of what constitutes 'an individual' are set into motion differently if one is using incursions into one's body strategically in order to expose the self's longing for openness, or if this self has to struggle against the multitude of metaphorical readings that cut into her flesh.

Spence's photos speak of flesh made to mean – made over into stories both by the medical regime and by the artist, by cultural narratives of women and appropriate behavior in aging, and by me, when I spin my own fantasies around the moment of the photo. Spence herself writes about the different knowledges and emotional investments at work in her photos – she is

> explaining my experience as a patient and the contradictions between ways in which the medical profession controls women's bodies and the 'imaginary' bodies we inhabit as women.
>
> (Spence, 1986)

The historical fallacy of the photograph – 'something happened' – grips my body and activates a temporal theater of fantasized encounters with this experience. By staging the photo, panopticity becomes visible as a mechanism: the transparency of visual truth as construct is exposed.

Performing reading

Acts of reading can provide different pleasures. On a basic level this pleasure can be seen to be caught up in the recognition of a culture's value-schemes and centralities – members of a culture have conceptual strategies that allow them to find a comfortable position in relation to the text, affirming their expectations and self-definitions. For a young African-American, Augustus Hill most likely signifies different than to a white, working-class boy. Affirmations of hope, respect, disgust, fear can all be made available through different readings of the presented scenes. Media studies have shown how media representations can become endowed with utterly unexpected meanings through ritualistic reading practices: for instance, Latin American filmgoers have created counter-readings of Rambo not as a neo-conservative vigilante figure of white supremacy, but as a fighter against the imperialist US system, and parts of the gay culture have recast Judy Garland as a figure of camp adoration and investment (Dyer, 1986). Jo Spence's body can be used in different contexts to provide multiple pleasures: as cultural capital in the form of an art text (Bourdieu, 1984); as sign of otherness for a woman eager to affirm to herself her body's health and shape; or as identificatory material for a woman getting ready to face mastectomy. All of the reading positions and pleasures outlined above find a niche for the image and affirm the user's position in culture by their interaction with the photo.

Disruptions of reading patterns can occur within specific parameters – the power of the grotesque in Jo Spence's diseased images can temporarily upset understandings of agency, femininity, physicality, by showing the slide of ascribed meanings into their opposites. Here, it is the patient who constructs the photo in teamwork with the doctor, it is the woman who displays her lived body with/out shame, it is the physical body which becomes articulate and expressive. The desires and mediations that constitute the meaning-making process can become visible at the edges of the picture, the procedural character of the reading as an act in time can become a performance as the photo answers back, intruding its own desires into the space of the spectator's subjectivity. The spectator is forced to pronounce the meaning, to become aware of his or her position within the theater of culture, and the panoptic scenario of ordering. The photo needs to be actively called to order, thereby opening up the registers of disorder and potential unruliness lurking beneath semiotic acts and phenomenological engagements.

The process of cultural stratification works upon all aspects of culture, it pervades language and bodies and their relationships. The 'cultural system' and its power to bind readings in specific frameworks cannot be located in specific texts, be they figures of authority, singular media-phenomena or direct political intervention. Instead, 'culture' perpetuates its meanings in negotiations, inscribing and re-inscribing itself into the smallest bodily practices. Disability, youth, age, race, ethnicity, sexuality – all aspects of identity formation and language which can be used to ascribe identity to one's self are part of the stratification machine which controls all positions towards it – accepting positions as well as oppositional stances. Spence's performative photo is bound by this pull of the system: there are no alternatives within representation, even to artists who, unlike the makers of OZ, might wish for a loosening of textual meanings. Any act of meaning-making has to move within the confines of this binding field, and has to arrange subjectivity in relation to these markers of identity.

Can the body of *Exiled* escape the objectification of photographic language, even momentarily, as readings inch away from panoptic distancing? Different forms of engagement move towards the frontier of subject/object by stretching the possibilities of Barthes' intertwining of text and reader (1977). Engagements such as the emotional investment with the victim-position or the affective phenomenological potential of 'shared embodiment' threaten to overcome the voyeuristic gaze at the disabled woman as Other. *Exiled* extends the questions about conventionalized readings of the relative power positions of masculinity and femininity, artistic agency and medical victimhood. It can map out the terrain for reading the woman's body: nature/culture, death/life, fertility/sterility, medical/personal, flesh/word. Binaries criss-cross over the exposed breasts, but the missing volume of the left breast, the 'heart-matter' (at the core of traditional significations of woman) opposing the head, cut-off by the camera, takes some force out of the clamour of binary fighting. The non-symmetrical body (and the non-symmetrical theatrical mask) allows peals of laughter on the battlefield, sounds of the earnest fun of accumulating the heaps of meaning.

Synaesthesia, colliding the texture with the look, the physical scream with the icons of writing, loosens up the boundaries of meaning in the photo. 'Breast' becomes unstable, loses its weight as the signifier of woman in the light of rolls of other fat connoting the warmth and expanse culturally assigned to the motherly breast. Displacements shudder any firmness of connotational placements. Irony locates itself in inadequacies: the theatrical West End's *Phantom of the Opera* (in the white half-mask) meets the Monster of culture, the striptease meets the surgical 'green cloth' – an icon of medical hiding and exposing. The discourses of low art and serious business are mixed. The physicality of the body is unique, staunch, present, disrupting the tensions of cultural meaning. Finally, the eyes of the object are taken out but are replaced by the gaze of the subject: photographer and model are the same, the tensions between seeing and being seen are momentarily confused by the apparent sameness of the two sides of representation. The reader encounters a whole, whose intimate communication is suspended, leaving only surfaces to be read.

The assemblage of readings amassed here acknowledges the binaries that construct culturally connoted meanings of female flesh, breasts, monsters and masks, but overloads the structuring binary, makes it visible in the disturbing breakdown of the symmetrical. By dislocating the center and its natural hold, the blind spot of the Panopticon once again comes into focus, questioning the validity of the system *as* natural.

Augustus Hill's persona modulates a number of binaries, and it is his position on the borderline of these discourses that gives him culturally the power to speak. He is not threateningly male, his masculinity being put under erasure, bracketed off, by his alignment with the disabled position. Like Teresias, the Greek seer, the prize for the ability to understand all those around him is disability and difference. Teresias lived for a while as a female, then reverted to the male position, and the Gods punished him for the extra knowledge he gained by blinding him. By being 'naturally' placed into the position of storyteller and analyst, Augustus Hill performs, articulates and incorporates the ideological binary of male/female. He performs the 'natural' meaning of disability as difference, non-masculine, non-threatening, tragic enough to lift him beyond the action-lives of his fellow inmates. His performance and position does not threaten established order, it reaffirms it (including the position of black in relation to white). For artists like Spence, who work outside the realms of popular culture, the stability of the binary sign seems fair game: in different ways, they overload the scales of the meaning-making apparatus, and an audience can witness the strain on the cultural system. Of the two performances and their citation of disability, it is Spence's work that touches me most deeply: in her work, the label of 'disability' transcends its secondary status, and acquires the primary, experiential quality of a fractured, complex mode of living.

Absences

The kind of alternative reading strategy that I am most interested in is one that disrupts the binary, the deep semantic structure, while acknowledging it, and positing an absence as a trace of life. The connotation disrupts the stability of the sign on a systematic, conceptual level. The sameness of object and subject that describes the interaction between Spence's body and Spence's eye 'exiles' the stranger, the eye of the spectator. The spectator might be addressed in the written sign, or willingly acknowledged in the theatrical gesture of the mask, but she is exterior to the core meaning of the body to the embodied subject.[9] Pride? Pain? Anger? Loss? Any reading of this body implicates the viewer more than the subject, lodges meaning more in the connotations of the 'extra-bodied' signs, the 'sememes' (minimal semiotic units – units of meaning) written on the flesh, than the flesh itself. The flesh offers itself as unreadable, without eyes – 'windows of the soul' – or a hand to guide our perception, to 'point' to the 'essential'. The mouth, being slightly open, reveals a darkness within and, in doing so, points to the general openness of the body.[10] The female body is ready for invasion, to have language put in its mouth, to be raped – but in another reading, the body is revealing itself to be dense, full of dark places, non-readable. Traces of past invasions are left as scars on the flesh. But the openness of the display points in its excess to the act of reading – the act of filling absences with presences. To read the photo is to invade a body. There is nothing to be found, just folds, crevices, holes and emptiness to be actively filled by the spectator. The discourses of public and private are activated by the orchestrated play of signifiers which do not have their equivalent in any stable 'real' of the body shown.

The double nature of address, the knowledge split between the helpless, incomplete body in the photo and the connotations of the title and signature, is another destabilizing force. The interaction between the two different systems, the visual and the written, is recognized by Derrida:

> It is not enough to *simply see* the work to decide what the subject is . . . at the edge of the work, neither inside nor outside, readable rather than visible, the title is our only recourse. As for deciding the subject, an initiative is always left to words.
>
> (Derrida, 1990/91, quoted in Phelan, 1993: 15)

Accordingly, Spence's authorship takes dominance over the visual signifiers. But the limitless nature of the body in the photo, this body that spills over the boundaries of the frame, the mask, which exposes itself under the surgical gown, comes close to re-appropriating the small white sign fixed on the museum wall next to it. The agency of the artist becomes the helplessness of the 'cancer-woman', just as the monster-image is broken through by the private, the 'real' of a time sequence and a name. No one position and name can be safely given to the work, neither Jo Spence nor 'monster'. This doubling of subjects through different modes of agency also points towards the theatricality of the photo. Ian Watson describes acting theorist Meyerhold's model of the layering of the actor:

> Wsewolod Meyerhold's algebraic definition of the actor, $N=A1+A2$ – in which N stands for 'the actor', A1 for 'the artist who conceives the ideas and issues the instructions necessary for its execution', and A2 for 'the executant who executes the conception of A1' (Meyerhold, 1969, p. 198) – highlights the major difference between the literary and the performance text. In the theater, the actor not only creates his/her performances . . ., but that creation only exists when the actor performs it. Similarly, the entire stage event only exists when it is in progress.
>
> (Watson, 1995: 136)

This triad can be further developed when N becomes the carrier of subjectivity as projected by the audience onto the multilevel (actor/figure) stage person. Meyerhold's formula also opens up the semiotic binary with its signified/signifier implication, and acknowledges the agency of performance work in destabilizing opposing positions. The body in performance is thus located in different positions, different subjectivities are at work at the same time, generating a multitude of responses from the audience, the witness. Traditional notions of intention, truth and artist are split open by this shifting scenario, which envelops the spectator rather than keeping her at a distance.

My approach to the reading of signs is deconstructivist. As I split up previous givens into contradictory and partial units, I show up the constructed nature of discourse, communication and culture. This absence and its momentarily realized, disruptive potential have been analyzed,[11] and become constitutive for important analytical approaches.[12] My approach focuses on the value of this potential for using silence within political representations. But the silence that I want to look for is not the silence of non-representation, the non-visible, but the glaring blank and empty noise of the present invisible. The invisible refuses the pat play of signifier and signified, and hints at that which is outside speech but not outside culture. Culture might have relegated this invisible to the sidelines, repressing political difference, but it has not wholly removed it into the non-culture spaces of which Barthes writes. This space for performances of meaning can acquire political power when mapped to protrude, like an absent breast, across the smooth surfaces of words, connotations and meaning. Its problematic materiality, held in a position of non-fixity by the excess of meaning it carries, threatens systematicity – the blind spot of an ordering schema becomes visible from its peaks and valleys.

Temporalities

Jo Spence's *Exiled* is undoubtedly a photograph, according to conventionalized definitions to do with the relationships of object, subject, technique, the 'natural' of light and bodies and understandings of artistic control and media-defined parameters of being. But content matter, intertextual position and formal attributes make this photograph a liminoid work, spreading itself out between performance and film. 'Liminoid' is anthropologist Victor Turner's (1982) term for a potentially disruptive, resistant activity, as opposed to a merely liminal, ultimately reaffirming activity associated with rituals, festivals and the carnival. Turner's liminoid refers to something happening at the level of communities, but I want to use the thought structure here to think not about a large social event, but the individual, limited intervention of a photograph/performance. It takes place not on the level of work or religion, but within the sphere associated with the private: the female body, the social non-sequitur of mastectomy, the therapeutic situation between doctor and patient, or Spence's community arts photography activities with working-class women. It is in such spaces that different structures might develop, challenging the established structures of seeing and knowing (Carlson, 1996: 23, 24). To create time-based performance out of photographs, the markers of stable historical moments of the self, is to question the unity, stability and place of the self within one assigned place. *Exiled* refers to a past event, a present event occurring within the cultural parameters and images available for a female object, a metacommunication about the spectator's ability to identify, and to the potentiality of inclusion as a temporal progression.

Performance is shaping, condensing, modifying temporality by creating behavior not 'natural' to the time of living. Rudolf Arnheim focused theatrical performance's existence in time and its effect on meaning-making by yet another split in the spectator's subjectivity: two different knowings, one knowing that develops at a moment in time, the pictorial, and one that develops over the span of time, the literal (which is the level at which the intentions of performers and directors are probed, the narrative is followed, and so forth). The two levels combine as an intertextual system. Spence's photo partakes in these two systems of representation, and meaning is shifted across different media. The photograph is *not* a time-based form of art. It is dead before it is seen. Like the word, it is a trace of an event. Like the word, it bears the memory of culture, the constant cleaving of subjectivity and world. The photograph enacts, according to Lacan, the traumatic scene of difference and loss (Phelan, 1993). The photo allows a distillation of the world into meaning-carriers, wrenched from the change of time. In a Foucauldian reading, the photograph acts as a zero-point of gravitational knowledges: it holds alignments of medical practice and aesthetic reframings, resistances and compliances, the dream of the individual and the desire to confess, to flow into a communality – to be legible to both self and the world. At the same time, the photo shows the knowledges as practices rather than originary 'truths': as a snapshot of alignments, the photo exposes the existence of viewpoints – and blind spots. Not everything is seen. The scene is not fully surveillable. The individual is not fully readable – to herself and to the world. The photograph *is* a time-based form of art. *Exiled* distils time. Like the medieval allegory, it holds meanings both past and future, crystallizing a complex scenario into an image of iconic value. The photograph can be read as a mug-shot, with the monster-letters taking the place of more abstract identification, numbers on a piece of cardboard. But the claim of 'realism', inherent in photography's early history, is disrupted: the wound has already healed, this is not a post-op shot. This photo is more than a witness, who is caught in one moment in time, holding that moment's specificity up to the flow of time. Spence's photo combines witnessing with undecidability, unknown factors of time and presence.[13] She can't be caught.

Exiled allows time to find visual expression in the folds of flesh and breasts, by the play of gravity, by the graveness of the situation. Like the Phantom of the Paris Opera, the photo exposes what shouldn't be: the effects of time on bodies, made monstrous in the eyes of those that demand an image of body perfection that doesn't allow for progression, distortion, the mark of desire stamped with acid into a face. By opening up the gap between the regulated body of femininity, youth and control and the agency of time, the photo locates time in the spectator's body – if you are young now, you will be something like this in the future. If you are masculine now, you can be culturally feminized by the indignities of medical treatment. If you are TAB, temporarily able bodied (for a discussion of this Americanism, see Wendell, 1996), you have to face up to the implication of the T.

> Under the disciplines of normality, everyone must fear becoming a member of the subordinated group; everyone who does not die will become a member of the subordinated group. Who does not suffer from these standards (of normality)?
>
> (Wendell, 1996: 90)

The frightening implication of assuming wordlessly the body standards of culture are made palpable in Spence's work with its orchestration of time as a part of bodily experience. The theatrical mask on Spence's face is an assertion of conscious agency, not the operation theater gas mask they use to lull that consciousness to sleep. This photo could be one part of a half – the after-pendant to a before-shot, laying claim to knowledge about effects, causes and developments. *Exiled* moves beyond its time-status of the death of an event by pointing to its self-directed agency, pointing towards a future of self-representation, not a future of 'pure' physicality, circumscribed by a helpless body before a camera. This body stages itself and confounds easy messages about the effect of operations.

The photo of Spence's body holds excess energy: a compression of time and being-in-time, a gravitas of life. A double showing is taking place: a being-in-space that fills its space, and a being-in-our-space, an extension across the temporal stage that materializes the body too close to me, and engages me in a play of meanings. What does it mean to feel these stitches? How does my body remember a breast? The photo enacts a phantom pain of energy on me.

Presence relies on a communication of energy in time, as the spectator in her reading of the actor receives kinetic energy. Spence's body is thrown at the spectator by the framing gown, held open to display. What is seen and what is not, is not left to medical scrutiny or a realist camera, but is formed and changed by work on the body – the mask on the face, the writing on the breasts. The 'natural' body, invaded by an operation, becomes an energetic body through this 'demonstration' (or ostentation, or framing). The agency rests with the subject, in a willing display, incorporating the monster. This agency of the subject points to the agency of the spectator, and the charged, energetic encounter happening in real-time during the witnessing of the photograph. The photograph posits a living body as a dead photo as an instance in a living spectator's life, pointing out of itself to the death in time of Spence (years later, of leukaemia). Spence's represented body becomes a presence in space and time. Her photograph enacts the instability of her subjectivity, refusing to be caught: Spence says about her work that 'there is no peeling away of layers to reveal a "real" self, just a constant reworking process. I realize that I am a process' (Spence, 1986: 97).

The presentation is done by the readable body – this is not the Salvation Army showing a reeling drunkard as sign for their theatrical call for abstinence (Eco, 1977). Rather, this is a self-directed act of positing the body as 'other-than-the-body', of making it speak and write legibly. Spence's body is not just written on, but written through, and clear agency (of self, other, time, place) is displaced.

Another story of time is left out of *Exiled*, is displaced into the connotative subtext, and upsets messages of both scientific and personal agency in the picture: the story of cancer. Cancer fantasies multiply, setting the human body in semantic binaries of human/animal, past/future. Cancer is the animal that walks backwards, that undoes agency with disruptive and stoic force. Bodycells revert to embryonic status, change time-course, and become undefined. Without the direction of timely behavior, they destroy the being in time. The monster that walks differently makes the woman look different, undoes time, slashes the breasts of maturity. If we destabilize time in our stories and fantasies, do we slash hope as an activity based on the forward motion in time, or do we instead open up different conceptualizations of time that might allow new forms of hope to emerge?

Thus, far from being a one-dimensional political statement about the exclusion of the different as monster, *Exiled* displays signs of a complex engagement with time. Its position within Spence's work further subverts the 'moment in time' character of the photograph: it is part of a cycle of work, not a progression from before to after, but an exploration of states in transition. *Narratives of Dis-ease*, by Jo Spence and Dr Tim Sheard, consists of five photographs (*Excised, Exiled, Expected, Expunged, Included*) that make up stories of maturity and childhood, of adolescence and interiority, making use of teddybears and stilettos. Formally, all of these images refuse to fix the body in time and frame: in all of them the body protrudes into the space beyond the frame. Only one of the five shows the head of Spence – after four ex-s, *Included* shows her, clutching a teddy, eyes closed, private, outside our grasp. But the photo is not easily read as a positive statement: it is also a rehearsal of the first one in the series, showing her dressed in a gown, holding the teddy bear, her head bowed, her face not visible shot from above.[14] The photo stems from a therapeutic session with a doctor, centring on aggression:

> I said: 'I want to show you what I think happens to a cancer patient when they go into hospital.' I displayed to him how I felt – literally I was a tearful child holding her teddy bear. He understood very well, and stood on a chair and photographed me from the dominating position of the doctor.
> (Spence and Solomon, 1995: 211)

The compositional liminality of *Exiled*, showing me a partial body, a glimpse of a whole that I cannot see, points towards the meaning-making of the time-based art of performance. The pictorially present whole and the literally continuous becoming combine in a deeply intertextual dance. The death of time that is the vanishing point of *Exiled* becomes the central protagonist in the performative art – every sign is snatched away, we are in the presence of dying, at the meeting point of the sign that it becomes and the finished sign.[15] What I take from performance is the dead body of memories, already laid out by my narrational drives, but what I receive is the affect of living flesh, of the actuality of presence. Jackie Stacey, in a book which merges a personal account of her fight with cancer and cultural analysis, posits Spence's photograph in the context of the political fight for a future in which the health system rewrites its demeaning and disempowering ways (Stacey, 1997).[16] The future beyond the individual body of Spence is referenced, a future which the photo is seen to change. Jo Spence is dead – a contradiction in terms.

Strategies of absence

This chapter discussed representations of disability in order to analyze the complexities of meaning-making, of performance, of life and death in representation. OZ presented disability as a conventionalized sign, something that can be mobilized in a number of ways to signify ethnic, sexual, and embodied otherness, and that can stem the tide of narrative long enough to carve out privileged positions – in OZ, disability is not part of the action, it is what allows Augustus Hill to comment on it, from outside, from a glass cage.

Exiled shows what culture exiles. By the photo's stake in issues of life and death, by its problematic status in between the 'real' and the 'staged' its representation of disability is deep and layered. It brings back what culture has shut away, and it makes me shudder before I can find a connection with it. This 'Dis-ease' is caused by my inability to posit the photo safely in one specific location in relation to my self. Once the discomfort is accepted, a cathartic moment of tragedy occurs. But the stability and acceptance that catharsis is supposed to achieve is broken and re-broken by the traces of agency that act on my reading of the photo. Once I can reconcile my body with the ravages of time, and the inevitability of losing control, I am forced to examine whether the scenario of acceptance is the only possible one, or whether the alignment of acceptance and the tragic is necessary. I end up thinking about the power of representation, the traditional power differentials between the object and the subject. I start thinking about Foucault's docile bodies and I start to question the tragic in Spence's stance. No God or Pantheon has declared that human bodies have to suffer. Spence is no victim, but rather a Cultural Sniper.[17] She launches her weapons against a system of representation and meaning-making that has taken up the position of regulator and mastermind. My thoughts, kicked into action by a photo full of contradictions, spool through diverse possibilities, positions, answers and questions. Exiled exiles me from easy answers about the human condition and the status of human agency. Too many gaps appear between the binaries of meaning to be ignored, even if I cannot fill the absences. But my self can align itself with the absences rather than the presences, if those presences are filled with non-viable options.

Minority representations, put into motion by the waves caused by the unrepresented act of experience, can make palpable previously excluded identities, or identities that cannot be represented in their complexity by the traditional instruments of knowledge. Binaries are forced open in the interplay between living bodies, modes of representations, desirous spectators, and a field of energy that hums with the charge of bodies caught in frames. The panopticon is stressed by this proliferation of practices, of ways of reading, of life. The prison of social alignments doesn't vanish under this encrustation of possibilities, but, as a politically engaged reader infusing her practice with desire, I can look for openings, listen out for groans and feel for cracks. As I hope to show in other disability performances throughout these pages, complex interactions between physical presence, lived experience and mediation through various technologies combine together in contemporary performance work in order to create encounters with difference.

Chapter 2

Freaks, stages, and medical theaters

No study should discuss disability performance without acknowledging the history of oppression that had for so long kept disabled performers away from the 'aesthetic' stage and its inducements of prestige, potential careers, and professional lives. Since the eighteenth century, disabled people's performances have been historically confined to the sideshow, the freak display[1] (where at least professional skilled work, i.e. paid opportunities and social organization was possible) and the medical theater (where no pay is offered, although precarious social forms are found). I want to start here, then, with the problematic placement of disabled performers on different kind of stages.

Mat Fraser is a UK performance artist who went on a journey from London to Coney Island, US,[2] and from the freakshow stage to an Edinburgh festival theater, in order to clarify for himself his position as a 'freak' performer: a man born with a highly visible physical impairment, who enjoys being on the stage, and who wishes to query the dynamics that pertain to his engagement with his audience. In his show 'Sealboy: Freak', he resurrects Stanley Berent, a.k.a. Sealo the Sealboy, a performer he feels an affinity with. Fraser was born with phocomelic, i.e. very short arms. He has a colorful and successful career as rock star, theater actor, film star, disability personality and public persona on the UK's Channel 4. In the creation of 'Sealboy', Fraser was searching for his historic role model, his roots, his heritage. Employing these terms (role models, roots) designates the disability experience not as an individual and singular fate, but as a cultural minority experience, similar to cultural production shaped by the black diaspora. In his research into people like him in performance situations, he found successful people with names such as 'Lobsterboy', who performed monstrosity and freakishness for sideshow audiences in the first half of the last century. Berent was a performer in US freakshows from the 1930s to the mid-1970s, starting at the NYC 42nd Street's famous Hubert's museum, and including 'David Rosen's Wonderland sideshow' on Coney Island, the US freakshow center, as well as Ringling Barnum, the travelling show. As sideshows were shut down in the 1970s in the US, a way of life and a way of making a living was taken away from performers all over the nation, and Berent was caught up in this dismantling. He retired to The Riverview Retirement Home for Old Showpeople in Florida, not far from a larger retirement community for sideshow people, and died in 1984.[3]

Figure 2 Mat Fraser as Sealo. Photograph by Ashley. (Reproduced by courtesy of the artist)

Fraser came across Berent in his research for a theater show for Graeae, one of the UK's most visible professional disability theater companies, who produced 'Fittings . . . The Last Freakshow' in 1999.[4] He writes in his program notes:

> In this one act, one man show Mat asks the question: Can a disabled performer ever be seen as anything other than a freak, irrespective of the 'liberal' or

'postmodern' attitudes of today's sophisticated audiences?, and then he becomes his predecessor, Sealo the Sealboy, as the audience is forced to confront their collective connection with the freakshow audiences of the past.

Containing feats of strength, drum'n'bass, sexuality, and class A drugs, 'Sealboy: Freak' is a show that takes the spectator outside the comfort zone and into the teradome.

(Fraser, 2001)

Sealboy utilizes an audience address on the boundaries of the 'aesthetic' theater (referenced by the existence of the program note itself, and its reference to complex artistic motives and strategies) and the freak spectacle (in the second paragraph with its enumeration of attractions, culminating in the 'teradome' – a term derived from teratology, the study of monsters).[5] In the following, I want to show the different framings of disability and difference offered by the stage of the freakshow, and the environment of the contemporary performance act.

In order to construct 'Sealboy', Fraser went on a research trip to some of the core locations of Berent's life. He met up with retired sideshow people, including 'talkers', or pitch men – people who performed the chatter that drew the audience into the tent, and who moderated the show-stage inside. Sealboy opens with one of these patters, and in it a number of tropes and conventions are brought together. The talk starts with an enumeration of descriptions of the freaks on display:

> TALKER : We told you we had living, breathing monstrosities, the curious the spurious the downright furious. Creatures so strange they defy belief and scare the soul to think that, but for the grace of god, you might be as they are, such terrifying examples of nature's catastrophes, and you've paid to see 'em so let's get on with the show.
>
> (Fraser, 2001)

Fraser researched this dialogue with people remembering the patter, and tries it out and makes it effective anew on the contemporary stage. The talk opens with a justification for the spectacle of the freakshow: edification and morality, mixed with commercialism and sensationalism. The patter references the movement from horror to satisfaction: a terror, a catharsis, that allows the viewer to newly appreciate his or her fortunate position. The mechanism is at work in the reception of Tono Maria, another sideshow act. Garland Thomson describes how a contemporaneous reviewer of an 1822 London act displaying Maria, a scarred Brazilian woman stuffing herself with food on stage

> learned a useful lesson: having previously failed to fully appreciate English women, he would forever after 'pay the homage due to the loveliest works of creation, enhanced in value by so wonderful a contrast'.
>
> (Garland Thomson, 1997: 55, quoting Altick, 1978: 272/3)

As Garland Thomson describes, the freak on this early stage becomes the other that serves to heighten self-identity, allowing the audience to disavow and suppress aspects of self, constructing themselves as happy, restrained, appropriate, normal.[6]

Fraser's patter opens up a window onto these historical moments of Sealo and Maria, but in the 180 years that separate Fraser from Maria's time, the moral tale has grown very thin indeed. The patter is formulaic, taking its power more from the rhyming and rhythm than from a serious address of moral or edifying issues. Fraser continues by letting his talker enumerate some of the kinds of freaks that the archives slowly come to recognize, to see as performers rather than merely victims. Watching Fraser, the freak, perform the part of talker in 'Sealboy', gives the act depth: a calling-forth of a family, making a living in the strangest conditions, but a working, living community:

> Folks we've already shown you the rubber faced girl Etta Lake outside, her skin stretches 6 inches in any direction that it is pulled, and still to come Millie and Christine the two headed girl, Jo Jo the dog faced boy, his face and body completely covered in long, golden hair; the half girl Jeannie Tomani; reaching only a height of 2 and a half feet, she is the smallest woman in the world Ladies and Gentlemen. Also, for your fascination and amazement, the one and only Schlitzy the pinhead, the Aztec children, the bearded lady, the midget family, the giants, and all the other strange anomalies that make up the sideshow on the midway in our Stern's Family Circus.
>
> (Fraser, 2001)

Watching this twenty-first-century memory of the sideshow stirs me strangely. Having read and digested the analyses of these events collected by Garland Thomson and others, I now find myself watching the spectacle as a moment of oral history, a calling forth of a lost history, of men and women who provide strange foreparents to today's disabled performers. Garland Thomson sums up her analysis of the kinds of shows dominating the nineteenth century, the heyday of the freakshow:

> In an era of social transformation and economic reorganization, the nineteenth-century freak show was a cultural ritual that dramatized the era's physical and social hierarchy by spotlighting bodily stigmata that could be choreographed as an absolute contrast to 'normal' American embodiment and authenticated as corporeal truth.
>
> (Garland Thomson, 1997: 63)

In this analysis, the focus is on the others – the non-disabled, normal, or at least normal enough to be able to construct themselves as normal apropos the differences presented to them. Policing normality is here transferred into the hands of popular culture: the kinds of knowledges that later on rest firmly in the hands of the medical sciences here work on the street, in the everyday life of American

Figure 3 Publicity card for 'Sealboy: Freak'. Design Dan Jones. (Reproduced by courtesy of the artist)

people, who can experience the boundaries between right and wrong, self and other, us and them, first-hand in the tent. The freakshow is a spectacle of certainty: even if in other areas of life uncertainty rules, here, one's position on the far side of the stage is assured.

By performing this ritual in a contemporary context, and by inserting his own body into the supposedly clear distinction between (rational) presenter, teacher of the masses, and (irrational) presented, object of the gaze, freak, Fraser breaks open the rigidity of certainties. At the beginning of the twenty-first century, certainties about the body's similarity in opposition to 'deviance' are no longer given.[7] The act of surveillance, self-discipline and focus on oneself as freak characterizes much of popular culture and everyday life – as we have seen in the discussion of OZ, in the fashion obsession of shows such as *Sex in the City*, in the proliferations of CCTV cameras, and in the rise of medical methods like Botox injections or cosmetic surgery used to 'normalize' bodies. The contemporary bearded lady performing at the only existing freakshow display on Coney Island today doesn't strike me so much with her essential difference to my self, but instead she appears as a 'performer' – someone who chooses to climb onto the stage, asserting her difference as a powerful and proud display (it is of course important to note that hirsuteness is a form of difference that is less stigmatized than short limbs, and relatively easier suppressed into passing). To an audience used to the myriad of differences that American culture has embraced in its proliferating entertainment scene (in opposition to the many others that it hasn't, including those created by specific race and disability differences), a woman sporting a beard on stage doesn't have the same disruptive power as a woman with a beard behind a bank counter, or a in a supermarket line. The freak stage has lost much of its power to amaze and excite. The freakshow has lost its status as a place of freedom from social norms – the live character of the event, and the social visibility of anti-discrimination legislation undermines the permission granted by the old spectacle to its audiences. We can no longer point and snigger, abuse and forget.[8] In hindsight, it is clear that many of the famous acts of the freak show had a say in their career, but at specific historical moments such as the Victorian stage, the ritual demanded a clear demarcation of able and not-able, rational–irrational, 'man' and animal. Researchers such as Garland Thomson (1996, 1997), Bogdan (1988) and Fiedler (1978) show that nineteenth-century freaks were presented as less than or other than human, allowing the difference between self and other to be clearly grasped. The slightly off-hand delivery of Fraser as Talker prepares the stage for an encounter of a freak performance that is at a later historical moment, where boundaries are blurred and rituals are familiar but no longer fully meaningful. Fraser's delivery disrupts the boundaries between pure object and active subject.

Fraser's show continues by introducing Sealo himself. This act touches on a number of discourses important to the history of disability performance, in particular the medical stare, and the desire to read disability – histories readers will encounter in multiple forms in this book.

> SEALO: Good day to you folks, my name is Stanley Berent, but mostly I am known by my professional name of Sealo the Sealboy, so called because of an extremely rare medical condition that I have, known to Doctor's and

scientists as Phocomelia. This literally means 'Seal-like limbs', and as you can see my little 'Handsies', as I like to call them, do in fact resemble the flippers of a seal more than the regular, human shaped arms and hands that you good folks have.

(Fraser, 2001)

No records of Berent's actual performance exist. Performance is hard to document, even if it occurs in the up-market venues of famous galleries and theaters, but if it occurs within the limits of 'lower' pop cultural scene and beyond mass marketing, documentation is particularly hard to come by. Fraser isn't Berent, and although he has researched the act with people who did see it and were part of it, Berent hadn't performed since the mid-1970s. As I am watching the show, I have many questions: would Berent have introduced himself by name, giving his stage name as his professional name? Doesn't this present a diversion from the idea of helpless, dominated freak performer, where professional role and private being were not separated out? Is this Fraser's fantasy, creating a space for his designated historical rolemodel to name himself, become visible as an actor rather than an exhibit, or is this a historical recreation? Whatever the answer is, the question opens up the desire to be recognized, to be seen as an actor, as controlling rather than being controlled, guiding the audience's gaze rather than being the immobile object of its stare.

Entering the medical world

In his opening, Sealo names his medical condition. This posits Sealo at the dying end of the freakshow as historical phenomenon: the rise of the medical system is often linked to the shut-down of the sideshows, as bodily difference becomes a matter of medical discipline, and displays become confined to the medical theater.[9] Another reason for the closing of the freakshow as a genre lies with liberal outrage at the impropriety of sating oneself on one's less fortunate fellow beings.[10] With this, and with his naming of himself as other than just 'Sealo', Fraser's representation of Berent can be seen here to be on the temporal limits of the freakshows' appeal:

> The showman offered economic independence at the expense of cultural normalcy; the medical man offered normalizing procedures that often required submission to bodily intrusion and painful reconstruction. In order to reap the showman's benefits, the person with an extraordinary body had to agree to total immersion in the freak role. But the doctor's normalization requires denying aspects of one's individual body as well as negotiating the risks and psychic compromises of 'passing'.
>
> (Garland Thomson, 1997: 79)

In Fraser's fantasy of Sealo, Berent denies total freakdom, other-than-humanness, by naming himself, inserting himself in the social order implied by the name. He also lays claim to the medical vision of his body, naming a condition of his hands, and thereby claiming 'normal' status for the rest of his body – in keeping with the particularizing gaze of medical knowledge, the fact that one part of his body is different doesn't invalidate, *invalid*, other parts of himself, including his ability to engage in socially acceptable rational discourse. But he complicates this entry into discursive normalcy by continuing his talk to present alternative knowledge models to the one put forth by medicine:

> Some people say my Ma must've had somethin wrong with her insides to make me like this, or she must've been a real bad sinner, others say she ate too much fish while she was pregnant with me, heh heh, but I say I'm grateful to my Ma, and the good Lord for givin me these Handsies, so as to make a decent livin, so let's show our appreciation to God for givin us the lives we have.
> (Starts to applaud back handed, like a seal, as well as 'arf arf'-ing)
> (Fraser, 2001)

The reasons that Sealo gives here are mainly Victorian knowledge patterns, ways of explaining deviancy by pointing to the weakness of femininity – impression theory or pre-birth patterning (eating too much fish, similar to the woman who, scared by a hare, supposedly gave birth to rabbits), moral issues (sinner, over-eater), or incompletely understood genetic patterns (something wrong inside her). They are all minor knowledges, competing with scientific explanations well into the twentieth century, and, in popular culture, beyond. In these explanations of disability, the need to read, make sense of and justify the intrusion of difference in the form of disability is paramount: making difference part of the same, allowing narratives to gloss over the eruptions of something else, are at the heart of these proliferations of explanatory schemes.

The medical theater

Beyond the freakshow, the other non-theatrical stage open to disabled people has been the 'medical theater' – a place with its own definitions of performance, symptoms, reading practices and audience relations. Most specifically, the 'medical theater' refers to the operating room, the operating theater. More broadly, the 'medical theater' is also used to refer to the places and practices that surround demonstration as a method of dissemination of medical knowledge. Patients, or corpses, were paraded or dissected in an amphitheater. The architectural form holds references to Greek origins: to public visibility and to a body politic. Historical studies of anatomy practice discuss the growing public attraction of these sites of 'learning', and Gonzalez-Crussi describes one such place, the Bolognese amphitheater in the seventeenth century, as a site of theatrical spectacle:

> magnificently decorated for the occasion: the walls were hung with damask, and two large torches, places respectively at the head and feet of the cadaver,

illuminated the working area. A crimson-gowned professor then appeared, ceremoniously followed by his attendants, and silence descended upon the amphitheater.

(Gonzalez-Crussi, 51)

The scene is set: the wealthy and the mighty assemble to participate in the spectacle, the ritual, the theater of death and difference.[11]

The everyday medical theater today has lost much of its grandiosity, although none of its authority. The diagnostic gaze of the medical practitioner can roam freely across the displayed bodies of patients, and only rarely are its intrusive and objectifying powers acknowledged in the everyday encounter.

Most disabled people have intimate knowledge of these visual and performative practices of the medical theater: in particular if they have rare congenital impairments, they might have been required to undress in front of doctors and their students, photos might have been taken, demonstrations held over their mute, or even their protesting, bodies. The medical theater is a place of public performance: a body performs its materiality and meaning to a doctor, a specialist, who is empowered to read hidden histories and signs (Foucault, 1994). As we have seen, the medical theater absorbed the performance encounter of the sideshow, supplanting it as the point of popular fascination. A number of contemporary performers have used the medical theater as their counter-point: most famously, Bob Flanagan, whose sadomasochistic performance work is often discussed as a commentary on the pain of his cystic fibrosis history and management.[12] Other contemporary artists working in this genre include Angela Ellsworth, whose shows make visible the labor at the heart of the meeting between medicine and individual bodily fantasy: in one of her shows, she enlists a large number of community members to physically enact the medical vision of blood-cells and cancer cells in fight with one another. She writes about this piece, and its complex relation between commentary on the fantasies that sustain public engagement with medical knowledge and the shamanistic performative action at work in it: 'by performing my illness I am an active participant in resisting preconceived notions of cancer, with the hope that I am staving it off' (Ellsworth, 2001: 148)[13] Claiming agency becomes here the point of resistance, the insertion of difference into a medical scenario which often casts 'the patient' as patient, as a passive stage on which medical personnel acts.

The alienating use of sexuality and eroticism can undercut power-relation, even if only momentarily, and encounters of the medical theater and performance have often focused on this relationship – most historically vibrant in the counter-readings of Jean Martin Charcot's psychiatric work with hysteria patients in the Salpêtrière.[14] One contemporary example of US performance artists can help to see alignments between Fraser's freakshow and the performances on the medical stage.

Greg Walloch is a contemporary US performance artist who uses performance modes derived from stand-up comedy and autobiographical narration as the basis of his work.[15] He uses underarm crutches to walk, and in one of his performance pieces, 'Walking Inspired', documented on the video *Crip Shots* (dir. John R. Killacky and Larry Connolly, USA, 2001), he choreographs his own specific version of the encounter with the medical stare in the performance of disability. Walloch's performance, delivered as a stand-up comedic turn, relies on a shifting tectonics of knowledge and desire. He fantasizes medical knowledge practices away from its disinterested stare towards an erotic encounter. In his performance, the diagnostic gaze becomes implicated in an erotic scene.

Walloch narrates a childhood experience: he is waiting to be seen by the doctor, the specialist, who is to pronounce on his body's development (the actual medical narrative is kept unclear – it is not the focus of the performance).

> When I got to the clinic I was asked to strip to my underwear, and after a while a nurse would call me into the main room. In the main room sat a panel of about thirty-five people [:] doctors, therapist, and student. The nurse would give me my cue to begin, and I would walk back and forth in front of a panel. Sometimes one of the doctors would stop me, and then move his hand down my back, grab my ankle, or poke at one of my ribs. I would wait until he was done, and begin to walk again as the panel took notes.[16]

His narration sets up cues for the 'genre' of this encounter: 'nurse would give me the cue to begin', 'I'll walk in front of a panel': the genre referenced in the way Walloch describes the medical encounter is the audition scene. This conventionalized scene usually sees the performer waiting nervously in the wings, waiting to be pushed on by a secondary character (here the nurse), and then having to perform to a darkened auditorium, in which people sit who will decide on one's fortune. Walloch mixes these two different biographical genres, the medical story and the audition gag, freely and fluently. The comical highpoint of the scene arrives: Walloch describes himself sitting alone, naked, in a small room, waiting for his entry, and he worries 'please, don't let it happen'. Audience expectation of agency and violence, power and sexual connotation are confounded when Walloch continues: 'I look down – and sure enough, I would have the biggest erection I've ever had in my my entire life.' Over the laughing audience, Walloch deadpans: 'Mr. Walloch, you can come in now'.

This short performance piece uses a staple of disability culture: the skit, the one-person autobiographical sketch of the encounter with the medical system, often performed with a twist (here the erotic charge), or with an unfamiliar generic framing.[17] In Walloch's rendition, the sketch re-writes the encounter with the medical, diagnostic gaze by turning it into a sexualized, fantasized erotic stage. Queer aesthetic and disability culture meet as the supposedly demeaning and dehumanizing encounter – where disabled people feel powerless and objects of the gaze – is turned on its head. Walloch breaks various subject positions. First, the position of 'object' of a stare is conventionally occupied by women (hysterics, prostitutes, porn models, advertising models, etc.). Here, a man occupies this role

– a gay man. The role isn't freely chosen – Walloch's delivery communicates an ambivalence,[18] but it is quite clear that the paradigmatic power-relation of cited object and citing doctor are still firmly in place. But Walloch thematizes the other dynamic that accrues to the viewed/seer position: the erotic dimension, the link between eroticism and (medical) power. The diagnostic gaze is subverted, its 'disinterested' and distanced stance is questioned, when an erotic exchange is project(able) onto the scene.

A historical cultural icon of this connection between the sexual and the medical can be found in the famous painting by André Brouillet (1887), *Une Leçon Clinique à la Salpêtrière*.[19] It shows Jean Martin Charcot at one of his famous lectures on hysteria, staging a fit for his medical audience (one of his methods to start a hysteric attack was to press very hard, with his full fist, into the ovarian region of these women, see Bronfen, 1998). In the image, Charcot is the focus of the gaze of his disciples, with an unconscious woman in his arms, barely held upright by him. The woman's clothing is disturbed, and her bare shoulders and general disarray stand in contrast to the tiered, regimented order of the onlookers.

The gender dynamics of these images of displayed female patients have been discussed widely.[20] Within the image, a definite staging is taking place: the chairs are indeed arranged into an amphitheater, and behind the professor two stage-hands are waiting to take the woman away as soon as the act is finished. The

Figure 4 André Brouillet (1887), *Une Leçon Clinique à la Salpêtrière*, showing Charcot demonstrating on Blanche Wittmann (Reproduced by courtesy of the National Library of Medicine)

theater space is clearly delineated by a swathe of light that cuts diagonally through the image from center front to a big window in the background, and it is in this swathe that the doctor stands and holds forth. Footlights are provided by the white pinafores of the persons next to Charcot on both sides, as well as the white bosom of the unconscious woman. The iconography marks out his lit face with its deep eyesockets, more clearly lit than the poor woman's hanging head.

In Walloch's performance, he is the stage manager, the person in charge. His careful timing manipulates his audiences's laughter. As a stand-up comedian, Walloch doesn't tend to use scenery, but his body, his gestures, his face become the focus of transformation and action. He is in the light, and the medical personnel become the shadow figures, only called forth at his will, on his timing.

The performance of the medical stage might disavow the effect that encounters have on people as sexual agents, but the repressed returns: a contemporary audience can hardly see past the performance of gender and agency in the Brouillet image – in particular given that contemporary spectators are well versed in law suits and accusations of sexual misconduct against doctors.

Walloch feels the erotic dynamic of the patient–doctor encounter, and presents himself as aroused in this childhood fantasy. The performance unmasks the supposedly clinical encounter and writes erotics and fantasy back into it, muddying its waters. The stage and its seedy associations of casting couch and den of sin intersect with the space of adolescent fantasy and occupation with one's physicality in the realm of medicine. This multiplicity of association undermines the certainties of the medical system, and confounds audience's expectations of 'bodily truths'. Walloch references performance and the ability of everyday situations to re-write scripts, to change the scenario in minute ways, re-reading power and agency: no 'real' emerges as he lets us see his earlier self fantasizing about his position. Even bodily truth is confounded: the only cue that Walloch describes in this sketch is his erection, the outer sign of his fantasy life, as an audience, we do not hear details about the physical difference of disability.

Freak sex, the carnival and the grotesque

In Mat Fraser's show, sexuality is also used to comment on the voyeurism, eroticism, and transgression. Fraser in his Berent persona indulges in sexual innuendo ('being able to do what all men do'), and horseplay (admonishing the ladies in the audience that he doesn't have 'those kinds of pictures' of himself). The function of these asides, pretty innocuous in Fraser's Berent act, become clearer when Mat Fraser's contemporary alter ego enters the stage. We meet Tam Shrafer as he is hyping himself up for an audition – talking a mile a minute, all psyched up and ready to go where his agent, on his mobile, tells him to go. Part of the nervous talk at the beginning of the scene moves from considerations of contemporary reactions to disabled people on stage to the realm of sexuality. The monologue rehearses the relative impotence of liberal theater politics in the face of deep-held stereotypes.

It's a funny old time I suppose, 20 years ago I wouldn't even be standing here, a disabled actor in a professional audition scenario; 30 years ago most directors didn't know that there were any disabled actors. There probably weren't that many, No role models . . . 20 years from now, maybe disabled actors will be a normal part of productions. At the moment we must be in the transition stage, well, it often feels transitional; awkward, ill fitting, painful sometimes, with most people too, what, scared? Unimaginative? Complacent? To cast us. And anyone who does have a real vision of drama, that includes us lot, hailed as either a visionary, a revolutionary genius, exciting and confrontational, or, a manipulative sensationalist, cruelly exploiting the freakish value of actual disabled people on stage, inappropriately cheapening the production ya ya ya ya – You know what? People are always gonna say shit like that, whether it's true or not, and isn't a conversation about all that better than not having one? Didn't narrow minded reviewers squawk, balk, and then finally accept female, black, outwardly gay actors before us? Is this a freak I see before me? – No, if you look again you'll see it's an actor! . . . Oh Shut Up Tam! . . . Sorry about that, I'm just trying to give myself strength with a pep talk before I go in to the audition.

(Fraser, 2001)

This part of Tam's monologue rehearses familiar arguments about liberal art politics, and the necessary changes in the expectation of audiences in order to make disabled actors part of the mainstream. The image becomes more complicated, though, when liberal politics intersect with internalized images of physical difference, and embedded attitudes towards freakishness. In the continuation of his monologue, Tam merges his acknowledgement of the power of the extraordinary body to overwhelm the narrative scenario, highjack the attention, by placing himself firmly in the tradition of the freak out to shock, to parade taboo subjects:

Thing is, when I'm watching myself on film, I think 'Fuck, those arms' . . . Although mine are familiar, they're even alien to ME when put into their rarest context, i.e., the performance mode. Of course I can make the necessary leap of faith to find my own arms and hands appropriate in a scenario that traditionally might find them alien, say in a love scene, I mean hell, I've never been that short of a shag in real life; maybe it's the way I was brought up, but I've never found it a problem to get a partner. OK sometimes I'm being freak fucked, but no more than the number of times I've been guilty of fancying a girl because of certain, um, physical attributes, I'm just the thick end of the same wedge. 'Big tits? Wahay! petite size 8? phwoar! Big fullsome bottom? mmmm!! Hairy armpits? nnngggg. Short arms? OOooh!!' . . . My hands may not reach all the way round someone, but they can be tender, loving, wanton even. It's not how far you can reach, but the way you do the reaching. (Damn, that sounds like an excuse for a small cock.)

(Fraser, 2001)

Openness about sexuality and sexual issues has always been a trademark of Mat Fraser's public persona in Britain (Kuppers, 2002). In this show, the foregrounding of sexuality takes on interesting aspects in relation to disability visibility. By breaking the ultimate taboo (and inviting the resultant titillation) around disability and sexuality, Fraser extends a structural similarity: like sex, disabled bodies are disavowed, shut away from the mainstream, locked into bedrooms.[21] Fraser's freak status results as much from his 'outrageous' behavior, his song-lyrics and his patter as from his physicality: he refuses to leave things in the bedroom, or the privacy of non-public environments. With this, Fraser doesn't embrace disability politics from the polite, liberal, rational, civil rights end, but utilizes freak tactics, disruption, destabilization and irrationality as his weapons to punch through assorted stereotypes and to establish his presence.

This performance strategy draws upon the disruptive potential of two figures with currency in representational theory: the carnivalesque reveller and the grotesque. Each of these figures holds different positions in relation to the status quo, and to spectatorial address. Both figures have historical power to destabilize the image of the Other to the dominant, and both are problematized by the history of disability performance, with its emphasis on visuality and the stare at the extraordinary body – the 'sock in the eye', 'the gaze intensified, framing [the] body as icon of deviance' (Garland Thomson, 1997: 26).[22]

The carnivalesque body has been theorized by the Russian theorist Bakhtin, who investigated the body at the center of carnival. Bakhtin's use of the term 'carnival' here is not a metaphor, but is grounded in historical practices, ritual social moments in European history where social ties are inverted and the body becomes the stage for disruptive practices. In his analysis of the French writer Rabelais' work, Bakhtin describes the crowd in the carnival:

> The festive organization of the crowd must be first of all concrete and sensual. Even the pressing throng, the physical contact of the bodies, acquires a certain meaning. The individual feels indisoluably part of the collectivity, a member of the people's mass body. In this whole the body ceases to a certain extent to be itself: it is possible, so to say, to exchange bodies, to be renewed (through the change of costume and mask). At the same time the people become aware of their sensual, material bodily unity and community.

> (1968: 255)

Unity and community are the concepts invoked to describe the field of the carnival. Within Fraser's performance, visibility, stage/audience distinctions, conceptual distinctions between self and other are the operating principles. His in-your-face politics of freak sex, with his repeated references to his dick, and to sexual acts, shore up the differences between the non-disabled crowd and the angry, disabled performer heightening the performance of difference to its extreme. Bakhtin's description of the physical locus of carnival presents a major difference: for Bakhtin, the carnival relies on the pressing of flesh on flesh – 'first of all concrete and sensual'. This carnival is not one where bodies are translated into images which are then able to carry the weight of social distinctions, contradictions and transgressions. Instead, bodies are physically engaged in this (temporary) re-writing of norms and roles – 'through the change of costume and mask'.[23]

The celebration of sensuality, in which the body becomes the center for group identification, is only achievable when no theater takes place. Theater relies on recognized boundaries between audience and stage, even if these boundaries are subverted and transgressed. The carnival does not know a spectator.[24] The experience is pre-modern, since it describes a society where the mechanisms of visual othering can be suspended. When the disabled, 'extraordinary', or other body is the freak, it cannot at the same time be a focus for communality. The history of the sideshow performance does not stress commonality between spectator and object: the shows are founded on the presentation of difference (even though, as we have seen above, the psychic effects of the freak spectacle have destabilizing effects, assaulting the boundaries of firm knowledge about self, but only to strengthen them again in a cathartic effect). The historical move from the sideshow to the medical theater also doesn't imply a loss of hierarchy and communal alignment: even more than in the circus crowd, the medical spectacle relies on distance (the scientific gaze) and particularization (the search for symptomology). In both regimes of visuality, difference is the core factor.

> As a cultural representation in the late nineteenth century, the freak belongs to the increasingly codified world of spectacle . . . More than merely an image or collection of images, the spectacle is a way of looking.
>
> (Russo, 1994: 79)

The grotesque image is different from the carnivalesque group-body: it is also an historic image category, but with a different relation to otherness and selfhood. It hasn't the same performative, living quality as the communal carnivalesque, neither does it describe a mode of living as an embodied being, but, like the carnival, it stands potentially in an interesting relationship to visuality and epistemological certainties.[25] The word 'grotesque' stems from the Latin of Rome's 'grottos' – hidden places, caves, places where the aesthetic eye can rest from order, symmetry, and can lose itself in the folds and baroque display of detail and ornamentation that characterizes the grotesque style.

The grotesque has been seen as a political tool that is implicated in that which it attacks:

> The meaning of the grotesque is constituted by the norm which it contradicts: the order it destroys, the values it upsets, the authority and morality it derides, the religion it ridicules, the harmony it breaks up, the heaven it brings down to earth, the position of classes, races, and sexes it reverses, the beauty and goodness it questions. The word 'grotesque' makes sense only if one knows what the 'norm' represents – in art and in life.
>
> (Kuryluk, 1987: 11)

Here, the grotesque is an oppositional image, an image that acknowledges its secondariness to the dominant, but that nevertheless holds the power to remind us that the status quo isn't all there is. Caught in this image, Fraser's performance is doomed to always be the 'other' to non-disabled performance, always be the degenerate, belated curlicule, ornament, baroque excess to normality.

But in other definitions of the term, the power of the grotesque can be greater than just binary 'otherness'. This power becomes dangerous, contagious, when it is not 'bracketed', that is, set in clear opposition. Geoffrey Galt Harpham's definition of the grotesque gives more attention to the non-visible, not clearly defined presence – his grotesque is more upsetting: it

> stands at the margin of consciousness between the known and the unknown, the perceived and the unperceived, calling into question the adequacy of the ways of organizing the world, of dividing the continuum of experience into knowable parts.

> (1982: 30)

The problem with this grotesque persona who breaks through representational categories is that this presence is strongest when it is not visible, but only hinted at, a figment of the imagination casting about for its threatening other. As Harpham shows, the grotesque is in the margin of paintings, frescos, manuscript, and its detail and ubiquity threaten the classical centrality of the center image – not by opposing it, but by inserting an oscillation, a moment between frame and center. The grotesque only threatens the center, it never ascends to being the main subject. As soon as the grotesque becomes clearly visible, it loses its power and becomes the mere other, the monster or freak. The freak, in opposition to the grotesque, represents a realm in which the contradictions of conflicting cultural norms are played out – the bodily reminder of that which society expels. As such, the freak holds a position of fascination and power, but not of structural disruption. Institutionally and aesthetically, all these histories of category confusion and specular/spatial location of difference come to bear on the performance of disability, making 'newness' and the attempt to communicate problematic.

Fraser's physical presence, his bodily difference, made dizzyingly present through his references to sexuality as the taboo desire, and with his ambiguous position as director/actor, leader and led, combine to destabilize the image of disability as physical other or weak victim. The non-disabled world has to take note of this wish to act, to be in potentiality, to not be known a priori. Fraser's performance presents a way of 'being in' disability, knowing Berent's history and his social framework, which doesn't fit into traditional binaries, and threatens to disrupt the dominant organizing knowledge of freaks and normals. In Fraser's show, the disabled body is a figure on the limits of the grotesque and the freak. It opens up the instability of the representational system – instead of joining the discourse of the human and the animal, the child and the adult, the foreign and the familiar, this grotesque points towards an unmapped, uncharted terrain. But the power has a price: this performer has no clear contours – we cannot really see him.

Fraser's performance tactics echo the strategies of theater practitioners who use excess and destabilization in order to move beyond the difference-denying polite frameworks of asinine sameness. One example of this performance of excess is porn artist Annie Sprinkle, who used a speculum on stage, inviting her audience to come up close and look at the female body. She questions the politics of the punter's gaze while exploiting it to create a network of desire towards the stage. Sprinkle turns the visual vanishing point of the female body and its workings as a self, rather than an object, into a subject position (Schneider, 1997: 65). She cheerfully winks at the people coming up to shine a light at the speculum inserted in her vagina. Can Fraser achieve a re-vision of disability, exposing the sensationalist gaze of the non-disabled audience by breaking taboos and playing with sexual connotation? He would need to refashion a vision machine that allows for a subject position for the disabled person. This necessitates breaking the 'naturalness' of the blind spot, that position that invisibilizes 'normate' bodies as originators of a specific gaze, and that keeps disabled people in their position of Otherness, keeps them from aspiring to agency. His alter ego, Tam Shrafer, acknowledges later in 'Sealboy': 'I read this book once that said the mainstream will only ever see disabled people performing in the same way that they view a performing seal' (Fraser, 2001). And while he continues to hold forth on the politics of the stage, and on non-disabled audience's inability to see 'acting' rather than spectacle, he rolls a joint with his short hands, perfectly timed to reach his lips the moment his monologue ends. What did the audience watch? The Berent-esque spectacle of rolling a joint, akin to Sealboy's shaving or wood sawing, marvelling at the facility of these 'little handsies'? Or did they listen to Fraser's critique, an actor who during his discourse engages in the nearly invisible act of getting ready to smoke: a conventionalized sign of theater, often denoting contemplation and meditation?

Conclusion

Disability theater exposes histories of 'looking at the disabled'. Fraser's citation of the freak show spectacle provides reasons for the failure of the disabled body to be seen as engaged in a social performance – the discourse of the freak stage was one where the performer was seen not as performing, but as a 'seal' – a non-human other, not as an act, but as a being *only* within the boundaries of difference. In that position, communication becomes problematic: if the act of communicating becomes the point of wonder, any other message of the communication gets lost. The image of the freak is too stable, too stabilized in social discourse, to enter easily into 'theater'. As an image, it is static: it provides a mirror for a changing society, having various values thrust on it, but it isn't easily the generator of narrative energy on its own terms. Thus, Sealo and Fraser occupy the same position, project the same image, engender the same audience reaction of wonder and frisson. But at the same time, life is asserting itself, undermining the stabilities. Fraser is addressing his audience from a theater stage, a different location than the heavily 'freak' framed stage of the sideshow. Walloch similarly takes agency through an erotics of play: he undermines the active/passive scenario of the medical theater and inserts his own fantasies into a space that threatens to reduce him to an unfeeling, de-individualized body.

In 'Sealboy', Fraser's physical presence and his 'otherness' threaten to undermine his discourse, a fact he is aware of and plays with – often through explicit reference to the carnivalesque, grotesque, disruptive bodily realms of sexuality – but how far the play can be taken depends on the audience's reaction to his difference, on their reading of his person as different on a sliding scale of humanity, or as radically different 'freak'. Walloch also allows for a sliding engagement with his self: as a stand-up comedian, he is both vulnerable and powerful, he opens himself to the gaze, and plays with its potential. By referencing the medical theater, he points to a place of abjection, of suffering for many people 'paraded for their differences', but his banter shows how the different engagement of the stand-up comedy and its use of sexual matter can reclaim this field.

The histories of disability performance are not disavowed in these performances: they become the material that fuel contemporary engagements with audience addresses, stares and gazes. The freakshow and the medical theater are important moments in the genealogy of disability work, and the notion of the freak, the passive patient and the grotesque are aspects of disability presentation that color any engagement with disability on a stage. In the following two chapters, these disability-specific histories of presentation meet two theater histories and their weight on contemporary stage work by and with disabled people: Brechtian alienation strategies and Artaud's Theater of Cruelty.

Chapter 3

Deconstructing images

Performing disability

The disabled performer is both marginalized and invisible – relegated to border-lands, far outside the central area of cultural activity, by the discourses of medicine. At the same time, people with physical impairments are also hypervisible, instantly defined by their physicality. The physically impaired performer has therefore to negotiate two areas of cultural meaning: invisibility as an active member in the public sphere, and hypervisibility and instant categorization as passive consumer and victim in much of the popular imagination.

Disabled performers have successfully and visibly taken up the medium of performance to expand the possibilities of images, spaces and positions for their bodies. In their work with bodies in public spheres, they attempt to break through stereotypes of passive disability. In the following pages, I discuss the relationship between disability and performance through the lens of performativity, that is, with an attention to the activities of re-inscriptions and interventions that maintain the cultural and material net of bodies and meaning. I am questioning the use of the 'natural' in relation to bodies, and the 'natural' connotations, the conventionalized stereotypes, that accrue to disability. I analyze performances by professional performance groups or artists: *Bilderwerfer* (Imagethrowers) in Austria, Bill Shannon's street-theater work in Russia and the US, and a filmdance made by the British dance company CandoCo, *Outside In* (chor. Victoria Marks, dir. Margaret Williams, 1995).[1] All of these performance instances occur outside the theater, off-stage, and present the disabled performer in the 'public sphere' of street-theater and TV respectively. *Bilderwerfer*'s performance *Einblicke* (Insights) took place in a shopping arcade in Vienna. Shannon's performance actions occurred on staircases and pavements. CandoCo's short film has reached wide audiences through its presentation on the BBC TV channels, and was instrumental in creating the image of CandoCo as one of Britain's most visible disability performance phenomena. This image is not necessarily embraced by the company itself – they seem to want to break away from the 'disability ghetto', normalizing their intervention into British dance (Benjamin, 1995). But our cultural practices do not easily allow for these break aways: the issue of disability and its cultural meanings remain strong in many reviews of CandoCo's performances. When disabled people perform, they are often not primarily seen as performers, but as disabled people. The disabled body is *naturally* about disability. The re-framings of this disabled body through the lenses of filmdance and performance analyzed in this chapter point to the *un-natural* body in discourse, and allow a different perspective on the active embodied person to emerge. With this, the chapter probes the relationship between disability performance and the theatrical tradition deriving from Bertolt Brecht, and his work in political theater. In Brecht's theater, alienation techniques are used in order to allow structures to become visible, to undermine the 'common sense', the 'natural', or 'what everybody knows'. Instead of presenting certainties on stage, the audience is challenged, questioned, seduced into engaging in a play of difference. But what 'everybody knows' about disability is institutionalized, sedimented, and controlled by a powerful social discourse. Before I continue to unpack disability performance, I want to investigate further some of these issues of disability as institution.

Fighting on

Identity politics debates surrounding race, gender and class have had to face the problems of the *natural*, this common-sense logic that fixes people in their relative positions and into clear narratives. As a feminist disabled performance artist and theorist, my own journey with critical theory demanded finding entry points for *de-naturalizations* of disability. Just as contemporary queer and feminist theories query the binary of male and female, the construction of disability as the other to normality needs to be investigated. Feminism has only relatively recently started to acknowledge disability as an important area of difference within its ranks. Previously conceived as an anti-issue – with women seen as the caring losers burdened with more work if disabled people were to get out of institutions – more and more women realize now that these easy conflations and assumptions are inadequate and stifling.

> It is not sufficient just to reconceive disabled people as active agents in their own right, as though all difficulties could be resolved by the move of simply re-evaluating the status of disability. So long as 'disabled' is seen as just another fixed identity category, an identity that we might carry with us into all situations, then the boundaries which separate us, one from another, are left undisturbed. Where postmodernism can come to the aid of a feminism attempting to end its own past indifference is in two ways: first in deconstructing all and every identity, and second in laying bare the ways in which the body is constructed and maintained as disabled.
>
> (Shildrick and Price, 1996: 96)

In relation to women caregivers, we need to deconstruct notions of women as tied to the home, and as the 'natural' nurturers, as well as disabled people as unable to contribute to a household and to another person's psychic wellbeing in other capacities than as carereceivers. When we have loosened these ties of 'natural' connotations, we can move on to discuss how the public images of disability and femininity continue to perpetuate the discourses, and how art (and other) practices can intervene and challenge the 'natural'.

With references to Judith Butler's deconstruction of the body as 'raw matter' (1993), and Foucault's disciplinary practices, Shildrick and Price are two feminists who claim the space between issue-based feminist politics and academic theories of deconstruction. The work emerging from this thinking points to the discursive nature of disability – rather than being a medical or a social construct, the category of disability enters the realm of appellation. Political theorist Gramsci conceived of the connection between self and institutions as a 'hailing': a policeman shouts 'hey, you', in the street, and the subject turns around, feels addressed, understands herself to be named, which means that she is actively involved in the construction of a reality where a policeman has the power to address a subject. Conceiving of disability as appellation means that a subject is hailed into the positon of disabled. Public narratives and images, social institutions and psychic structures that emerge out of our embodied being, together with bodily practices and ways of learning of how to be a 'normal' body in our social world, work to create images of disability that go deeper than a temporary 'social construction'. A disabled subject is hailed as disabled, she understands herself to be addressed by the term, and what it stands for. The status of disability demarcates a way of life, a social position and a way of being that isn't easily abandoned, given the ideological and institutional anchoring of the concept in everyday life. The way ahead is clear:

> It is – to brazenly paraphrase Judith Butler writing on heterosexuality and homosexuality – as though disability 'secures its self-identity and shores up its ontological boundaries by protecting itself from what it sees as the continual predatory enchroachments of its contaminated other', ability. . . . The task of postmodern feminists is to lay bare and contest the discursive construction of all seemingly stable categories.
>
> (Shildrick and Price, 1996: 111, quoting Butler, 1991: 2)

So how can we give up these stable categories without denying the existence of current realities of oppression, division, subjugation and exclusion? What do these explosions of stable positions of difference, of clear distinctions between disabled and non-disabled with their attendant social consequences, mean for disabled performers? For the disabled person, the project of expanding and delimiting the stereotypes of disability through entering the 'other' of various abilities, is problematic. I see the problem here in the psychological stereotype of disability. The psychological stereotype says that disabled people want to be 'normal'. The stereotype denies disability culture as a positive experience. Given this assumption, to slide towards the other (from disabled to able) is always already too easy to conflate with the desire to be other-than-disabled. Too easily, the performance of difference becomes caught in the binary described by Shildrick and Price: disabled people as tragic cripples/disabled people as heros ready to take on the world and become 'honorary able-bodied'. Respect for difference is hard to come by. Self, subjectivity, privacy and a position somewhere in between these extremes are easily denied to disabled people. Mary Duffy is a highly visible disabled performance artist, using her own body as model for her work. She states her desire for a different representation, one that escapes from the 'Ties That Bind':

> I have been surrounded all my life by images of a culture which values highly physical beauty and wholeness, a culture which denies difference. My identity as a woman with a disability is one that is strong, sensual, sexual, fluid, flexible and political.
>
> (Duffy, 1989: 6–7)

This statement frames Duffy's performances as an armless Venus of Milo not as meditations on loss or tragedy, but as attempts to install a positivity to her different body. Born without arms, her body fulfils Western beauty criteria by aligning itself with Greek statues of women without arms – marble statues whose arms are lost. By using the idiom of the Greek ideal body, Duffy both points to the violence the Western gaze has perpetuated on women – using incomplete bodies to signify ultimate female beauty – and the ableist aesthetic that makes that reading possible, an aesthetic that sees 'without arms' as broken, incomplete and passive. Her way out of the conundrum is the presence of her living body, a body clearly complete on its own terms. Out of layers of negativity and critique emerges a position of challenge, a living presence that breathes fluidity and change into encrusted aesthetic frames.

In the following pages I analyze how disabled performers challenge narratives of disability, and how the use of theatrical intervention in the everyday and in the mundane medium of TV can play along these boundaries of representation. But first, it is necessary to re-visit one of the most visible critical events in recent years, an event which continues to frame performances by people perceived to be 'trapped' in culturally undesirable positions of otherness: the victim art debate.

Disability and choice

> In theater, one chooses what one will be. The cast members of *Still/Here* – the sick people whom Jones has signed up – have no choice other than to be sick.
>
> (Croce, 1994/5: 54)

With these words, Arlene Croce famously refused to review Bill T. Jones' dance show *Still/Here*, which featured as part of the stage scene videos of dying people talking about their experience. She did not want to see 'victim art', and thus, she refused to go and visit the show. In the same controversial non-review in *The New Yorker*, Croce grouped under the heading 'Victim art' 'dancers with physical deformities who appear nightly in roles requiring beauty of line'. The core of Croce's argument against 'putting these people on stage' rests with 'choice'. Our culture denies choice, body control and self-determination to disabled people (as well as dying people, people of size, PWA). Croce merely parrots this demeaning, conventionalized stereotype in her refusal. This cultural situation relies on a specific understanding of 'the body', an understanding challenged by contemporary theories of representation.

The quote by Croce homes in on an underlying cultural assumption: people who are defined by their bodies are trapped by them. Bodies are made readable to allow cues to the 'inner state'. This vision of a direct relationship between visible freakishness and inner qualities is expressed in a number of historical practices. Phrenology, skull analysis, was a nineteenth-century practice that attempted to map character and intelligence onto specific regions of the skull, and thus create a chart of valorized types, with an 'ideal' white European skull at the top of the hierarchy, and features such as large noses or thicker lips as clues to less brain development. To read the scale of humanity on their skulls, ordering mankind culturally and politically through exterior factors, was the aim of this 'science' born at the beginning of modernity and its quest for order in a more and more disorderly world. Other attempts to read interiority through exteriority, and to categorize people, included anthropological studies that tried to read (non-white) women's sexual drive by measuring their vaginas (for a discussion of this relationship between science and gender ideology, see Gilman, 1985). In all of these attempts to structure the West's image of itself and of its others, the need to read the inner depth through the outer surface was paramount. Popular culture in the twentieth century has maintained this desire 'to know', as contemporary case studies can show.

David D. Yuan (1996) discusses Michael Jackson as a freak who attempts to stay in control by denying the scrutinizing gaze. Jackson's control rests on mystery and ambiguity. Discourses surrounding race, freakishness, difference, sexuality and surveillance come together when Jackson's body is 'scientifically' measured and recorded by the police department in order to establish evidence regarding the allegation of child molestation. Michael Jackson fought successfully against having his penis measured – a critical moment in race relations. In our cultural history, the 'secure' knowledge of another person's physical otherness was enough evidence for (in the case of black people) condemning them, categorizing them, pointing to their heightened and frightening sexuality. Yuan chronicles how Jackson's journey as public persona can be seen as 'the struggle to control his image, avoid static enfreakment, and maintain his aura of mystery' (p. 381). Jackson isn't white (which would valorize the power-differential between black and white), and he isn't black (and therefore easily kept in the 'black box'). His performance is potentially dynamic and plastic:

> If the static curiosity is that which has been fixed, frozen, stuffed, or pickled, the 'plastic freak' by contrast is free to move and moves to remain free. The plastic freak seeks to elude fixity and definition: his 'true' identity remains hidden as he weaves images and stories around himself to arouse curiosity.
>
> (Yuan, 1996: 371)

Jackson's strategies in many of his most successful musicvideos underline this desire towards non-fixed difference: in the videos, his persona mutates into animals and sleek cars, his most famous 'moves' in his dance routines focuses on various isolations of limb movement, which challenges conventional notions of human movement, and he utilizes 'border-technologies' such as prosthetic locomotion devices in his stage shows. Through a plethora of difference devised, Jackson keeps his mystery afloat. Jackson's case points to a dilemma at the heart of 'being different' and 'performing difference'. Minority members have to negotiate cultural representations which threaten to fix them. The mobility and choice open to the center is not open to the center's 'others'. Michael Jackson performs white-face, but historically much more common was the practice of black-face: white people acting black. Their whiteness is invisible, normative, mobile, 'able'. The 'other' is held in place by an overwhelming, defining physicality.

These issues apply as forcefully, if differently, to disabled people. Similar to black-face actors, non-disabled people can prove the 'mastery' of their craft by 'acting disabled', whereas disabled actors are often denied work opportunities. One reason for this is the continuing marginality of disability to mainstream narratives. But another, equally powerful reason is anchored in our understanding of acting and performing: as Croce showed, the ability to choose and play a role is valued. And thus, while male, white and heterosexual become invisible, attributes such as old age, disability, non-white race are too visible to allow full mobility. Dustin Hoffman's publicized and celebrated stunt as a disabled person in *Rain Man* (dir. M. Johnson, 1988) is hailed as a *tour de force*. In his role, the non-disabled Hoffman is still visible – his presence is the palimpsest that allows the audience to engage in the movements of make-believe. The 'presence' of autism is held at arm's distance. To 'be' autistic would mean not to be able to be 'a performer'. This dynamic, playing disability because one can, and shining through its excellent execution, has become a familiar device in the annual quest for Hollywood Oscars: from *Forrest Gump* to *A Beautiful Mind*, to play disability is an excellent way to be recognized as a consummate actor.

The performance of disability relies on the understanding that disability is transparent, uni-vocal, easy to see, and wholly reproducible in theater. Disability functions as a master sign in our culture by dominating other discourses of identity. Its connotations cannot be escaped – to be disabled thus means to be profoundly excluded from self-representation. It means that new strategies need to be found to perform one's own image. This emphasis on the 'natural' disabled body puts the disabled performer in a position similar to, but not the same as, lesbian performers/theorists eager to find expression for their position of difference from a heterosexual mainstream. Theorists such as Sue-Ellen Case (1996) or Jill Dolan (1993) have explored mechanisms that move away from the inescapable hetero-sexual woman-image, mapped on the female body. They struggled with a situation in which particularly the role of the lesbian 'femme' again and again means re-absorption into non-self-defined images. These confinements lead to an effort to break out of cultural stereotypes.

Performance groups such as Split Britches have found ways of working with this blind spot called lesbian desire (Case, 1996). Using masquerade and role-play, their strategies of dislocating familiar stereotypes have been adopted by women of color, lesbian women and other peoples in position of cultural oppression. In order to destabilize conventional readings, they piled on the images, multiplied the narratives, documented, sang and enacted many herstories. The strategy dislocates any subject presented on the stage. The performance strategy echoes Brechtian techniques that undermined the certainties of naturalist theater, where the spectator's sense of self, sense of location in the world, self-identity and knowledge could be seen to be shored up by the stage spectacle.

> Brechtian theory posits a theater of knowledge, but without realism's focus on the private secret, the explosion and recontainment of difference, or the satisfaction of narrative closure.
>
> (Diamond, 1997: 44)

The Brechtian *Verfremdungseffect* or alienation effect, requires the audience to rethink its own stereotypes and assumptions: 'a representation that alienates is one which allows us to recognize its subject, but at the same time makes it seem unfamiliar' (Brecht, 1984: 192). No image holds, and what becomes visible instead is the constructed nature of all images.

When one image meets the edges of the next one, both become unstable. Judith Butler describes this destabilizing moment for gender politics: lesbian is to straight 'not as copy is to original, but, rather, as copy is to copy' (Butler, 1990: 31).[2] The copy (with no reference to the 'real') upsets the universality of the 'real'. Irony is the mechanism by which the tools of representation are turned against representation in a conflicting, problematic but nevertheless empowering relationship lying between the complicit and the confrontational.

Lesbian performers are faced with cultural stereotypes that see their desire as 'deviant' from the heterosexual norm. They counter by showing fulfilled, real, complex, interesting, annoying, unsuccessful and successful pleasurable lesbian relationships on stage – within the multitude of stories, the easy binary of lesbian as the Other can loose its hold.

The main cultural discourse which governs the disabled image is frustration, tragedy, tears and struggle. I want to suggest that the reason why traditional feminist theater approaches to performance do not really function for the disabled performer is because her image is already loaded with the desire to be other, projected onto her by the audience. If she whizzes around on stage, she becomes open to a reading where she momentarily 'overcomes' the wheelchair. This narrative of 'desiring to be away' overshadows any representation performers might put forward on the stage. Therefore, an enumeration of different images would not be read as a succession of possibilities, of structurally similar positions of identity, but as stages in a flight away from a caught body dreaming about difference. For the disabled performer, the hold of the 'bodily' as a supposedly transparent, natural entity needs to be challenged, and reconfigured. In the mainstream, the experience of disability is not seen as broken, negotiated, performed in itself. It is this second, more elaborate concept of disability as complexity that David Hevey (1992) tries to bring to the fore in his political photography with disabled people, and that guides many disabled artists' attempts to destabilize their cultural image. These performed identities are not about free choice,[3] but about a destabilization of certainty that goes beyond the social positioning of disability and that embraces certainties about the matter of bodily knowledge, as well.

These issues of 'performing' versus 'being' are central to the public evaluation of disabled performers. The tensions surrounding their performances mirror the different discourses surrounding the body in culture. On the one side, disabled performance is seen as therapeutic – the relationship between body and performance is unproblematic, performance is an 'opportunity' for disabled people to discover themselves as 'whole' and 'able'. The focus is inwards: aimed at the disabled person doing the performing, not the wider community. The performance is 'authentic': it connects to the 'true being' of the performer. On the other side, disabled performance can be seen *as* performance: challenging dominant notions about 'suitable bodies', challenging ideas about the hierarchy between (led) disabled people and (leading) non-disabled people. Here, disabled performance is seen as a political intervention, aimed at the whole community. A split can be created between performer and performance, body and presentation: the 'truth' of the bodily expression is manipulated, cited and rewritten by the performer. This does not imply a level of agency that manages to actively *rewrite* the fabric of bodies, but an agency that acts out of the pain that the alignments of language, knowledges, physicality and matter continue to create. The show is an act. As Carrie Sandahl writes about her performance and research work as a disability activist, dealing with the metaphors of disability: 'Instead of compliantly inhabiting metaphors, my work attempts to expose their constructedness, impairing their naturalizing power' (1999: 16). It is time to investigate the cultural narratives, opportunities and stagings of this act.

Performance and disability

One of very few sustained discourse analyses of disability and dance is provided by Ann Cooper Albright (1997). She compares images of 'normalized' disability in dance, subjugated to the discourses of ballet, where the disabled body is 'fitted into' the balletic discourse, with the emergence and acceptance of the grotesque body in contact improvization.

Contact improvization (CI) emerged in the 1970s and has always been used in a variety of settings, and by different people (including disabled people; see Bruce Curtis and Alan Ptashek (1988), other reports in the magazine *Contact Quarterly*, and the group Touchdown). Specific body shape and sensory access have been less important than the mechanics of the living body, with the universality of touch and gravity as the prime movement impetuses.

Awareness of touching the partner and following the 'point of contact' provides the impetus for movement, which adheres to no preset pattern and relies on a general vocabulary of falling and rolling varying from one individual to another. . . . No ideal physical type for contact improvization exists, nor is there a single physical prerequisite for skilled performance. Willingness to coordinate one's efforts with another person and to give up control over one's own movement could be called prerequisites to learning the form.

(Cohen Bull, 1997: 276/7)

In the performance context, which is different from the jam context, the successful CI dancer is in control of sequences of movement, and can externalize this bodily control in the display of acrobatic sequences in which dancers throw each other through the air apparently defying gravity through the intricate manipulation of it. This skill of control is in evidence in Steve Paxton's discussion of Emery Blackwell's dance. Paxton is credited with the 'invention' of contact, and is a strong voice in the field of contact improvization. Blackwell is a dancer and workshop leader resident in Eugene, Oregon, who performs and workshops around the world. He has cerebral palsy and uses a wheelchair. Paxton writes about Blackwell:

Emery has said that to get his arm raised above his head requires about 20 seconds of imaging to accomplish. . . . And we feel the quandary and see that he is pitched against his nervous system and wins, with effort and a kind of mechanism in his mind that we able-bodied have not had to learn. His facility with them allows us to feel them subtly in our own minds.

(Paxton, 1992: 14)

The good dancer is here measured according to the skill with which dancers manipulate their bodies and interact with other bodies. Albright values Blackwell's dancing as opening new ways of relationships between disabled and non-disabled people:

What intrigues me about Blackwell's dancing . . . is the fact that his movement at first evokes images of the grotesque and then leads our eyes through the spectacle of his body into the experience of his particular physicality.

(Albright, 1997: 89)

These statements reveal for me a search for authenticity, a way to 'share' the disabled dancer's embodied experience: Blackwell's dance communicates the physicality of his experience. As Paxton's review shows, this 'true' experience is one of labor and hard work. I feel uncomfortable with an aesthetic of disabled dance which values dance by wheelchair users because of the effort they have to put into it, how far they overcome their 'nervous systems' – although at the same time, I am seduced by the openings into other people's forms of embodiment. Fantasy, desire, seduction and play are the mechanisms at work in the unanchoring of certainty, where 'knowledge' shifts into a physical dialogue.

Albright's emphasis on CI's ability to show 'becoming' rather than fixed images is intriguing, but I think that there is more to explore in the question of how far Blackwell's evocation of the grotesque is a 'natural' presentation or a 'performed' representation of his body.

Tactical performance

In order to find entry points into subversive performance aesthetics, the meaning of the body itself needs to be challenged. This distinction between natural and performed can be seen at the heart of some performances, and can articulate a core critique of conventional images of disability and the 'natural' body. This destabilization occurs for me in the problematization of presence. Suddenly, the sharing with the performer's distress, effort, pain, exhilaration or ecstasy is no longer given. Strategies derived from alienation techniques and Brechtian epic theater insert barriers into identification and firm, unquestioned knowledge. These dynamics still give energy and power to the performance, but are no longer transparently readable. We do not know what it means to move in that body.

The concept of performativity can elaborate these concerns. Disability studies scholars Mitchell and Snyder (1997) critique contemporary theorists of the body for their non-attendance to the lived quality of the disabled body. In the discourses of many contemporary body theorists, all bodies are limited, disabled by language – a metaphorical understanding of disability which can be seen to diminish the actual lived oppression and experience of many groups. But philosophies of the body and the mind pay attention to the way that discourse aligns the 'inferior' to the bodily.[4] The problem lies with the discursive space of physicality. Disability functions as a concept of otherness – it is a name for widely different impairments, and widely different embodied experiences. Disability is structurally similar to gender and race – they are all defined by a mythologized physical difference. Mythology does not necessarily point to the absence of the difference 'in reality', but to both the over-forming of this difference into value-laden binaries, and the 'creation' of this difference as an important dividing line between differently valued groups. As a strategy for disabled performers, that binary which locates the disabled body in 'the body' – tragic, passive, inert – needs to be made visible and tangible before spaces can be found to explore what Derrida called 'incalculable choreographies' of non-binarized otherness (Derrida and McDonald, 1995). We need to revalue the body as a source of experience and difference, before we are able to move forward with identity politics.

Performativity points to the ambiguities, the multi-valent nature of discursive actions: we are inscribed in subjectivity and culture through power, and yet we also wield the power to transform these relations. Disabled performance can be seen as powerful, active incursions into the conceptual space of art: neither disabled nor non-disabled performers just 'are' – they position themselves on stage and in discourse. The very act of being positioned/positioning themselves is working against the view of the disabled person as merely passive, 'incarcerated by an overpowering body', 'tragic victim' of a pre-discursive physicality. Performativity balances between activity and passivity, locally and specifically: Judith Butler's analysis of different cultural works shows less clear-cut strategies than interventions which throw up questions, destabilize certainty. Butler is concerned with the political situation of embodied identities here and now. She sees the reiterative, performative force of power at work in the public grief monuments surrounding AIDS, which brings to the fore the unspeakable, the disavowed, the presence of the 'other' sexuality. She describes the function of the AIDS Quilt, the stitching together of memories, of names and traces of the dead:

> The NAMES Project Quilt is exemplary, ritualizing and repeating the name itself as a way of publicly avowing the limitless loss . . . insofar as (collective institutions for grieving) involve the publicization and dramatization of death, they call to be read as life-affirming rejoinders to the dire psychic consequences of a grieving process culturally thwarted and proscribed.
>
> (Butler, 1993: 236)

This reference to the quilt as a public act is not a static moment of holding on to the dead body, but is charged with the force of performativity. This version of performance answers back to Arlene Croce's aesthetic of dance which rests on choice. The choice made by AIDS activists in the face of a disavowal on a cultural level, of not having any spaces and cultural conventions for the grieving over homosexual love lost, is the choice to perform the grief publicly. Balances of visibility and invisibility change through these choices. But we have to be aware of the complexity of the bid for change. This intervention of AIDS visibility works by relegating the 'private' – traditionally feminine – space again to public unimportance, at the same time as 'quilting', a traditionally female activity in the US, is given center stage as a public, political intervention. The connotation of quilt-making, which is associated with the private, the homely, the feminine, preparation for heterosexual marriage, and often communal working, are in productive tension with individual voices and graves, public visibility and a sexuality without positive cultural images. All performative acts are balancing acts.

Bill T. Jones's dance show, *Still/Here*, about dying people dared to cross a similar line, to perform the private publicly. Croce slammed it, but the reverberations of the performance are still ongoing. Interventions and transgressions are tactical; they destabilize discursive fields only one at a time, but they can create communities and discourses that work on and effect change. For disabled performers, the task ahead is to destabilize in different ways. This task can be to challenge the 'anti-choice nature' of the disabled body.

Denied insights

Disabled performers can perform a dance of theory. The Austrian performance group *Bilderwerfer* understands training in philosophy and theory as a necessary part of their training regime. This approach creates intricate encounters of bodies and new spaces in their work.

In the performance '*Einblicke* (Insights)' 1995, a wheelchair user, Elisabeth Löffler, performs her movement sequence inside a shopping window in a busy Viennese arcade. She frames and re-frames her work, making it and herself unknown. In her performance, she is dressed in 'street-wise' clothes, made-up and ready to go clubbing – disrupting the image of the passive, tragic disabled victim. Her concentration is on her movement sequence: she is on the floor, next to her chair. She drags the chair over her body, aligns herself with it on the floor as she swings around it, puts it into new spaces. Her face is concentrated, unreadable – no emotional relationship to her wheelchair (and, later in the performance, her crutches) is discernible, merely an exploration of potential and space. The audience, some walking past, some sitting on chairs, having entered into a 'performance contract', watch her from behind the glass window. Her performance is private, unreadable, and public at the same time. An easy fit between action and thought is broken through various mechanisms: while she performs her private movement with her chair, personal narrative fragments are piped out to the audience with the help of loudspeakers. The fragments do not stand in any easily readable relationship to the physical actions, and the mediation of loudspeakers, shop window glass, and recording devices open up more spaces for unstable references. What is this woman's story? What is she thinking? These questions remain unanswered. The situation is made far too complex for easy

Figure 5 Elisabeth Löffler in *Einblicke*. (Video-still by courtesy of Daniel Aschwanden)

narratives such as 'she enjoys moving', 'she wants to escape her chair', or 'she hates her crutches' to emerge. By drawing attention to the mechanisms of meaning-making, the performance can manage to disrupt the 'natural' connotations of the disabled body. Insights are denied, and instead exploration is stressed: exploration of space, of bodies in relation to the mechanisms such as the spinning wheel of the chair, and explorations of the multiple narratives that make up a person's life.

Löffler's performance in the city puts her body as a readable sign to others in new spaces, and opens up new conceptual meeting places for theatrical performativity. The 'purity' of the presence of the body on stage is broken by its positioning or framing: a whole array of different connotations and interactions between disabled experiences and narratives are opening up through the unusual space of the performance – in a shopping arcade. Just as the stability of dance as a familiar concept is questioned, the stability of the disabled body as 'other' is undermined by simultaneously appearing in the 'normality' of the shopping arcade, and in the 'abnormality' of the role as performer. The 'truth' and the physical experience of the performer as social actor and as embodied dancer are opaque to the spectators: the complexity of signs allow us no one guiding metaphor with which to capture her.

This attention to the performativity of any appearance in any situation in any space can create encounters which break through discursive frameworks. But meanings are hard to overcome: our performance language of physicality is constantly under threat from the binaries that structure cultural meaning-making. When this performance took place, members of the Viennese public phoned to complain: they felt it necessary to 'protect' disabled people from 'being made' freakish spectacles in the city. The delicate play on the borders of agency and passivity, of positioning/being positioned, is always in flux, and cannot easily be pinned down into clear political statements.

Involving the public scene

Bill Shannon is a performance artist who uses crutches in his movement-based work. Within the New York club scene and beyond, Shannon has reached visibility through his work as the 'Crutchmaster', combining hip-hop aesthetics, breakdance and skateboarding skills with disability performance. Shannon is highly aware of the structures and nets of gazes and expectations that suffuse social contact, and in his street-performance work, he addresses these structures in ways that confound the 'natural' disabled body. He attempts to make visible the 'everybody knows' framings that pertain to encounters in the street scene. With this, he creates a form of epic theater in the street – the positions of performer and audience become unstable, attempts at identification are thrown back onto the body of the spectator, acts are repeated and held open to receive meaning in dialogue with spectators. Knowledges about disability are tested and brought to the fore. During 1999 and 2000, Shannon created street happenings in a number of places, including cities in Russia and Boston, USA. During these events,

Shannon performed a number of everyday tasks, and recorded, through observation and through secretly placed cameras, the reactions of members of the public to his tasks. These one-on-one or public performances are then relayed through lecture-demonstrations and videos ('Regarding the Fall', 2000), which Shannon tours internationally.

In one of these street actions, set in a Russian street, Shannon creates a highly sophisticated and complex action out of walking down a flight of stairs with his crutches, developing this everyday action into a ballet of swoops and falls, graceful and comic, clumsy and artistic at the same time. In another action, he stands on the pavement and attempts to pick up a water bottle standing on the pavement in front of him. He uses two underarm crutches, and, as many crutch-users know, picking up objects can indeed be tricky – but Shannon has developed highly sophisticated crutch-skills. In the street action, though, the emphasis is less on acrobatic crutch display then on the audience's reactions to the spectacle of disability. As Shannon balances precariously, unwitting street performers draw near and become involved, sometimes through the decision *not* to be involved. Shannon calls his work 'invitations' rather than interventions:

> The reasons why I call it invitations is because I don't really intervene in other people's path, I retain my own path and other people are welcome in that path. . . . People will come into my pathway, with well and good intentions but not understand the level of complexity at which I am able to . . . negotiate particular situations that I am in. People who look at me go 'Oh! That's so sad!', so part of the invitation is to invite the projected narrative of . . . assumed sadness, or assumed sort of failure or awkwardness and invite it in so that I'm not subject to it but the host to those.
>
> (Shannon, 2000)

In the stair scene, people offer their bodies as prosthesis, creating new constellations for movement. Some of the people intervening are so unskilled in the reading of movement and weight transference that the 'helpers' hinder Shannon, or even lose balance themselves. Movement competence becomes destabilized from 'known' differences between disabled and non-disabled. In the Boston street, some people pick up the water bottle and pass it to Shannon, but at least as interesting are people who are hovering on the periphery, trying to decipher the social script: should they intervene or not, engage or not, does he need help – or not? These hovering side performances create lines of tension and energy that link Shannon and his unknown co-performers: one woman visibly reacts with a shudder to the culmination of Shannon's elaborate movement, as he finally reaches the bottle on the ground. Emotions and kinaesthesia create vibrancies in the street scene.

In his lecture-performances, Shannon frames these everyday performances through an elaborate and sophisticated analysis of coding: he draws his audience's attention to the small choreographies of gazes, reactions and non-verbal signs that

Figure 6 Bill Shannon. Publicity still. (Reproduced by courtesy of the artist)

make up reactions to disability, and to a disabled person infiltrating the street scene. This analyzing gaze further removes the actions in the street from the 'natural' disabled body: Shannon's presence on the street is the presence of an anthropologist, a reader, an analyst, a host whose performances enables scenes of disclosure of subconscious social scripts. Similar to Löffler's performance, 'purity' is inaccessible here: Shannon's street actions are not performances of disability, but a performance of the readings, visceral effects, social embodiments, and public nets surrounding the meeting of different bodies. Watching the videos as part of the lecture-demonstrations, it remains unclear if the street spectators' narratives of disability and their perspectives on disabled bodies are challenged by being caught in his web of performances. The street sediments everyday knowledge, and Shannon's slightly weird spectacle is only a small part of the street scene. At the same time, Shannon performs an inscription of the public disabled body that repeats the disabled difference as difference: he confounds disability stereotypes by simultaneously heightening potential dis-abledness (in the literal sense) and displaying an uncanny ability to play with weight and gravity. Shannon's everyday audience has to be active, has to make a decision and choose an action (walking by, helping, or just staring). Through this audience address that asks to go beyond the visual and towards an interactive, kinaesthetic experience, Shannon's contortions and excessive crutch-play destabilize any easy readings of the 'normal' disabled body.

Multiplying frames

Another example of this kind of complex, framed performance can be found in the British filmdance *Outside In* (1995). The term 'filmdance' points here to a performance which could not exist outside film – techniques such as montage and image manipulation create non-naturalist spaces, where landscape paintings can become a row of heads, dancers breathe underneath the grass, and wheelchairs (without people) roll through walls. The film employs two strategies of representation, freakishness and shared embodiment, and between them the fixities of the disabled dancer begin to crumble.[5] The tactics of filmdance allow a form of representation which destabilize both the invisibility of disability (by bringing it into the public sphere) and the hypervisibility of disability as 'other' or 'freak'.

In *Outside In*, the filmic interacts with the conventional dance performance as a framing device – a device that can estrange the spectator from the 'easy truths' about the performing bodies. The hypervisibility of the disabled body becomes displaced, is played with and explored rather than denied by a range of dancers using the camera as their surprising (and surprised) dance partner. This move towards reclaiming the disabled body and the agency of representation has been widely explored in the visual arts within the disability arts movement.

It is most appropriate to investigate filmdance in this discussion of the performance of disability: the physical freak and early cinema shared historic spaces and cultural position not too long ago. At the birth of cinema, the peep show, the freakshow, and the first brief reels of naked ladies all shared the space of the fairground. The entertainment value of the freakshow and the early cinema was similar, no matter how much people tried to exonerate either spectacle by making it 'scientifically important'. The structurally similar fascination with cinematic practice and medically derived imaging techniques is discussed in Cartwright (1995) – she finds the desire to see 'life' at the center of an early cinematic aesthetic. Capturing the 'other' body of disability created a history of visualizations in medicine, a tradition subverted and played with in some photographic art that emerged from the disability rights movement (Evans, 1988; see also Halford, 2001). The thrill of the other, be it the other of 'normal perception' or the other of body and shape, lies at the root of disability representation and early encounters of audiences and cinematic material. This historical interpenetration is explored by film theorist Studlar (1996). She analyzes the star persona of Lon Chaney, who was the child of disabled parents, and shows the traces of the cultural history of the sideshow spectacle in the connotations of his various film appearances and their linkages with various impairments. Similarly, Norden (1994) in his study of the representation of disabled character in cinema, finds the freak, the other, the spectacle as one root of Hollywood's fascination with disability. Another aspect of the use of disability in cinema is narrationally driven: the disabled person in film is a stereotyping device that manages to convey narrational meanings economically and emphatically.

In *Outside In*, the strategies of freak spectacle are used in parallel with film's historical aesthetic reliance on visual curiosity. But since the presentation under discussion is a filmdance, the affectual resonances set up by the interaction between music, kinaesthetic reaction and shared embodiment destabilize any easy reading scheme.

Film historian Tom Gunning re-introduced readers to the pleasures of the cinema of attractions, where visual curiosity and stimulation were dominant over the narrative pleasures of later cinematic practice. He writes about the pleasures of early cinema:

> The cinema of attractions directly solicits spectator attention, inciting visual curiosity, and supplying pleasure through an exciting spectacle – a unique event, whether fictional or documentary, that is of interest in itself. The attraction to be displayed may also be of a cinematic nature, such as . . . early close-ups, or trick film in which a cinematic manipulation (slow motion, reverse motion, substitution, multiple exposure) provides the film's novelty. Fictional situations tend to be restricted to gags, vaudeville numbers or recreations of shocking or curious events.
>
> (Gunning, 1990: 58–59)

Outside In is both an extradiegetic spectacle (offering the shocking view of disabled people dancing) and a spectacle through the filmic mechanisms used: the attractions of a cinematic nature, film tricks, special effects. The fixities that place disabled people into cultural narratives of 'freaks' and tragic victims are under-mined by the spectacular, counter-narrational elements of the film.

One of the dancers in the video, David Toole, can be seen to employ strategies of 'enfreakment' (a term used by Hevey (1992) to describe the mechanisms by which disabled people become the 'other') to escape the perceived immobility of the disabled body. Toole has incredibly strong arms, and big hands, but no legs. The choreography uses the shock effect of his dancing: he gets out of the wheelchair, walks on his hands, jumps on them, and displays astonishing acro-batic feats. His accomplished range of dynamics, controlled facial expression and presence in the video and in live shows challenge any reading of his performance as scripted for him by a non-disabled social worker or choreographer: he is seen as in control of the situation. Frequent close-ups of his concentrated face underline this authority.

Within the UK, Toole, more so than any other dancer in the group, transformed the image of disabled dancing. Although many disabled people have strong reservations about the use of 'freak' tactics, and although Toole had to give up dancing for a while because of the destructive strain on his joints, his performances of disability – of some, but not other discourses of it – had a wide effect inside and outside the disabled community in the UK.

On the cinematic (or, in this instance, televisual level), the film employs 'tricks', special effects and other means to distract from forming narratives and instead solicits an interest in the present. In one scene, one dancer (Jon French) is sitting in front of a landscape painting. His chin rests on his hand, and he gazes out at

Figure 7 David Toole in *Outside In*. (Reproduced by courtesy of MJW Productions)

the landscape. Since he is sitting in a wheelchair, the spectator well versed in cultural narratives can quickly decode the narrative situation: the 'cripple' is longing for a run in the fields. But this narrative, reliant on my knowledge of cinematic narrative conventions (access to inner space through reading longing gazes and the *mise-en-scène*) and disability stereotypes, is arrested, as my focus switches. The painting of rolling hills transforms into the facial profiles of a row of dancers, including the on-looker's face, dispelling clear distinction between utopian, communal image and lonely reality. As one of the performers in the 'painting' sneezes and upsets the landscape formation, the play with bodies, spaces and non-realistic configuration is taken up again.

The spectator's attention switches from 'here is a story' to 'how do they do that' – no coherent narrative emerges. This form of audience address is more closely aligned with Gunning's cinema of attractions and Brecht's epic theater than with conventional Hollywood or avant-garde representation.

It is important, though, that the building block of this spectacle is still the human body. The beginning of the video shows how a breath is blown from one dancer to the next, accompanied by strong rhythmic music. The breath sets up different physical reactions: it is 'handed on', blown across by a kiss, poured into an open mouth, and thus sets up an intriguing performance of everyday gestures. A 'small dance' emerges. Steve Paxton paid attention to the complexities of movements that go into the act of simply standing – the intricate play of breath, muscles, balance and blood stream. The first choreography of every body is the act of living itself. The 'difference' of the disabled body as cultural other is under-mined by these choreographed acts of living and breathing – the choreography here is accessible to non-trained bodies, and relies on familiar, everyday gestures which are shared by the spectator community.

The reliance on bodily cues for camera movements and cuts is also present at other moments in the film: a dancer's clearing of the floor with her sweeping hand motivates a cut to a new scene. Another dancer (Toole) starts to move his hands on a tango-floor pattern (the black shoe prints used in dance books to teach ballroom dancing). This interaction between body and space (the painted floor) cues tango music (the scene starts in silence and then the music starts up as a response to the rhythmically moving body) and motivates a tango scene with the ensemble dancing. The structure of the filmdance reacts to the bodily cues, to breath, movement, and physical contour (in the landscape painting). This reliance on the relationship between body and filmic elements allows for a sharing across the spectacle, and across the freak connotation. As a spectator, I am drawn in by the rhythms, the echoes of movements translate themselves into my own body, its breath and its movements. The 'freaks' (disabled people and professional dancers with extraordinary bodily control) are brought closer by this combination of physical performance and film technique, and breach the gap between them and the spectatorial community. The movement set up can be seen as a moment of affect – as music, rhythm, physical echo and filmic close-up combine to share in the physicality of the 'other'.

As this reading has shown, *Outside In* uses cinematic spectacle and freak techniques to make a filmdance with disabled people. The non-realist aspects of the filmdance allow a disruption of conventional narratives while heightening the sense of physical sharing through close-ups and strong rhythmical echoes. By thus combining the elements of technology and the presence of physical bodies, *Outside In* is for me a progressive film: it shows the disabled performer as a motivator, manipulator, and mover outside her and his 'cultural baggage' as disabled, passive victim, but not outside his or her own body. The performer's emphasis on physicality is retained. The narrative of disability that equates the disabled dancer as victim, fixed and without choice is undermined. Simultaneously, the disabled body as site of presence and action is reclaimed: disability becomes graspable as performative, as its meanings slide and lurch. In an elaborate dance between freakishness and familiarity, the complexities of the performative balancing act again become apparent. These disabled performers cannot be fixed, but each physical act of dancing inscribes new meanings, makes the unfamiliar appear in familiar environments, and the familiar appear strange.

Occupying all bases

In CandoCo's, Bill Shannon's and *Bilderwerfer*'s performances, the physicality of the disabled body, its ability to take space in the public sphere remains at the forefront of the aesthetic strategy. The performers do not exhaust themselves in images and narratives, but point back to an embodied living, in shared spaces and bodies working in shared ways with their audiences' bodies. This emphasis on embodiment and communality can allow them to go beyond freakishness – a tentative move, which is always at risk of being recuperated by a public eager to maintain its boundaries. Their bodies do not remain in the safely 'other', but can challenge their audiences to investigate the familiar. Disabled dancers can challenge what it means to dance every time they take the stage – they perform the mobilization of the 'trapped body', which disability as discourse of tragedy enacts so powerfully in our society. But this mobilization does not occur only at an individual level – the fodder for 'tragic cripple smiles again' publicity – but on a discursive level. Disabled dancers confuse non-disabled people's concepts of what dance can be, what bodies are supposed to do, and what disability means. As a consequence, critics like Arlene Croce lose their safe grounding and get angry. The ambiguous decision to perform one's body, to enact a drama of activity and passivity within one's physicality, opens up new chapters for disability narratives – and for dance. These performances occur on the scene of unknowability: the acting is more important than the being. The performing body is present, and makes its presence felt, but the body denies insights into its truth. Disability *is*, but isn't clear. Pain and muscular effort *is*, but isn't readable, and knowable, and able to be put into pat narratives. Once we have opened up these labilities of binary identity, we can hopefully move forward to explore the specificities and richness of differences in embodied living.

The Brechtian tradition relies on alienation techniques to distance audiences from an identificatory or 'knowledgable' relation with the performers, from the established modes of seeing and knowing that developed in the safe zone of naturalist theater. By inserting difference, the social constellation that shapes the performance character as a cultural agent can become visible. In these pages, my aim has been to show the deepening of these concepts, soaking down to the matter of flesh and bones, as cultural inscription at work in the minutiae of bodily habit and shared physicality become temporarily visible; also I charted how disabled performers have taken up the challenge to de-naturalize disability. In the next chapter, another important performance tradition will be the object of investigation, another tradition that developed out of a rejection of the naturalist Western stage: the undermining of social rules, categories, knowledge and structure by an encounter with an Other that explodes the boundaries of the theater. Taking my cue from Artaud's theater of cruelty, I discuss a different strategy used by disabled artists to wield their bodies as weapons to undermine the status quo.

Chapter 4

Outsider energies

I do know that
space, time, dimension, becoming, future, destiny, being, non-being, self,
    non-self,
are nothing to me;
but there is one thing
that is something,
one single thing that is something
and that I know
wants to COME OUT:
the presence of the pain in my body;
the menacing, indefatigable presence of my body.

and however hard people press me with questions
and however vigorously I refuse all questions
there is a point at which I find myself compelled to say no,

NO

then, to negation.
                (Artaud, *To Have Done with the Judgement of God*, 1948)

Languages, cultures and societies are relatively fixed systems, based on underlying if shifting understandings of basic difference and identity. For many thinkers, the other holds a fascination because it challenges and plays with the criteria for 'being human' that act as gatekeepers of the rational. In Greek mythology, the minotaur, the man-bull, holds such a place between the human and the animal, a place that is characterized by violence and surprising tenderness. The minotaur is the result of a pairing of a queen and a bull, cunningly engineered by Daedalus, the inventor of the labyrinth, the robot and the flying machine. The space of the minotaur is the labyrinth: a dense, dark place in which meanings become unclear, and the Greek sun of rationality dims and falls away as young men and women are sacrificed to elemental appetites.[1] The minotaur is the other side of the clarity of Greek discourse, of safe and familiar family trees that speak of linearity and purpose, and of bounded gender roles. Its very existence undermines the clarity and light of people who understand themselves to be rational and 'pure'. The minotaur also represents mythical knowledge: a reality beneath the everyday, beneath or beyond that which is validated by the constructs of 'realism'. And myth holds alive a life force of creation that fuels the stories and discourses of meaning-making.

In this chapter, I want to show how disabled performers use the strategies of embodying the outsider to challenge social certainties. They employ the mythical and psychological energy of transgression and taboo as means that threaten to destroy the spiderweb of rational conventions. But wielding the power of otherness comes at a price. As the meaning of political intervention changes, its effects on contemporary political frameworks are hard to chart. Before I describe how the minotaur becomes the disabled person, though, I want to investigate the meeting of human and other in another un-human place, deep under the sea.

Anthropologist Alphonso Lingis describes his encounter with the sea as a phenomenological theater of moving into otherness. Here, the borderline between animal and human, and between agency and engulfing oceanic sensibility is referenced by the disabled other:

> Laden with air tank, regulator, gauges, I went into the sea. The belt of iron weights dropped me through the strong current of the surface. Below there was no current, but there was surge, water compressed to three atmospheres throwing me back and forth thirty feet, so that I fought it violently to stabilize myself, afraid of being dashed against the coral cliffs. Something then told me to put off struggling, to free my body from human posture and swim strokes, to use my limbs only like some thalidomide freak able to make but the slight movement necessary to avoid the prongs of elkhorn coral and steer into canyons. I drowned the will to move myself, consigned myself to the movement of – what? . . . And then the bliss came, as though being suspended in this cosmic movement and losing the motility that comes from taking a stand and taking hold, I had found what I went down in the sea to find.
>
> (Lingis, 1983: 5)

Lingis becomes other in the sea – the 'thalidomide freak' stands in as an absolute other to agency, control and rationality. As he moves on to describe the sea surrounding him, Lingis shows a careful and poetic attention to language in his description of sea animals as part-organs, read in relation to humanity, their colors displayed in excess of any eye to take in, or mind to decode. In this woven universe, physical posture and metaphor, body being and body name, become one: various connotations of 'taking a stand' interleaf in his description. The encounter with the deep loosens, momentarily, the hold of the unifying self, and other forms of embodiment, referenced by the 'freak', become desirous and voluptuous.

> Without a posture for holding myself upright, without that inner diagram for holding myself together and appropriating the detachable things outside, organs separated in me too, skin that made contact with the anemone, eyes

still full of marine water making contact with the eye stuck on the ganglions of the octopus. A sponge put in a blender and reduced to broth, and then poured into an aquarium, will reassemble itself after a few days; in an hour, on the beach, my inner ingredients, or most of them, would reassemble themselves into that aleatory clustering I call my psychophysical integrity. Like the algae in the sea anemones the bacteria and enzymes that drift in the thermoclimes and currents in my tubes and that I call 'me' are perhaps animals only looking after themselves and parasitic on me. There are plankton and krill, sponges and gorgonians within. There are tadpoles and eels by the millions, swimming in the testicles. There are animals occupied with secreting the ribs and the vertebrae, the inner coral reefs.

(Lingis, 1983: 12/13)

The sea visit provided Lingis with the vicarious thrill of self-dissolution, a pushing at ego-boundaries, an encounter with thrilling difference (mediating his male, non-disabled identity). Lingis goes on to analyze the eye as erogenous gaze – it becomes an organ of touch, losing its control function, and instead becomes subsumed in the activity of caress. But this eye, losing its hold on unity and agency, is also the primary object that the self is looking to encounter – being recognized by the other, seeing oneself in the eye of the sea, finding affirmation of identity and being for the subject.[2] But instead of finding a recognizing look back on his self, Lingis encounters the frisson of dissolution in his fearful encounter with a shark, that 'biologically perfect' ancient animal. Under the surface of the sea, Lingis goes to look for the gaze of the other on him, and finds a shark. But the shark turns away, and the eye gliding away holds the horror of the non-returned gaze:

[The shark] turned slightly, its color and contour vanished, and the eye that had been on the lookout was detached from its look, from the seas, caressed by the cold look of the monster.

(1983: 15)

The monster inserts itself – it takes over the relation between self and other. The monster here is the absolutely other that is not in any relation to the viewing self: this shark is for itself in such a way that the self gazing upon it feels its own emptiness, feels the impossibility of reciprocity. The universe, the sea – in the moment that the fish's eye shifts from potential other to absolute other, the self feels the shiver of the sublime – that understanding that the world is bigger than the self.

Remembering his own fear, Lingis quotes Heidegger:

Fear, Heidegger wrote, is inauthentifying, disperses out of reach whatever powers are one's own, detaches one from a being that is one's own, disintegrates. The one that goes down to the deep goes for the fear.

(Lingis, 1983: 14/15)

Lingis's analysis of the pleasure of self-dissolution, the 'Rapture of the Deep' which gives the title to Lingis's chapter, phases the self out of its own skin into the realm of otherness. Loss of agency and loss of motility makes the living of this moment a lived experience of 'the monster', 'the freak'. This pleasure of both sensual encounter with multiplicity (as the body-in-pieces he describes) and psychological encounter with the absolute other links also to ways of looking at disability. As Lingis metaphorically links the disabled person, the thalidomide freak, to his experience of bodily otherness, so disability has often functioned as placekeeper for a radical otherness that allows distance from the everyday self of normality. The signs of disability become the corals, fish and water pressures that remind 'man' of 'his' vulnerable, transitory, precious and wondrous fleshliness at large in a world of other forces.

The minotaur fusion of human and animal flesh, genetic freakishness and metaphorical expulsion from the realm of polite society can provide such a nexus of energy, desire and repulsion, fear and catharsis.[3] With its production *Le Labyrinthe*, the French group Compagnie de L'Oiseau Mouche picks up the heritage of the outsider's tale, and creates a visually and kinestethically strong ritual on European stages. In L'Oiseau Mouche's version of the minotaur's story, the bull is the hidden center of a society that defines itself by its foundational violence. L'Oiseau Mouche and their directors, Jean-Michel Rabeux and Sylvie Reteuna, work in Roubaix, France, and consist of around twenty performers, all of whom have developmental disabilities. The group is professional, paid, and provides rigorous performance training for its members.[4] Their style of work relies on a form of performance communication that circumvents realist roles, and embraces movement and strong visuals in the creation of ritualistic events. Impairments such as Down's Syndrome are not thematized in the performance work, instead, in *Labyrinthe*, an archetypal narrative exposes exclusion and the practices of definition as fundamental mechanisms of social groups.

The performance opens with the bull, a man with a bull's head, clad in brown trousers, his upper body naked, being led onto the stage by a group of people in flowing red costumes. The bull is held in tension between a network of ropes – he is the center and the point of energy, strength radiating outwards along these tethering lines. The struggle between center and periphery ends with the minotaur bound and immobilized on the ground, muscles bulging with contained power.

The people in red trace a chalk labyrinth on the floor, like the alchemist's pentagram, designed to keep the demons bound within their circle. In measured steps, the performers move across the stage, erecting stakes until a forest of markers, like an alien graveyard, bristle on the stage. In a stunning display of visual transformation, the people in red race around these stakes with an industrial-size paper role, wrapping the stakes into an intricate and instantaneous labyrinth. A woman in red, carefully moving into the labyrinth, eventually frees the bull at the heart of the labyrinth. There is no text, no psychology to the woman's action: the audience provide their own memory of ancient myths of Ariadne. Within the universe created on stage, the woman's action is merely necessitated by the energetics of the spectacle, and by the forces that bind the group and the outsider together into a continuously looping cycle of violent encounter, submission, build-up and release. A naked bull is washed, slowly, respectfully, folding funeral rites and reincarnation rituals into one. After the bull is loose, and wandering in the prison, the red people cluster around, venture into the paper world, and taunt the beast. As the rhythm of the taunts, hammered out and percussive, builds to intolerable levels, the minotaur breaks out – abandoning the paper corridors, he smashes through the walls, destroying the elaborate building and undoing the tension that maintains the labyrinth. In the silence that follows, the bull-man slowly, mesmerizingly, lifts his human hands, and rips the bull mask from his face. He laughs, laughs at the proceedings, at himself, at the audience, laughs himself out of the story. And then, he begins to dance with slow grace. One by one, all cast members join his flamenco, and in this release of physical energy they thus end the cycle of violence – for now.

L'Oiseau Mouche's performance takes the form of a ritual, a carnival play that uses the mechanism of archetypes, percussive sound and chant, strong visuals and the energies of moving and still bodies to allow a sharing of theatrical energy that goes beyond words or structural arrangements. When I saw the performance as part of a festival in Hamburg in 2000, the audience was filled with disabled and non-disabled people with, I assume, widely different experiences of art and theater, all engaged in different ways by the stage language. The performance put the gap of learning disability under erasure, but the gap hadn't vanished: the strong elemental images affected many powerfully, but at the same time, other voices wondered about the stereotyping of people with learning disabilities as animals, radical others, or idiot savants.

Within the disability arts community, developmental disabilities hold their own status: historically, the struggle for equal rights within liberal discourse frameworks, articulating a rhetoric of independence, found little place for the rights and needs of people who do not enter the rhetoric field as masters of political language. But feminist and disability scholars question this notion of the independent, rational

Figure 8 Compagnie de L'Oiseau-Mouche, *Le Labyrinthe*. Photograph by Bruno Dewaele. Publicity postcard

individual as the only way of figuring agency. The works under discussion in this chapter join in this questioning of the notion of the individual in control of his/her own destiny.[5]

L'Oiseau Mouche presents in *Labyrinthe* an image of a society as an interrelated circulatory whole, within whose dynamic polarities actions occur and develop on a path that seems guided by principles of energy rather than psychology. Even though the mode of audience address harks back to the carnival, and its celebration of community, no essentials seem present on the stage: the bull is a mask, and can be discarded – the positions of outsider and insider, beast and man, are arbitrary. As an audience member, I can make inferences, and apply the scenario to the position of disabled people within society: outsiders due to the structural requirements for opposition and violence, not essential outsiders *qua* their impairments. Watching L'Oiseau Mouche's *Labyrinthe*, the spectator can gain a sense of the movement of life, and its mastication of individuals within its ever-moving jaws – jaws that echo the shark rather than the human-shaped rationale of the built machine. This quasi-celebratory, affective and mythical theater that shows life's movement rather than naturalist fully formed individuals on their path towards rationality recalls Antonin Artaud's calls for the Theater of Cruelty:[6]

> With this mania we all have today for belittling everything, as soon as I said 'cruelty' everyone took it to mean 'blood'. But a 'theater of cruelty' means theater that is difficult and cruel for myself first of all. And on a performing level, it has nothing to do with the cruelty we practice on one another, hacking at each other's bodies, carving up our individual anatomies, or, like ancient Assyrian Emperors, posting sackful of human ears, noses or neatly dissected nostrils, but the far more terrible, essential cruelty objects can practice on us. We are not free and the sky can still fall on our heads. And above all else, theater is made to teach us this.
>
> (Artaud: *The Theater and its Double*, 1993: 60)

Pointing to a non-individual, non-human objectness of the universe (the non-gaze of the shark in Lingis's adventure) and its momentum can activate this cruelty beyond the singular. 'Bloody' storylines help to open the sensibility of audiences to the assaultive theater mechanics Artaud sees at work on his stage, but his prime organ of cruelty is the actor stripped of his acting – 'the actor is a heart athlete' (88): emotions are created through the expenditure of energy and effort, not through a metaphysical connection to ideals or truth. By this total presence on stage, a field of magic emerges between spectator and actors (95), as the audience is swept up in its physicality by an onslaught of images that affect beyond the rational, that are not allowed to become abstract, divisible from the acting bodies.[7]

> Artaud's theater is one of the phenomenal body, not only because the body is the center of the mise en scene, but also because the function of this body is not to identify layers of signification within operative cultures

(i.e. the domain of semiotics) but to aim to discover 'language beyond words', a meta-physics of the theater via an immersion in the physical. . . . It is this attempt to find the idiom of theatrical metaphysics which leads to the now famous metaphor of theater and the 'plague'.

(Sanchez-Colberg, 1996: 43)

This tempting, seductive vision of a theater of ecstasy and empathy has been widely explored in the happenings and performance art of the 1960s and 1970s, but to many it has proven politically empty – its challenge is too easily deflected. The spectator can flee the implications of the presented communal event by extricating herself, by making the witnessed event into a spectacle.[8]

Breaking down the individual and rational subject of theater into an assemblage, a machine, a field of forces and energies, has currency in contemporary performance work through these heritage lines of Artaud and, later, the philosophies of Gilles Deleuze. Accordingly, performance artists make use of echoes of Artaud's audience address in order to create powerful presences for disabled people in our shared public life. Aligning the disabled body with non-rational, affective and energetic states is a dangerous motion: too easily, the Artaudian magic is not achieved, and what emerges instead is a confirmation of the 'animalistic', 'natural', 'non-rational' stereotypes surrounding disability. Hahn describes in his investigation of the relationship between disability and beauty how disabled people have been linked to a form of subversive sensualism – giving as an example people of small stature working as jesters at medieval courts, sometimes entertaining their lords naked (Hahn, 1988: 28). Transgressing taboos, they were allowed a measure of satirical freedom 'reflecting on society in ways prohibited to normal people' (Whyte, 1995: 286). These forms of transgression always fall back on the semiotic register set up for the Other: the unbridgeable difference, the connotation of 'rawness' and 'nature', and the alignment with the irrational. The naked jester will never be allowed to marry the princess. But the tactic remains seductive: using the affective character of disabled forms of embodiment and their social taboo status as keys or catalysts for the holy terror of magical involvement.

Deleuze and Guattari write of a different kind of visuality, linked to a reference field of phenomenology that particularizes sensual encounters, and that doesn't posit unity as its core value. Their work helps to focus this problematic of the seductive versus the reductive without reference to a romantic magic. In *A Thousand Plateaus: Capitalism and Schizophrenia*, Deleuze and Guattari differentiate between smooth – engaged, embodied, surrounding, immersive knowledge in a haptic, touch-oriented field, and striated – distant, categorizing, abstract knowledge in a visual, distancing field:

The Smooth is both the object of a close vision par excellence and the element of a haptic space (which may be as much visual or auditory as tactile). The Striated, on the contrary, relates to a more distant vision, and a more optical space – although the eye in turn is not the only organ to have this capacity.

(1988: 493)

The eye and its sense-informations stand here in different relation to knowledge projects. In Chapter 2, I discussed the historical move from the partially invisible grotesque to the visible freak, focusing on different models of visuality as my frame of reference. In the distinction between the smooth and striated, the object of knowledge is everyday practice, not necessarily just historical succession (although Deleuze and Guattari chart the knowledge of the sea, maritime knowledge, as a gradual striation, a mapping project).

Authors such as Anna Fenemore have applied the knowledge of smooth and striated spaces to the performance encounter (2001), and to the different forms of knowledges available to actors and spectators in the theater space. The emphasis of this form of theater analysis is not on the socially bounded space of pre-modern carnival, in which a community celebrates itself, but on a form of engagement that oscillates between abstraction and intense encounter, but that doesn't rely on commonality or even humanity to function.

> The first aspect of the haptic, smooth space of close-vision is that its orientations, landmarks and linkages are in continuous variation; it operates step by step . . . one never sees from a distance in a space of this kind, nor does one see it from a distance; one is never 'in front of', any more than one is 'in' . . . Orientations are not constant . . . There is no visual mode for points of reference that would make them interchangeable and unite them in an inertial class assignable to an immobile outside observer. On the contrary, they are tied to any number of observers . . . nomads entertaining tactile relations among themselves.
>
> (1988: 493)

The smooth space can be a theater stage for adventure and immersion – encountering performances that are in proximity and relation to oneself. This relation is not a psychological relation of identification, but a relation of shared, continuous space. Intensity is not a function of recognition of sameness, but of a haptic recognition of a spatial energy that enmeshes the *field* of spectator and performer. In a performance encounter, the meshing of smooth and striated spaces allows for a way of thinking about categorization (the inescapability of difference that so haunted Mat Fraser's search for a role) and difference *together* as a machine for energy.

One of the predominant performance troupes feeding from the legacy of Artaud and using Deleuze's vocabulary of the schizophrenic scene are Soc̀ìetas Raffaello Sanzio (SRS), a *nuovo teatro* group who work out of Cesena, Italy, under the direction of Romeo Castellucci. Their performances involve the audience in a laboratory of exhausted language, post-Heiner Müller's theatrical exhaustion, and a ghosted presence of the traditions, recycled and fragmented. This theater moves towards the body-without-organs, that is, the Artaudian actor who is not an authored sign, but an index. But, ultimately:

> There is no theater in the world today which fulfils Artaud's desire ... the 'grammar' of the theater of cruelty, of which he said that it is 'to be found', will always remain the inaccessible limit of a representation which is not repetition, of a re-presentation which is full presence, which does not carry its double within itself as its death, of a present which does not repeat itself, that is, of a present outside time, a nonpresent. The present offers itself as such, appears, presents itself ... only by harbouring its own intestine difference.
>
> (Derrida, 1978: 247)

The theater exhausts itself by attempting to find a point of presence, of finding a place to stop, only to repeat, again and again. In keeping with their forefather visionary Artaud, and his philosopher, Deleuze, the destruction of mental health becomes a metaphor for contemporary life and communication, as does energy and energy flow. Thus, at the beginning of SRS's *Hamlet: The Vehement Exteriority of the Death of a Lazybones, or, The Vehement Superficiality of the Death of a Mollusc* (translations vary in different countries) (1992), the Shakespearean play is nothing but a vague memory, held without connection and emotion, repeated by the 'autistic' survivor Horatio who is alienated from language and its meanings, and reduced to defecate waste and words. Humanity, if *Hamlet* stands for the human condition, is reduced to reflexes, pattern, feeble attempts at connection (Lehmann, 1999: 378). The lone male telling a story at his dead comrade's request is a vulnerable presence amidst a scene of debris, an old bedstead, a brown misery of space. Car batteries are lining the wall, ready to provide a cathartic glow of energy, but energy that goes nowhere. Later on in the show, in a brilliant piece of theater machinery, the iron bedstead glows red-hot: this self-defeating energy expenditure is all that Horatio is able to accomplish. Charge and discharge take over as dominant themes of the emptying of self into public space. This model replaces the model of the role as translatory function that charts psychoanalytic functions of meaning on the actor's body. The actor is here the physical battery cycling. Although *Hamlet* uses a traditional proscenium stage as its space, with its attendant histories of perspectival vision and survey knowledge, a range of devices seem to invite a smooth spatial knowledge: the smell and heat of the iron bed, the (imagined?) smell of feces, the long, tense quiet that can communicate itself to the spectator. All these haptic encounters can be read (striated) and/or experienced (smooth) – I hesitate to call any show that is clearly marked as such, and that one has paid to visit, a smooth event. Deleuze and Guattari's model invites thinking about modes of knowledge, it is not a model that lends itself to a mapping of our social world. But the 'boredom' of the long duration in the presence of the actor invites the move from reading to being in a way that can be aligned with striation and smoothness.

The condition of autism becomes a master trope for both the theater and the formation (and unmaking) of self. The theater of the monumental, including the monumental presence of energy, is always inviting the meaning of striation: a mapping of the world. But the mapping doesn't hold, any symbol is created on the back of a diminished, silent, broken figure who, different from those waiting for Godot, hasn't even an empty spiritual frame to hold on to. The border of incommunicability questions the fundamentals associated with humanity. Artaud infuses his theater vision with 'first principles':

> If theater is as bloody and inhuman as dreams, the reasons for this is that it perpetuates the metaphysical notions in some Fables in a present-day, tangible manner, whose atrocity and energy are enough to prove their origins and intentions in fundamental first principles rather than to reveal and unforgettably tie down the idea of continual conflict within us, where life is continually lacerated, where everything in creation rises up and attacks our condition as created beings.
>
> (1993: 71)

Deep energy vouchsafes the 'first principles', communicable through the presence of energy. The principle itself is the presence and vulnerability of life beyond the condition of 'reality', but on a level that embraces dream *and* created world. Theater, here, becomes the renewal of life in a ritual vortex that points to energy as the base.

In SRS, this energy of theater figures as an attempt at communication, deploying all strata of bodily discourse, ransacked words, and the tired images of wombs, machines, engine rooms and beds. The symbols are empty, and stand as indexes of the world-machine inventing its dreams. With the references to the disability label, and psychoanalytic discourse, theater also becomes the attempt to create a unified self out of ill-fitting debris. Gordana Vnuk describes SRS together with troupes such as the Bak-Truppen and artists like Branko Brezovec as 'iconoclastic' theater (Vnuk: 1998). Vnuk associates the breaking of images with a bodily felt, deeply engaged search, but a search that flounders in its inability to construct a full image.

In other performances, SRS reference schizophrenia and autism, war-induced trauma and hysteria (*Voyage au bout de la nuit*, 1999) as backgrounds for their theater works. Beyond these metaphoric uses of forms of embodiment, SRS have created much-publicized art with actors that can command a contemporary theater audience's attention as icons of a post-sense world: in various shows, people with developmental disabilities have been present on stage, as have people so thin as to invite the label 'concentration-camp victim' by the press (in *Voyage*, a version of Celine's novel, in which these people stand for the 'broken bodies' of post-World War I modernity). These displays have outraged liberal sensibilities, but the company follows a rigorous philosophy, where body/mind states are the very matter of meaning-making – a moment at which rhetoric based on the rational independent subject of liberal political discourse is suspended, and all forms of embodiment and the interfaces between physicality and meaning are caught in an exhausted set of electric discharges. In this field of energetics, Garland-Thomson's extraordinary body is merely quantitatively, not qualitatively, different from the 'norm', and all body-beings are caught in a post-carnivalesque theater of remnants. In SRS's theater, no one plays theater – theatricality is replaced by the index, the human body holds itself upright (or not) in the theater space, no role exists beyond its brutal and elemental presence. This theater combines aesthetics and ethics in a fascinating and disturbing quest for a metaphor for contemporary life. With this, SRS goes back to Artaud's theater of cruelty – pure presence, nightmares, the evil and beautiful beast-man.

Alien bodies

Other contemporary performances of disability also reference the theater of cruelty and its passionate index and radical anti-theater. I want to show how in these performances a withholding, a moment that doesn't allow the full consumption of the 'other', the disabled person, acts as index of an overwhelming physicality. This process of moving up to the edge, but withholding full knowledge or full disclosure, can break, put under erasure and into uncertainty the romantic sublime and the holy terror. The closure of realigning self and world, self and God, restructuring the world after the cathartic effects of disruption, cannot easily happen. With this, pre-modern concepts of theater as ritual sharing and magical opening can emerge in a contemporary world of different sensibilities.

In the previous chapter, I presented this move in relation to performativity's distancing of body and meaning, dancetheater's ironic framing devices, and street performance's play with the public. All of these devices are at work in the three performances I want to discuss, but the performances hold distancing mechanisms in abeyance by a magical, mystical but non-illusionary presentation that invites a form of physical contemplation, a sharing of space with that which is other than the self.

In *Sensation of Motion in Time* (2000), Japanese performance artist Erika Matsunami created a public event at a gallery opening with two performers of the Theater Thikwa in Berlin, Germany, a well-established disability focused theater group. Matsunami and her two performers, both of whom have cerebral palsy, performed task-based actions among spectators in the Kunstlerbahnhof Westend, an old train station re-functioned into an art space. In the show, they walk or slither closely by their audiences: some spectators decide to move, making way for the performers taking space, others seem to enjoy the close contact, the permission to stare and to see in close-up. At times, Erika Matsunami, Martina Nitz and Tim Petersen are noticeable in unison: with Matsunami's (who is non-disabled) 'normate' motion in a form of echo or counterpoint to Nitz's spastic impulses. The 'rawness' of huddled spectators sitting on concrete benches and on stair steps, watching the writhing of Nitz on the floor at their feet, is off-set by large

Figure 9 Martina Nitz, in *Sensation of Motion in Time*. Photography by Christa Zauner. (Reproduced by courtesy of the artist)

video projections on the top floor of the old railway station. These projections present the performers in a more ethereal light, giving an aesthetic frame to their unfamiliar physicality. The video projections allow for a different perspective on both Nitz and Petersen: not as live presences of disabled bodies in a public space that isn't designed for them as valid citizens (the stairs are a constant reminder of this), but as signs of beauty, shapes and lines in movement. With this, the presentation sets different sets of understandings of disability in tension: As Overboe reminds us,

> The identity of disabled people who experience cerebral palsy is reduced to their appearance that is, according to Young (1990: 124), the antithesis of the controlled being associated with rationality, linearity, productivity and normality.
>
> (Overboe, 1999: 18)

Here, the appearance, the visual encounter itself is manipulated, creating a temporal difference that translates what appears uncontrolled into an elegiac dance. Mediation, difference, the space between performer and spectator become visible as they double up between live performance and video. The space between projection and live presence allows for many details to emerge: different rules of visual engagement apply to the two forms of communication.

The video presents Nitz in slow-motion, with beautifully colored tones, and the spectator can gain a different relation to Nitz's see-through shirt showing off her muscular upper body and allowing vision of her breasts, and to her private and triumphant luxuriating smile at the execution of her movements. In the live action, the same kind of 'aesthetic' appreciation becomes more complex through the abrupt quality of Nitz's movement, more 'alien' to many observers, and her position at the feet of most spectators, echoing uncomfortable social realities rather than 'value-free' art spaces.

Energy, circulating clearly like shocking currents through the three different live performances, is transformed into a more elegiac and expansive pace in the interaction between camera and bodies captured on the screens. But the quality of energy as motion binds all elements of this site-specific work together: spectators and performers, architecture and videos. The train station is a place of coming and going, of traversal lines, of lines shooting off to elsewhere. Train timetables and the geometries of railway lines create striations in a field of reverberating departures and arrivals. The movement energy creates smooth pockets of encounters, where the directions of erotics and fascination, disgust and upset are arrested and set into 'tactile relations among themselves'. Beyond the visual distance between extraordinary and normate body,

> the eye itself has a haptic, nonoptical function: no line separates earth from sky, which are of the same substance; there is neither horizon nor background nor perspective nor limit nor outline or form nor center; there is no intermediary distance, or all distance is intermediary.
>
> (Deleuze and Guattari, 1988: 494)

The happening doesn't model a larger social homogenization, or a carnival celebration of shared space. But it focuses attention on the living quality of encounters, on the quality of disabled bodies as carriers of live energy, and as engaged in a journey between life and mediation, art and everyday. The vulnerability of the body is present, and pressing onto the sensibilities of the spectators so close in contact with bodies usually held at bay through the 'disabled' label. But the vulnerability (imagined and otherwise) pairs with strength and resistance as presence. I am not sure whether I should read the performer's presence in their bodily difference as openings into the possibility of sharing social space, or rather as monsters, as Lingis's sharks that destabilize vicariously the 'normate' nature of non-disabled viewers. I want to read the immersion into an ocean of bodily difference in the tank of the train station as a moment that can overwhelm the escaping striations of categorization into an encounter with smoothness.[9]

A similar tightrope walk between the spectacle of the disabled body as alien, vulnerable, potentially disgusting player in the theater of cruelty and the disabled body as herald of a seductive encounter takes place in *Body Distance Between the Minds*, a dance performance by German choreographer Gerda König. As in *Sensation*, essentializing the disabled performer in its outsider role is a danger in any presentation of the disabled body as a sign on the limits of signification. But at the same time, it is not only the certainties of representational categorization that are questioned by these maneuvers between theater and index, but also the representation system as such is put under erasure. Smooth space explodes the system of striation. Every act, every performance undermines by its dynamic quality the rigidity of order: 'Smooth space is filled by events . . . far more than by formed and perceived things' (Deleuze and Guattari, 1988: 478). The dream of first principles is alive when boundaries are transgressed, and life emerges as movement in itself.

In *Body Distance*, König and Marc Stuhlmann begin their piece by lying side-by-side on the stage floor. The image is striking: both König's and her partner's upper bodies are naked – it seems. The light is falling on them from stage right, showing a landscape of flesh, but flesh painted blue, made alien, leaving a soupçon of doubt alive – are they naked – or not? What this there/not there of their bodies reveals in this long-held opening image has created controversy around DIN A 13: König lives with spina bifida, and her body is small, with a curved back, an asymmetrical chest, delicate arms and fingers. Presenting her body naked disturbs a number of taboos surrounding both the female and the disabled body. Different from Mat Fraser's laddish freak tactics, König's careful revelation doesn't seem to espouse the shock of Brechtian alienation, but rather the different shock of Artaud's cruelty: the unveiled presence of life *qua* life, its struggles, its energies, its dynamics, its intensity.

Her body begins to move soon, and engages in an intimate and tactile exploration with her partner's equally naked and blue body. Her body negates dance's perfect bodies: like Nitz's proud see-through black net shirt, König's blue paint wouldn't be scandalous on ballet-normate bodies, where we are well used to seeing the small breasts of thin, upright dancers. My reading of König's intervention into the more conventional dance aesthetics relates to the workings of the striated and the smooth:

> The striated is that which intertwines fixed and variable elements, produces an order and succession of distinct forms, and organizes horizontal melodic lines and vertical harmonic planes. The smooth is the continuous variation, continuous development of form, it is the fusion of harmony and melody in favor of the production of properly rythmic [sic] values, the pure act of the drawing of a diagonal across the vertical and the horizontal.
>
> (Deleuze and Guattari, 1988: 478)

König moves – she breathes her body into a rhythmic encounter with conventional aesthetics, with the spectators' predominantly normate bodies, and with the taboos of sexuality and disability. Rhythmic waves of living drown rules and tame images. The disabled performer here uses her outsider status as a means of breaking (cruelly) through the great polite 'harmony and melody'. But the price to be paid is the embrace of her body as outsider. And literally, the exclusion of her body

Figure 10 Body Distance Between the Minds, Gerda König and Marc Stuhlmann. Photograph by Jo Kirchherr. (Reproduced by courtesy of the artist)

from the polite stage – DIN A 13 have experienced censure for their display (like *Bilderwerfer* did, as members of the public complained about the 'use' of disabled people in the city performance). Cutting across the harmonies of the known is a risky business, but new rhythms, new ways of knowing social space and public bodies, can emerge in it.

Language machines

In *Hearing Things*, performance artist Aaron Williamson employs speech recognition software to create an oracle machine of new meetings of bodies and language. If the minotaur is one version of the outsider as animal/man, as suppressed and exiled Other, an other outsider is the venerated god/woman, as exemplified in the metaphors surrounding the Delphic oracle. The priestesses of the oracle sat on stools over toxic and hallucinatory fumes, which created states of trance and shamanistic vision in them. Being half in this world, half in another, they pronounced insights that were not of this world. The utterances needed interpreting by scribes: they were not in the language of humanity.

It is into this complex of metaphors and constellations of difference that Williamson inserts himself. He is profoundly deaf, and in his highly physical performance work, he wrings sounds out of his body – sounds that do not resemble 'speech', and that are highly affective, muscular and visceral.[10] Beyond his body, other sculptural elements inhabit the installation space: a large plaster ear, a tripod stool echoing the Delphic priestess (as does his long, white garment), mirrors, projected text, and a stone. With these elements, Williamson creates sounds and feeds them to a computer listener. He writes:

> Playing with and challenging the computer to interpret sound as speech often produced an incredible, accidental response that was, if not exactly fully coherent, entirely original or uncannily prescient. I was reminded, as the computer 'recognised' my distorted, non-verbal vocalisings, of the phenomenon of the 'oracular language', of language appearing from nowhere, in response to a mediumistic enquiry.
>
> (Williamson, 1999: 17)

The spectator becomes a body in space, a location of wild signification in the installation, as sounds produced in the act of spectating are channeled into the computer's meaning making. Williamson describes how loud footsteps in the gallery are translated by the software, and spewed out in strange form, projected on the floor: given the computer's

> intentionally ill-set probability models of linguistic recognition . . .: Going going going through Achilles Tendon to Broadmoor, Broadmoor and the Wrath of Zeus, Going where? Going low, lower . . .
>
> (Williamson, 1999: 17/18)

The text of *Hearing Things* is created in a human/non-human encounter, between biology and digitality, between interpretation and 'being'. Openness – the wild, indiscriminate search for sounds – and closure – the programing at work in the computer – create new sounds in their encounter. Circular interpretation opens up a vision of a desire towards meaning, and text is produced not as an authored, directed production, but as a machine where new constellations can emerge. This production can be aligned with Deleuze and Guattari's schizoanalysis,[11] where

> a text is never a scholarly exercise in search of what is signified, still less a highly textual exercise in search of a signifier . . . [but rather] a productive use of the literary machine, a montage of desiring machines, a schizoid exercise that extracts from the text its revolutionary forces.
>
> (Deleuze and Guattari, 1988: 106)

Williamson explores the machine character of language: its nature as an alignment of forces, rules, and chance, openness, in complex relations to bodies and their movements, and spaces and their echoes. Exposing language as machine deconstructs the 'natural' of meaning. The body as creative and energetic source is set at full gain, but we are held at one remove from unproblematizing its presence. It feeds its energy into coils of meaning-making, and the presence of this mechanism holds at bay the notion of the 'natural'. This disabled body isn't the raw matter preceding the fully arrived, evolutionary pinnacle of linguistically communicating 'normal man'. Instead, the disability divests itself from its connotation of loss, and enters into a creative space where the mechanism of linguistic communication itself can be exposed as a ritual machine. Our communication environment, telephones, answering machines, email, TV and their translatory practices are exposed, and our bodies become visible as soft tissue working in a giant machine of meaning generation. 'We are not free, and the sky can still fall on our heads' (Artaud, 1993: 60) – as individual authorship and agency are undermined, and the great desire machine that binds us all into compulsive meaning-making is exposed, the theater of cruelty shakes its spectators out of their certainties.

The performances discussed in this chapter undermine traditional meanings of 'the political' – they pose interventions into the realm of representation that are structural, but that do not necessarily find new positions for disabled people in our shared reality. Instead, the challenge to the structure of meaning and matter can be twisted back on itself, relegating disabled people into the negative position of the binary that keeps disabled and non-disabled apart. Aligned with incomprehensibility, with the 'natural', with the pre-linguistic and irrational, the physical, corporeal, abject, the politics of materiality can glide off the certainties erected in the name of the rational. But their force isn't easily ignored: the energy of the 'first principle' and the inauthentifying fear in the face of the alien shark can insert a wedge of doubt, exposing the construct of the rational and its judgments as historically contingent, local and non-universal. Wielding their forms of embodiment like weapons, the disabled artists presented here embrace the discomfort they have so often witnessed in their presence to push through to a different way of seeing social interaction. Beyond the polite, the cruel and its intensities becomes a vibrant if problematic option.

Chapter 5

Encountering paralysis
Disability, trauma, and narrative

The experience of disability is often figured as a moment of rupture, as a tragic loss of certainty about bodily status, social and economic future. Popular culture provides us with endless images of disability as a narrative impetus, as reason to set a story in motion. The reliance of narrative on disability as driving force has been called 'narrative prosthesis' by David Mitchell and Sharon Snyder. This prosthesis doesn't primarily create highly complex, differentiated images of disability as much as stories riven with their own status of incompleteness. They write:

> This defining corporeal unruliness consistently produces characters who are indentured to their biological programming in the most essentializing manner. Their disabilities surface to explain everything or nothing with respect to their portraits as embodied beings.
>
> (2000: 50)

And yet, disability narratives upset narration itself – the disability theme's traces of the bodily exceeds and challenges the neat progression of story. Disability narrative is seen as the attempt to overwrite, compulsively, the gap that opens up between bodies and difference.

> The effort to narrate disability's myriad deviations is an attempt to bring the body's unruliness under control . . . disability's representational 'fate' is not so much dependent upon a tradition of negative portrayals as it is tethered to inciting the act of meaning-making itself.
>
> (Mitchell and Snyder, 2000: 6)

So how does this literature-dependent model of narrative apply to bodies present in other forms than narrative texts? For Mitchell and Snyder, disability narratives provide a valuable function: 'Within literary narratives, disability serves as an interruptive force that confronts cultural truisms' (Mitchell and Snyder, 2000: 48). This force is dependent on the foundational difference between language and the body:

> The body's weighty materiality functions as a textual and cultural other – an object with its own undisciplined language that exceeds the text's ability to control it.
>
> (Mitchell and Synder, 2000: 49)

Setting up and perpetuating this binary between the body and the word creates problems for disabled performers, both on stage and in film – as I have discussed in the debates surrounding the 'natural' of disabled bodies in the previous chapters. Performance is the medium of the body – performance relies on the complexities of presence for its aesthetic drive.[1]

How disability metaphors and their narrational effects, and living bodies and their excessive vitality can move together and undermine the certainties of the medical label of trauma is the topic of this chapter. Through an analysis of videodance, I want to investigate the relationship between disability as a disrupting experience on the borders of the personal and the social. Videodance, or filmed performance, holds an interesting structural similarity to disability. Disability has a complex status – on the one hand, it references lived experience and its alignment with a bodily 'real'. On the other, it is used in much popular and high culture as a metaphor-generator, and a ready source for quick stereotypes.

In videodance, performance, textuality and history come together: 'liveness' and 'recording' create a strange dance that can unanchor conventional notions of the 'truth-status' of the live performer. A video can 'trick us' – it can show its function as projection, fantasy machine and construction of narratives in powerful ways. Video and film function as referents of a pre-textual history: something has occurred before the camera eye.[2] But this historical alignment between the camera as historical recorder, snapshot photography as marker of personal history and hand-held video as marker of live presence in TV coverage is at odds with contemporary vision machines: film machinery as a special effects creation, computer graphics and their potential for manipulation, even the red-eye adjustment that every computer user can effect on her computer, disrupt the old stabilities, the 'historical fallacy' that aligned photography and its successors with reality. Like disability, video and film are structurally on the limit of a pre-textual real and a hyper-textual fantasy. In the examples discussed here, this problematic status is further complexified by the liminal nature of dance, which rests in between 'natural' expression and codified, highly social behavior.

Trauma is a topoi well suited to this dual focus on private, bodily, 'real', 'true', 'natural' narrative and 'constructed' social meanings and stories. Trauma refers to a rupture: the word can both pertain to a physical injury, the effects of a blow on soft tissue, for example, and to a psychic phenomenon – the inability to narrativize, to integrate an event into one's personality, one's lifestory. Trauma is both private effect: paralyzing a person's ability to cohere her own story of herself, and public effect: trauma is diagnosed by an other – psychoanalyst, reader, interlocutor, the one who can see the discrepancy between the person's story with the socially accepted history.

Cathy Caruth's explorations of trauma and memory detail trauma's status in relation to reference, namely the relationship between immediate experience and language. With this, Caruth intervenes in 'the concern that the epistemological problems raised by poststructualist criticism necessarily lead to political and ethical paralysis' (1996: 10). Caruth refers to the issue of difference: poststructuralist theory presents language as always alienated from its subject. Language is seen as a self-referential system, and doesn't allow for an understanding of the 'other'. For instance, by endlessly repeating the binary structure of 'man' and 'woman', 'able', 'disabled' one term is always seen as the negation of the other term: neither 'woman' nor 'disabled' are terms in their own right, but are determined by their language opposition to the central term – 'man' or 'able'. Since these later terms are 'central' they easily become invisible: 'able' and 'man' come to be seen as the norm. Our language structures knowing – if we learn in oppositions, we are not able to grasp the 'other', that which falls outside the center, on its own terms. In this way, poststructuralist theory with its insistence on our inability to grasp the 'real', and its emphasis on a world where language always slides off and misses its referent, alienates earlier political projects. If we cannot speak 'for the other', since to do so does violence to it by pressing it into dominant schemes thinking, how can we think politically, how can we change the world? Caruth uses thinking about trauma and its disruptive effect on the individual psyche to open up a space for a way of thinking that falls outside the dominant framework, a way of understanding that opens up a path for difference. She posits that trauma allows for us:

> a rethinking of reference [that] is aimed not at eliminating history but at resituating it in our understanding, that is, at precisely permitting *history* to arise where immediate understanding may not.
>
> (1996: 11)

Mediation, distance, repetition – these processes which intervene in the 'immediate understanding' – allow for a different path towards the 'other' and her story. In traumatic narrative, the story is not fully there, not fully owned by discourse and is not within the mastery of the individual. In place of the masterful narrative, a new communication can emerge in and through the sites and bodies of trauma, a communication in which shared distances, not sameness, act as points of connection. Caruth analyses the film *Hiroshima mon amour* (Alain Resnais, F, 1960) as such a narrative of missed immediacy, of translation, passings and mis-understandings:

> It is indeed the enigmatic language of untold stories – of experiences not yet completely grasped – that resonates, throughout the film, within the dialogue between the French woman and the Japanese man, and allows them to communicate, across the gap between their cultures and their experiences, precisely through what they do not directly comprehend. Their ability to speak and to listen in their passionate encounter does not rely, that is, on

what they simply know of one another, but on what they do not fully know in their own traumatic pasts. In a similar way, a new mode of seeing and of listening – a seeing and a listening from the site of trauma – is opened up to us as spectators of the film, and offered as the very possibility, in a catastrophic era, of a link between cultures.

(1996: 56)

Social history can become obliquely accessible through the halting narrative of the personal, the physical, the individual, the positing of gaps in meaningful, but not fully owned places. In *Hiroshima mon amour*, the rupture in the life of the film's individuals occurs when they arrive too late: the Japanese man is absent from the bombing of Hiroshima, the French woman arrives to find her lover dying. But what happens to places of trauma and the relationship to time when the trauma is the violent rupture *within* one's body? How can a story be told across the bodily difference of disability, a difference marked as 'tragic' within narrative economy, and a difference full of social meanings of exclusion? How can a communication be established across this divide of cultural and physical difference, allowing a story of pain to emerge without drowning it out with known references?

This chapter tells a story about the relationship between time, rupture and narrative in a dancing and disabled body, that is made accessible through the medium of film. The body, a woman's body, a disabled body, a dancing body, a body in a film, a person – these are some of the meeting places of the personal and the public that are touched upon, queried and ruptured in the images, communications and translations of film.

Trauma, disability and narrative

The body and its states act as powerful meaning-carriers in discourse. The Caruth quotation above spoke of a 'political and ethical *paralysis*' [my emphasis]. Many tropes of language rely on these physical references of visibility and mobility. Paralysis (and blindness, 'crippling', amputation, abortion) – these words resonate beyond the 'abstract' order of language and literary analysis, and have meaning in the order of bodies and the psychic. These meanings are reiterated in discourse and practice through the use and re-use of their negative connotation in communication, for instance in film narrative. This marking of disability as negative within the cultural narrative economy undermines social attempts to revalue disability, and to bring disabled people out of the ghetto of abjection.

How can the unknowability and individuality of the physical and psychic experience of another being be safeguarded against language's power to determine and name? To unfix the physical experience of paralysis from its known parameters without undermining the psychic and social effects of disability is a task similar to the dilemma facing feminists in their quest to mobilize 'woman' as an identity category without losing a communal, identificatory political base. The disruption of disability to an individual's life can be (but not need to be) physically and psychically painful, but is most likely painful in its encounter with the social. The social narrative of disability sees it as negativity, and the social world excludes disabled people through environmental and attitudinal barriers. Language and narrative re-present disability as pain and tragedy. These markers and meanings help to determine the 'knowledge' of disability in the disabled and non-disabled individual's psyche and physis. As we have seen, disability, like trauma, is a concept on the borderline of the private and public, an experience that is problematically represented in language.

Trauma and disability therefore articulate related problems in the referential nature of narrative and language – the inability of narrative and language to access and express immediate experience. While trauma studies explores the non-narrational nature of trauma – holocaust historians have battled against the containment of horror in safe structures – disability studies (like identity politics/representation studies) battles against narrative overdetermination.

Trauma is that which cannot be incorporated, the disruptive break, the horrifying immediacy, which becomes the focus for memory-work and compulsive attempts at narrativisation. Trauma is a moment out of flow – a moment out of time, unable to be smoothly reintegrated into the flow of time. Trauma exists within discursive practice on the horizon of narrativity: it is the block which does not allow full narrative, but which nevertheless sets it (and its repetition) in motion.

The experience of disability is often figured as a traumatic personal history, culturally marked as 'private' tragedy. Within literature and film, disability often becomes the symptom of trauma: like Freud's hysterical women, disabled actors are ready to carry the stigma of their personal histories as readable signs on their bodies. Moments of the symbolic nature of disability characterize film narrative.[3] The stereotyping of Victorian melodrama and its use of innocent blind maidens live on in contemporary film-making.[4] One carrier of this narrative device is the little lame boy in the different film and story versions of *The Secret Garden*: as soon as he is able to face his loneliness, his captivity, and grow more 'adult' in his relationship with others, he is able to walk again. As soon as the knot is undone, the trauma re-integrated and narrativized, the disability can vanish. Disability can act as a readable sign – it can be used as a dramaturgical device, a shorthand, in film or performance. The inner life of a character is expressed in his limp, her 'sensitive' blindness, his muteness. It can provide a recognizable 'trauma moment' – a defining point in a character's life, open to all to read, and a start to a good yarn.[5]

Paralysis is the theme of a short film about moving bodies, *The Fall*, by Darshan Singh Bhuller. This ten-minute long film was first screened by the BBC in 1991. What makes it particularly interesting for my investigation into disability and performance is that the protagonist of this film, Celeste Dandeker, has gone on to co-found CandoCo, the highly influential integrated professional dance company discussed elsewhere. The story told in *The Fall* has become part of Dandeker's public persona, as every article ever written about her testifies: the origin and effects of paralysis on her dancer's life. *The Fall* can be read as a symptom for the desire for narrative and narrative's instability in relation to 'immediate knowledge' of physical history. The film works with relational knowledges from different kinds of speech: film knowledge about the conventions of memory and flashbacks, awareness of TV genres such as docu-dramas or the 'fly-on-the-wall' documentary, and the knowledge of selfhood and body-truth that accompanies the 'common-sense' response to both a disabled body, and to the activity of dancing.

The Fall is a film in constant motion, not allowing either its characters or its spectator to rest peacefully in one place. The narration recoils, points forward and backward, distrusts itself. A synopsis of the film is useful, despite as well as because of the riskiness of the synopsis as a paralyzed form:

> In the name of the law, I shall take the calculated risk of flattening out the unfolding or coiling up of this text, its permanent revolution whose rounds are made to resist any kind of flattening.
>
> (Derrida, 1992: 234)

The undoing of narrational condensing by the coils springing up to halt motion is the subject of this chapter. The film is set up as a relatively conventional narrative: we see a woman in a wheelchair, who is working on a clay sculpture. As she switches the radio on, she overbalances and falls backwards. A man in another room rushes to her help, but while she is on the floor we hear a radio program, probably about her life, and we see flashbacks showing moments of it. The first flashback shows a carefree child dancing with a male adult. Then we see a young dancer exploring the space by herself, later joined by a male partner. Next we see the woman as a 'broken body' in a back brace, moved to music by the tender partner, and lastly on her own in a wheelchair, moving herself, but twisting her face and body in anger. Finally, the man reaches her and lifts her up again. She looks at a photograph of herself as a non-disabled dancer. Over the end credits, we see her laughing and moving in the wheelchair.

The woman in the film is played by Celeste Dandeker, a dancer who became disabled after a fall which occurred during her dance work. But whether the film's story is a 'true' story, or even 'her story', is never clear. The knowledge of Dandeker's personal history comes to the spectator from outside; nothing in the film conflates character and actress beyond the mechanisms of transparent film-narrative. This narrative is complicated, doubled, over-determined and questioned through various mechanisms, as a careful textual analysis of its opening shots shows.[6]

Filming narrative

The film opens with an evocation of narrativity and the placement of disability, trauma and therapy. The connection between these concepts, and the way they are invoked and kept in tension emerges out of a shot-by-shot analysis. The first

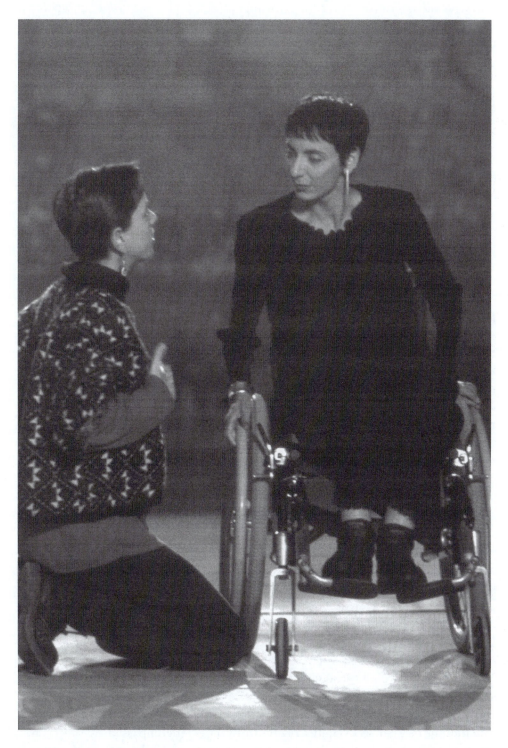

Figure 11 Celeste Dandeker and Margaret Williams, director of *Outside In*. (Reproduced by courtesy of MJW Productions)

shot is of a wet, glistening clay sculpture of a human head. The meta-genre of narrative allows us to expect a beginning: a temporal crisis. Tzvetan Todorov (1977) structured narratives into equilibrium, disequilibrium and new equilibrium: the clay may point to the solidity of matter, but a matter endowed with the ability to change (and therefore narrational). This matter is the unmaking to a form, the dis- to fixity, the becoming of something else. This clay, formally at the beginning, seems to equate the principle of narrative in general as well as the narrative in particular: the film will, following conventions, tell the story of a shaping of a human life. In particular, it tells the shaping of a particular life, of a young dancer who becomes paralyzed, but moves through paralysis.

The enunciating force of the film finds expression in a movement on screen – two hands appear in the film frame. They enter the frame and shape the clay head. The clay is shaped by external forces, it is not the shaper. But neither is the flesh autonomous, non-metaphoric, and stable in itself. Just as the hands shape the clay, the camera shapes the images of the hands (and the body, the flesh), and our reading shapes the video image of hands into shapers.[7] The reference to art-making, coterminous with the making of narrative, points to the artifice in the artefact. Making narratives, re-integrating the traumatic moment, is one therapeutic response to trauma.[8] Art therapy can use various avenues to integrate experience into the psyche, and clay modelling is one of the methods used. But by referencing (potentially therapeutic) art making in the framework of the film, *The Fall* points to the nature of shaped, worked-on, experience as neither wholly personal nor wholly public. The structures of meaning always exceed the personal, with the individual coming belatedly to them, and the personal always exceeds the public, allowing no full expression. The film-ness of the film about the moving body inserts a sliver of difference, of distance to the moving body. The first few seconds of *The Fall* already present us with a fall from the Garden of Eden, or a fall into Babelian confusion: translation and non-immediacy announce themselves in the images of making and reading. Full presence and transparent communication are questioned and undermined.

The clay head is framed in profile, lights bouncing off its slick, wet, unformed surface. As the camera tracks gently backwards, another nose edges into the frame, along with eyes, a chin. Just before the hands come up to mold the other head, to start the mold of the narrational agency, a mirror moment is briefly established: a head of flesh is looking at a head of clay. The new head is female, a quality not apparent in the first, unfinished head. Here, in the generic clay head, non-displayed gender reads male: a strange dance of gazes and display accompany this little dance of heads, camera and sculpture.

The Fall's initial shots articulate complicated positions: the woman is the (first) shaper of the sculpture, she is the creator. But the narrative of a woman artist is contravened by the movement of the shots: it is the clay head which is first seen looking out, with the woman's profile only later encompassed in the frame. Agency, in the guise of the gaze, moves from the unspecific head to hers, and the camera surveys them both, clay and flesh head, in profile, retaining the ultimate hierarchy of filmed object and off-screen spectator. They do not gaze back at the camera, only at each other.

As soon as the hands move into the frame, new meanings are spawned: the hands which mold the head are thin and wasted. They are the hands of a disabled woman. The weight of the disability as traumatic invisibility disturbs some of the possible paths that the spectator could potentially travel at the beginning of this narrative. The narrative encounters paralysis – the possibility of becoming firmly lodged in one reading. Disability (culturally) denies positivity – the body signals its (cultural) meaning of tragedy. The making of a head is the spectacle of the film: it is the woman's life which becomes molded and shaped into a sculpture just as her body acquires a new molding – a back brace and a wheelchair. But the initial instability of agency, of the gaze, of the hands, and the weight of disability haunts the narratives of the film, as the spectator is constantly denied access to a 'true', personal understanding of the woman's narrative. Her body throughout oscillates between being flesh and being clay – not resting in either materiality.

Repetitions

Todorov's disequilibrium is corporeally enacted as the woman reaches away from her sculpting to switch on the radio. In order to reach the radio, she levers herself up by holding onto the clay head. She overbalances and her wheelchair falls backwards, with the clay head falling on her. The fall is cinematically presented through a montage of repeated slow-motion elements. Somewhere else, a handsome man looks up, his face slowly contorts in the moment of realization, a scream 'no' renders the air. High drama is signalled in this accumulation of Hollywood signs and codes. Life is all too short, and must be held back through slow-motion to allow us to grasp its significance: the film announces its presence. The connection between the use of slow-motion and other technical devices and the mechanics of signifying time have been usefully described as 'the discourse swelling the time of an event that occupies a considerably shorter time in the story' (Stam, Burgoyne and Flitterman-Lewis, 1992: 121).

A female spectacle accumulates signs and connections. Over-determination, swelling, and reiteration out of control are the signs of traumatic experience – a traumatic narrative controls a psyche by forcing its structure of repetition into psychic continuity. This fall is the point of trauma in the film. Trauma in the film becomes doubled, mirroring the public/private character of trauma in language. A physical trauma has befallen the character in *The Fall*, and is never represented in the film – no images of her disabling experience are shown, as her trauma remains unrepresentable. This woman owns her story, and we do not know whether her personal life story in turn haunts her as trauma. The woman playing the character, visibly disabled, equally shrouds her own story. But their combined presences, in the film narrative and in the visual image referencing 'the actress', they create a trauma of reading for the spectator. The spectator cannot access the 'truth', a truth that is layered with the cultural meaning of disability that insists on the traumatic character of the experience. The film's progression offers no way out – images of instability haunt the meaning-making process of narrative. The narrative as presented to and created by the spectator is endangered by paralysis, and the referencing function circles endlessly into nowhere, or just back to the preconceived knowledges of the spectator. The non-immediacy of the film-narrative works as the trauma of the spectator.

The fallen body will be the image the film comes back to, again and again. The traumatic, thick, repeated and reiterated image refers to physicality on two levels – on physicality in narrative, and on physicality in sexual difference. The image of falling conjures up the possibility of injury (and the potential source of disability). At the same time, formally, the repeated, drawn out moment of falling signals the femininity of the fallen woman – the representation becomes 'hysteric', melodramatic, too much – in a word, coded female. But both of these references are made unstable, as they point in their ubiquitousness to the artificiality of a story created without the referent of (body and woman) truth.

Just as the woman of the film is both issuing source of change (sculptor) and matter to be molded by (diagetic) life and film, the effect of the fall reaches me as spectator on two levels. The slow-motion heightens the drama of the fall, and makes me feel with her the hardness of the floor, the disorientating experience of falling: the flesh of the fall. In the phenomenological flesh an intersubjectivity, a knowing is established – a connection which is denied, again and again, on the representational level. This affectual knowledge is combined with knowledge of the signifying practice of film as a semiotic system. As a spectator attuned to the genre of narrative film, I can read the conventions signalling a break with the 'normalcy' of transparent narrative. Brian Henderson describes how cinema codes transgressions from straight chronology:

> Classical cinema reacts to a tense shift as though to a cataclysm; the viewer must be warned at every level of cinematic expression, in sounds, in images and in written language, lest he/she be disoriented.
>
> (Henderson, 1983: 6)

The excessive use of filmic conventions, both on the level of formal practices (slow-motion) and conventionalist images, conveys this rupture to the spectator: a glass bursts apart twice during the elongated moment of falling, water runs freely. An audience trained in popular Freudian analysis can decode this sign – we are witnessing a moment of epiphany, linked to a release of emotions and acting as a pointer towards (female) sexuality.[9]

Genres, categories, conventionally separated aggregations of signs are mixing in this build-up to the narrational hub of the short film. The center of the film, the woman, has reached us as an aggregation of opposing signs: object and subject of the gaze, maker and made, active and disabled. The hands that reach up to mold the clay head are thin, twisted and weak – they are the hands usually on view in charity advertising – trying hard to guide a dripping spoon to a desperate mouth. Their position of agency is changed, but the meaning of the disabled body as passive, compensating figure is not easily destabilized. The oppositional potency of the two introducing images, the artist – self-controlled and agent – and the disabled – needy, dependent, tragic – give us no 'new narrative', but point us to the problematic nature of representation. Both images are well-used in the cinematic genres of 'artist's biography' and 'victim narrative' or 'woman's film'.

The predefined narrational values of these images dislocate the woman. She is caught between different narratives. She falls from one discourse set up by the conventional images to the other. The very excess of imagery and meaning destabilizes the signifying scenario. The structure of meaning is touched, not the content of any one of the images by themselves.

Before falling, the woman manages to switch on the radio. Thus we hear a pleasant female voice, imbued with the privileged position given to the voice-over in classic cinema at moments of temporal transgression. The status of this voice-over is hybrid: it is both intra-diegetic, since its appearance is linked to the radio, and extra-diegetic as it stands as the privileged source of narrational knowledge at a moment of shift. This hybrid, transgressive nature of the voice-over is further underlined by its being female and disembodied. Kaja Silverman describes the interesting position of a disembodied voice in an embodied representational scenario:

> There is a general theoretical consensus that the theological status of the disembodied voice-over is the effect of maintaining its source in a place apart from the camera, inaccessible to the gaze of either the cinematic apparatus or the viewing subject – of violating the rule of synchronization so absolutely that the voice is left without an identifiable locus. In other words, the voice-over is privileged to the degree that *it transcends the body*. Conversely, it loses power and authority with every corporeal encroachment, from a regional accent or idiosyncratic 'grain' to definite localization in the image. Synchronization marks the final moment in any such localization, the point of full and complete 'embodiment'.
>
> (1988: 49)

The radio voice shifts between the realm of embodied (in the radio) and disembodied (with its connotation of privileged knowledge). But since a space for it is opened in the diagetic world of the film through the woman's movement of switching on the radio (corporeal encroachment), the exact nature of its 'privileged viewpoint' is made unstable. Being female further undermines clear distinctions – disembodied means non-bodied, general, disinterested, which culturally has been coded 'male', whereas female conventionally means specific, subjective and individual – not qualities associated with the neutral position of an interviewer or anchorperson (or a generic clay head). Equally, the message of the voice-over also shifts between transparency, that is, the 'narrational truth', linked to a clear identification of the wheelchair user as 'real person', and artifice, destabilizing the representation.

The voice tells us about a 'successful performance artist, whose career has been nevertheless fraught with difficulties that most of us' never encounter. The scene is set for an encounter with the stereotypes of 'tragic' disability, but already made complicated, unstable, through the use of 'successful'. The remainder of the film consists of flashbacks, or snippets of a life, narrated in its traditional core stages: childhood, adolescence and love, tragic disruption with the onset of disability, and the journey towards living with the disability. The flashbacks, presented in black-and-white, insert a new level of abstraction or distance between the spectator and the unknowable woman presented on the screen, nearly drowning in conventional but excessive markings. The filmic narrative switches from a transparent, naturalist mode into a new gear – the life-stages are danced.

The dance of death: The paralysis of body trauma

Once upon a time, in the history of representation, the body's movement through time found a strong and resonant image: the dance of death. The dance of death and cultural studies' preoccupation with the living body can function as two tropes with which to grasp the mechanisms of paralysis and movement that govern *The Fall*. Hans Holbein's famous sixteenth-century depiction of the dance of death paralyzes one moment in time. It is the act of paralyzing the moment that demonstrates the passing of time. Just as trauma brings personal pain into the view of narrativity – the block as the precondition of the obsessive narrative – the freeze enables the vision of life.

In the dance of death, people are caught in the middle of life, frozen out of their social relationships and material surroundings. They have to hold the hand of a skeleton that leads them in a circular dance – the dance of death. Through the act of freezing and paralyzing, that is, holding in time on the canvas, life becomes apparent as a journey, a timed enterprise. Time is passing. Time is running out. But it needs the action of holding life, of capturing the moment and taking it out, which brings out the timed nature of life. 'Memento mori' is the message of the baroque dance of death – your life is but a passage, a journey, a timed event, with an ending waiting for you.

The action taken by the artist in paralyzing an image of a metaphorical dance of death puts life into a narrative. A beginning, middle and end are structured into the everyday existence of the painter's subjects. Narrative structures the time of life. Narrative provides the focal points which define life. Points of rupture, trauma, non-flow are the markers by which we present the flow of time and its effects.

Escape attempts from the prison of this narrow view of the body in art often take the form of celebrating the body triumphing over narrative. The dance of death is replaced by a dance of life – a dance of moments, freedoms, flow, expansion. Excess can be seen as a challenge to the structuring potential of time, specific traumatic moments and narrative. In some recent cultural theory, the body becomes a refuge of individuality, lived experience and value, and asserts itself in the face of the disembodying effects of structures, external knowledges, schemes of surveillance, etc. To dance on the grave of logocentrism, binaries and rationality – this is a dream that many of us may well share.

But is dance the appropriate medium to break through the narratives of bodies and time? Dance addresses its spectators in specific ways. One of these relates to its production of affect – when we see somebody dance, the kinetic energy can translate itself to us, and moves us. This is part of the authenticity of dance – its appeal has been read as going beyond traditional narrative and meaning, relating directly to 'the body'. In *The Fall*, a dance of differing and competing addresses is enacted. The spectator is faced with competing and contradictory versions of temporal bodies: bodies whose relationship to pivotal moments is questioned.

After the arrest on the floor, the end of the fall, a memory emerges, or is presented to us. It is a moment of harmony, happiness, corporeal and utopian well-being. We see a young girl, her ethnic affiliation unclear (and therefore easily read as 'white'), playing amidst a field of balloons. She is joined by a kind, beaming South Asian man. Together, they proceed to run energetically, taking space and enjoying their freedom. The girl is lifted up by the man and is twirled about in an image of childhood joy. The exuberance and kinetic experience is translated to the spectator through a highly mobile camera, allowing our senses to join into the new spatial configuration of an involved camera, entering the space of its subjects' bodies.

This image of ethnic harmony is followed by one of gendered harmony in the second flashback. As the radio voice proceeds to the words 'student days, young, independent, Chicago', we view a black and white, slightly grainy image of a female dancer. Sophisticated jazz music accompanies the dancer's movement around classical columns, as she is taking her space. She is joined by a man, and by the beat of percussions. They 'naturally' dance together, in an image of pulsating life.

But the authenticity of these danced moments is immediately put into question – in each instance, the 'naturalist' environment of the frame is replaced with the dreamscape of balloons (in the childhood scene) or stylized black-and-white photography (in the romance scene), referencing the generic, representational nature of these images. The freedom of dance movement, which can affect the viewer bodily through its translation by the mobile camera, is queried by the framings and filters distancing us from the images. Instead of merging with the woman's memories and entering fully the filmic path into identification, we are jarred back into the color-stock 'present' of a close-up on the woman's face, still lying on the floor, her face unreadable, not cueing us into the emotions potentially evoked by the flashbacks. The fragments of happy dance bring us back to the 'death' of meaning: to the refusal to signify clearly. This death is positive: it is out of time (the time of repetitions), and yet woven into the fabric of the film's time. It is a death that allows a becoming, by not cutting us off completely from the bodies and objects of time. This woman does not allow us to read her body's narrative (the story of her life) through traumatic repetition of past moments. The trauma of incomprehensibility is not the understood inner life of the woman, falling into place; instead it is the trauma of the viewer, as this story does not evolve and integrate. The body of the viewer is implicated in this teasing, frustrating death of narrative – the flashbacks with their dancerly audience address have gripped my viewing body and swung it into (inner) motion. Now my body has to recover from this fall into paralysis opposite the image of the woman's face, not giving anything away. The images do not dance into the set circle of the dance of life. Instead, the positive, generative paralysis of meaning hovers over interpretations, steps and stories.

The last two flashbacks seem to show us the time after 'the disability'. We do not hear of any fall, any reason for the physical impairment, or see any images that could give clues to this traumatic, disruptive, life-changing event. All we see and hear are the effects – the radio tells us of 'difficult times, restrictions, adjustment'. A new flashback shows the dancing man from the previous scene, dancing alone. He is now the originator of movement. As the camera moves, the female dancer enters the frame, held up by a frame, a brace encircling her whole torso. She stands stiff, upright, any motion she makes is broken by the brace's support, not allowing a full movement to emerge. The man loosens her brace, takes her out, the brace is viewed close up, suffused with shadows, a melodramatic dungeon. The music is tragic and mourning. The woman is moved by her partner, her head sometimes leaving the frame, while his head remains in the center of it. She is helpless, immobile, dependent. But the stability of agency is questioned: the woman moves her hands slightly, and his larger movements echo the spatial directions of her smaller dance – again, the relationship and power balance is not clear.

At this point, the flashback ends, and the fall comes full circle into recovery. The man, now identifiable as the male dancer of the flashbacks, has arrived, and moves the wheelchair and the woman up. As he tries to touch her, she shakes her head, but still, no definite emotion registers on her face. A final zoom moves into a photo on a desk, of the woman as a young dancer in a modernist dance company.[10]

To complement this array of images, the credits roll over footage of the woman, sitting in her chair, dancing with her arms, bending her body, a definite smile on her lips. Do we see a pre-filmic moment of a woman breaking through her confinement in the moment of private dance? Or is this a character, still part of the diegetic universe of the film, still part of the narrative?

Clay, flesh, radio, dance, photos and films: many different media give testimony to the life of the woman in front of us. Still, we do not know what her life means to her – what life means to her with her disability, with her dance, with her partner. Instead, the life is made paradoxical, caught up in conventions and film 'tricks' – the chronology of who photographed whom when, in what story.

One of the aspects of trauma that fascinates Caruth (1996: 66) is the enigma of survival, and the structure of personal and public that reveals itself in the witnessing of trauma – 'the theory of trauma, as a historical experience of a survival exceeding the grasp of the one who survives, engages a notion of history exceeding individual bonds'.

The film *The Fall* works on a similar trajectory – the individual experience of disability as bodily and psychic trauma is shadowed, veiled and made unknowable. What emerges instead in *The Fall*'s multiplying questions and stories, is the story of disability's problematic status within representation as a meaning device that fails to reference and instead injures the individual experience. If personal pain is unrepresentable, it is the signals of the traumatic rupture in narrative through narrative overload which can make witnesses out of spectators – witnesses for the impossibility of knowing, and for the generative potentials of a paralysis of meaning. In the impossibility of knowing, a sense of living can permeate graven images.

Dancing

> For in a question like this truth is only to be had by laying together many varieties of error.
>
> (Virginia Woolf, *A Room of One's Own*)

The Fall is at first glance a redemptory journey through a biography, with a tragic moment, the fall, which mirrors some accident in the past, and which now sets up a chain of memories waiting to be consumed, ordered and worked through. After this cathartic journey of an individual through her life, she is free to dance again. But any easy reading is complicated by filmic devices and the structures of narrative. Many varieties of error are laid together to allow a new story to emerge – a story of being-not-quite-sure, of moments when immediate reference breaks down, and a new respect for the other woman can emerge out of paralyzed fragments of meaning.

The truth claim of *The Fall*'s flashbacks is problematic. The present has the most vivid colors. The flashbacks depict stereotypical images of a life lived in and through dance. Is this a biography? Is dance emotion? Is the gaze the privileged site of knowledge, or does the foregrounding of the clay molding and the radio point towards other ways of knowing? The final image of the woman's liberated dance occurs over the credits – a nowhere land, precariously lodged outside the narrative, on a different textual level.

The viewer is forced to reassess her reactions to the film: the disabled woman traditionally signals body-truth – 'the disabled' are defined by their bodies. Against this stand the sequences of her as a young dancer: is this her, in old documentary footage? Which means, is this biography really the actress's herstory? Is she only faking her disability, and has she also shot this part? Does someone else dance this part? The temporal sequence of making *The Fall* as a recount of a life reveals a document of fakery.

What live dance performance accomplishes through affect is made problematic in filmdance. In film we do not have the unquestionable presence of the living body of the performer, both authenticating *and* disrupting the performance. The post-modern viewer is surrounded with a realm of technological simulacra, special effects, digital art, particularly in TV work, which complicates the consumption of 'representations experienced as perceptions', to use Jean-Louis Baudry's famous phrase. The truth-claim of the dancing body, engaged in 'natural' expression, allowing a 'true' inner life to be read on a 'true' physical shell, is subverted by this nagging incongruency regarding the origin of the various scenes. Thus, the spectator cannot witness the truth of another person – the other person is a representation which too often brings to the fore its own artificiality. Witnessing the other being would re-create a smooth story, a time of healing, a reintegration of the person witnessed into the social space of the witnesses. In *The Fall*, instead, a witnessing of the spectator's own trauma is called for – what is witnessed is the impossibility of narrative emerging out of the encounter with 'other' physicality. Disability becomes unknown. The dance and its affect reference the bodily, the flesh, even as the representational and narrational communication highlights the clay. These problematizations of authenticity subvert any reading of the woman as a tragic figure, and of dance as a clear bodily communication.

Beyond all these unclear markers of meaning rests the woman's immobile face. Our block is not removed – and we do not even know about the existence of her trauma. The private resists the most insistent readings of trauma, the most persistent attempts to narrativize. She doesn't let us know. As spectators, we have witnessed a traumatic moment: a re-enactment, and potential solution, to a potential earlier fall (from ability). This personal body-story can be accommodated within the range of cultural narratives available to us as cultural readers – including the trauma narrative, so proliferated in Post Traumatic Stress Disorder discussions in the popular media. Maybe a talking or showing cure will exorcise the block that stands in the way of us reading the woman. But maybe the block resists – maybe the horizon of narrativity is itself traversed by the traces of a private experience which remains out of reach.

Time is manipulated, pleated, folded, twisted in this encounter of female, disabled, artistic, dancerly, filmic, psychological narratives. Time as narrative is burst apart by the multi-valent images and the multi-stranded familiar narratives. Instead of being able to read filmic images as ordered in sequences, and connected in ways that Hollywood has taught us to read, the spectator is left with many different moments. They do not come together in a clear, univocal narrative, but create an image of lived experience of time which isn't graspable by sequential and causal rules.

Dance and its privileged position in relation to body-time, true time, embodiment, direct experience and affect has become unstable in my reading of *The Fall*. We are fallen from the grace of a stable focal point of 'real-ness'. Dance no longer means 'authenticity', an access to a clear and unified self. In a similar vein, Janet Wolff critiques the vogue for using dance metaphors in feminist and cultural studies, and reminds us of our mistaken trust in dance to free us from the narrational and logocentric straitjacket:

Dancing may well be liberating, and the metaphor of dance may sometimes capture the sense of circumventing dominant modes of rationality. But my concern about this particular trope is that it depends on a mistaken idea of dance as intuitive, non-verbal, natural, and that it risks abandoning critical analysis for a vague and ill-conceived 'politics of the body'.

(1997: 70)

In my reading of *The Fall*, my narrative of falling, dance becomes just one narrative of bodies in time – not a 'natural' one, not one that is privileged, but a complex form of being in time and space. From the point of view of a disabled woman, the 'naturalness' of dance is as confining, constricting and oppressive as the 'naturalness' of marriage or children. The body and its expression become enigmatic. What I find fascinating about *The Fall*, about wheelchairs and about dance is their potential for upset, tilting and falling. Narrativizing the specific other, the woman, and the general other, the disabled community, becomes problematic as the psychic structure of trauma reveals itself as a narrational tool to grasp the other with. It is only in the shared acknowledgement of the disruption of *all* narrative by the unknowable personal that a communication is achieved – a communication with narratives as masks which need to be picked up and discarded, used and recycled, if any story is to emerge. These 'reading scenes', encounters between embodied texts and spectators on the edges of the public and the private can work by oscillating us between narratives, rather than forcing us to abandon narratives altogether.

The Fall leads on from the dance of death. Instead of halting, paralyzing the moments of life into elements that demand narrative, that demand significance, constant movement of meaning keeps us on our toes. The narratives, frameworks, contexts, images of the film keep dancing to no measured step. Since this trauma cannot be cured, it remains the traumatic block in the reader, a block that doesn't allow integration into smooth known images, and which allows the representation of a private, non-readable other woman to dance.

Much artwork by disabled people has chosen similar avenues to undermine the over-determined narrative of non-disabled perception of disability. The question of how to show the personal through the veil of cultural meaning has moved artists such as film-maker Ann Whitehurst. In Whitehurst's film *Denial* (UK, 1996) she enacts a refusal to speak, to show and to confirm. The film presents a long-held shot focusing on a woman sitting in an electric wheelchair. She is refusing emotion to register on her body and face, while an off-screen interviewing voice asks intrusive questions about the nature of her impairment, her experience and her way of living. The film is a powerful indictment of the diagnostic stare, the medical and popular cultural intrusion in the experience of disabled people – their narratives are pre-cast, and individuality and voice is lost. At the end of *Denial*, the physical presence of the woman in the wheelchair asserts itself – she moves into the camera, closer and closer, taking space, pushing out the invading gaze, confusing it with her materiality. She is still denying engagement on the level of words and language. Like in *The Fall*, no answer is given – but the many varieties of error are laid bare as such by pointing to their narrational nature. Some parameters of the invisible, untold social histories of disabled people and of disabled women can become visible, not in the laying bare of the personal, but in the witnessing of unknowability.

After the story

How to end without paralysis? This close reading of a film remains in tension – the film is not seen, its immediacy and affect, mined in these pages, remain only paradoxically accessible in these words. Disability as a cultural placeholder of trauma is querying its status as originator of narrative. The phenomenological, immediate experience of disability remains covered up, but the storied covers point to their own existence as the translators of the immediate into the accessible. The images that dance in these pages are the clay of stories that are formed in the spaces between the text and the spectator, the text and the reader. The horrifying disruption of trauma can allow a tentative movement from the personal to the public – one culture talking to another – in the acknowledged ignorances, the reflective translations and repetitions of a story which spins out of the control of both maker and reader. These uncertainties translate the story of a woman from an individual story into one about the workings of difference and sharing.

For Caruth's reading of *Hiroshima mon amour*, the stories of individuals and cultures are linked into a history through what cannot be understood. In a similar move, readings of films such as *The Fall* and *Denial* can point to failure of language to reference the immediate, the private in the public realm of language. This failure, though, is only the beginning of a story, not the end of one. Stories continue to excite curiosity, and to forge new connections between one person and another, between disabled people and non-disabled people, between cultures. In saving stories from paralysis, the future of communication moves into view.

Chapter 6

New technologies of embodiment

Cyborgs and websurfers

In *Body Provisional*, a performance installation created by Sophia Lycouris and myself in 2002, we told stories of the body's interior. Our materials were movement, X-ray photographs, rhymes, interviews and the stony, semi-organic material of shells and sand. In the performance, we handed a small digital video camera to our spectators as we engaged them in one-on-one performances. On the camera was a small, LCD display, showing close-ups of crashing waves and sand traversed by traveling feet. Peering at the small display cradled in their hands, the screen lit up in the dark performance space on NYC's Lower East Side, our participants were invited to feel the pull of our movement. In this performance, we used digital technology to present a form of intimacy: the camera became an addendum to living bodies. Traces of embodied living became part of the formal elements of the video: in the recording of movements on a beach, the camera operator's movements were recorded, as well: we breathed while holding the camera to our eye, so the camera shifted slightly, as our feet moved across sand, the camera recorded the instability of our hand's grip. In the performance space, the camera and its LCD display remembered these movements on the beach, offering to our spectators vague sensings of our embodiment.

In our preparation to this show, cameras which today are conveniently small and easy to deal with, became normalized extensions of our vision apparatuses and our moving bodies.

This chapter attempts to read contemporary performance practices that create such alignments between 'new' digital technologies and living presences. The performances I want to discuss center on bodies with addenda: disabled and non-disabled people meeting on a technological interface, the computer screen, the keyboard and the mouse. At its core, this chapter proposes to read Maurice Merleau-Ponty's insights into the embodied nature of vision, and the consequences of such an intertwined conceptualization of the senses, and the corporeal nature of knowledge, for mediated performance work interested in difference.

Merleau-Ponty has used disability and disability-technology as case-studies that can present the workings of embodied perception.[1] He uses the example of the blind man and his cane, who becomes a cyborg being:

The blind man's stick has ceased to be an object for him, and is no longer perceived for itself; its point has become an area of sensitivity, extending the scope and active radius of touch, and providing a parallel to sight.

(1962: 143)

Merleau-Ponty's point here is that the body image, the concept of the body, is malleable, and open to change. Our orientation towards the world is not one of separation, but of immersion. He continues:

To get used to a hat, a car or a stick is to be transplanted into them, or conversely, to incorporate them into the bulk of our own body. Habit expresses our power of dilating our being-in-the-world, or changing our existence by appropriating fresh instruments.

(1962: 143)

It is this sense of 'fresh instruments', acting as addenda to our body, that I want to bring, in this chapter, to a discussion of new media. In particular, I want to think through the implications of Merleau-Ponty's later work in creating a political encounter with disability on the Internet.

How can a politics of connection work in new-media's image-rich modes of address? It is a challenge to create a visceral address in these media of immediacy and speed – to create a form of contact that doesn't just glance off a swiftly moving surface of colors and shapes. In all of the works discussed in this chapter, a variety of access channels (images, sound, kinesthesia, performative presence, etc.) are activated in order to grab the audience, arrest the endless flow, and create an encounter. Through the analysis of a range of webwork created by and with disabled people, this chapter will trace merging points between visualization and physicality, between (distanced) sight and intimate touch.

Distances

Twentieth-century poststructuralist performance theory taught us a sobering fact: bodies get caught in webs of texts. They only come into visibility in frames, in relief against the spectator's search for her self, in moments ripped out of flight. The gap between being embodied and being seen has troubled performance work and body theorists. On the one hand we experience the act of living: we are consciously and unconsciously aware of the multiple centers of movement, becoming and energy. On the other hand, we enact and re-inscribe the act of structural categorization: man/woman, here/gone, disabled/non-disabled, black/white, reading/being, text/presence, other/me, me/other vision of me. How these two ways of knowing oneself are interwoven, in the coherences created out of this multitude of impressions, memory, and glimpses of possible futures, over time and in dialogue with history, is less accessible to us.

Performance art is often characterized by the wish for, or play with, affect in relation to the image. Performances hinge on mechanisms that break through the distanced, categorizing viewing, and speak differently of life and death. In Eduardo Kac's performance installation *Genesis*, spectators on site (in the gallery) and on-line (via an interactive website) are faced with a petri-dish of bacteria, and a mechanism that allows the spectators to irradiate these bacteria with light-rays that cause cancer, mutating the bacteria's genetic coding. The highly aesthetic presentation of beautifully lit abstract patterns echo science illustration, or modern art – material to be viewed at a distance, living apart from the everyday in the sanctified atmosphere of the gallery. But the context of both artist's and spectator's manipulation of living cells make the gallery space and its actions a laboratory of life and death. Language plays an important role in this installation: using technology similar to the kind of gene-splicing that allows scientists to create bacteria that make insulin, Kac's bacteria are encoded with a Bible passage, and once the installation is ended, the accumulated effects of the irradiation are tested by decoding their genes back into English. Domination, power differentials, and the enormity of cause-and-effect are all referenced. Medical sciences's role as the gatekeeper of 'normality', and the judge of interventions into and creations of life is forgrounded as the realms of genetic scientific endeavor and art practice merge in Kac's work.

In this chapter, the edges of multiple forms of spectatorial and witnessing engagement become disturbed as the boundaries between public and private, live and media work are questioned.

My concern in this chapter is with disability's position between self and other. Disabled and constructed bodies have been present in Western stories for a long time. One myth about the origin of gender difference emerges from the Greek pantheon: the limping blacksmith-God Hephaistos created Pandora, an artificial woman, as punishment for the presumption of mankind. In romantic literature and in the ballet *Coppelia*, we find the tradesman Coppelius and his artificial dancing puppet Olimpia, who threatens the sanity of her suitor by appearing to him as the fantasy of the perfect woman.[2] Other artificial/semi-human characters can be found in the tradition of science fiction: the inventor's black, hard hand and his female robot in *Metropolis*; the disabilities/addenda of *Bladerunner*'s cyborgs, the X-Men and other comic heroes. In all these examples, technology comes as a threat – new technologies disturb what it means to be human. A fascination/repulsion with the bodily other, and with that which is extra to the human body, characterizes the viewers of freaks at Barnum's circus and the sideshows as much as it fuels Cronenberg's *Crash*, fanclubs of amputees,[3] and, of course, the ongoing fascination with Bob Flanagan's and Stelarc's performance art practices.[4] Disability and its companion, prostheses, are indeed not marginal to popular culture, but are often central to it, and to the fantasies of storytelling. But storytelling demands novelty, although it relies on recombination. In our accelerated media world, disability can explore its glamorous and public potential in (potentially) different ways from those open to disabled people in the ghetto of the sideshow.

The politics of immersion

The digital field and artworks generated in its purview have often been described as adhering to a new aesthetics and a new reception. In the digital frame, the image 'abandons the exteriority of spectacle to open itself to immersion' (Pierre Levy, 1997: 179).[5] It is this fantasized immersive quality of new media art which I find fascinating – its fantasy of a utopian embrace of a horizonless information world, the fantasy it offers of conceptualizing the infinite, the gaze moving on from link to link, never able to stand still in the surveillance of a whole.[6] Bodies are strangely aligned with the cyberfield:

> Cyberspace, we are often told, is a disembodied medium. Testimonies to this effect are everywhere, from William Gibson's fictional representation of the 'bodiless exultation of cyberspace' to John Parry Barlow's description of his virtual reality (VR) as 'my everything has been amputated'. In a sense, these testimonies are correct; the body remains in front of the screen rather than within it. In another sense, however, they are deeply misleading, for they obscure the crucial role that the body plays in constructing cyberspace. In fact, we are never disembodied. As anyone who designs VR simulations knows, the specificities of our embodiments matter in all kinds of ways, from determining the precise configurations of a VR interface to influencing the speed with which we can read a CRT screen.
>
> (Hayles, 1996: 1)

In order to continue thinking about unknowable but interesting bodies, I want to engage phenomenological thinking in relation to cyberpresence, and the interfaces that are created as performance encounters by disabled artists. As we have seen, Merleau-Ponty's phenomenological thinking focuses on the perceiving body. An emphasis on the body as a way of being in the world doesn't order the world only in terms of representation and meaning, but also in terms of sensual encounters and extensions. Given disability's problematic status within representation, its simultaneous absence and presence, hypervisibility and invisibility, these phenomenological approaches to the embodiment of disability are useful, as long as they don't glide into the personal, the individual, without a sense of the shaping forces that structure a particular form of embodiment.[7] The historical and institutional dimension is important:

> As a research method, phenomenology calls us to a series of systematic reflections within which we question and clarify that which we intimately live, but which has been lost to our reflective knowledge through habituation and/or institutionalization.
>
> (Sobchack, 1992: 28)

To point back to the example at the beginning, the blind man with his stick does not need to think about his stick, but a non-disabled person watching him move in the street can take the ease of his passage as a sign of a form of embodi-ment that troubles negative stereotypes of tragic disability. This passer-by might be able to access the sense of wonder that might have met the turtle walker: certainties become uncertain, the 'natural' body becomes an object of strange spectacle.

The sedimented, lost aspects of embodied meaning are paramount for an understanding of disability that goes beyond the immediate, private experience, and that links disability to the wider social realm. The personal isn't the political for disabled activists: it too easily becomes a narrative of overcoming, of living *in the face of* disability, rather than living *with and through* a disability and its historic and institutional placing. Phenomenological approaches to digital art are very appropriate in this framework: being-in-the-world, immersing oneself consciously into the stream of sensate impressions, is the premise of Merleau-Ponty's phenomenological investigation, not survey or mastery. The mind cannot be outside the body and outside the flesh of the world. The aim of phenomenologi-cal approaches like Merleau-Ponty's is to reach out away from the all-encompassing self to the other, that elusive presence which is hoped for, felt in different, diffuse ways, and intuited by the fact of immersion, that being-in-the-world.

A number of contemporary performers work on this edge of the immersive – some with specially designed devices that are strapped onto spectators,[8] some by employing holographic representations that create strange encounters between virtual presence and flesh world.[9] In the examples I discuss below, the surface/screen remains the interface of performer and spectator, but embodiment and difference are evoked in multiple ways.

Merleau-Ponty's late meditations on self and other in visual relations drafts an understanding of visibility which is interestingly picked up by contemporary, digital age visual aesthetics. First, in his late work, Merleau-Ponty does away with the primacy of vision. Our vision is always located in the world of material presence, and is intricately engaged with senses of locomotion, touch, and kinesthesia:

> It is a marvel too little noticed that every movement of my eyes – even more, every displacement of my body – has its place in the same visible universe that I itemize and explore with them, as, conversely, every vision takes place somewhere in the tactile space.

> (1968: 134)

Merleau-Ponty begins to think of vision and touch as intertwined and co-existent in every act of being-in-the-world – 'since the same body sees and touches, visible and tangible belong to the same world' (1968: 134). It this sense of a sensible mass that then moves him forward to think about the wider relation between one body and the world (the things):

> The body unites us directly with the things through its own ontogenesis, by welding to one another the two outlines of which it is made, its two laps: the

sensible mass it is and the mass of the sensible wherein it is born by segregation and upon which, as seer, it remains open.

(1968: 136)

This conception as a body immersed in the world, and part of the world with an existential openness towards it through the senses, brings us to the notion of 'flesh', an extra-human possibility of the world as connection:

When we speak of the flesh of the visible, we do not mean to do anthropology, to describe a world covered with all our own projections, leaving aside what it can be under the human mask. Rather, we mean that carnal being, as a being of depths, of several leaves or several faces, a latency, and a presentation of a certain absence, is a prototype of Being, of which our body, the sensible sentient, is a very remarkable variant, but whose constitutive paradox already lies in every visible.

(1968: 136)

He continues to explain the difference between this conception of the 'visible' and the purely visual, emphasizing the sensorial quality that connects individual being to the flesh of the world, the possibility of sharedness.

What we call a visible is, we said, a quality pregnant with texture, the surface of a depth, a cross section upon a massive being, a grain or corpuscle borne by a wave of Being.

(1968: 136)

The 'one' of the self is always a thickness. This thickness is a fold – but the material of the fold extends beyond itself, beyond the self-touching/seeing of the self. Self and other are united in a non-specific flesh, the materiality of the world.

Within this experience of living, politics can be rethought:[10] moving to 'the register of subject/object relations unknown to modern rationalists' (Coole, 2001). The phenomenologist's charge is to engage and interact with the world, 'composing' a representation 'as an experienced pianist deciphers an unknown piece of music' (Merleau-Ponty, 1964b: 93), interpreting with full awareness of one's own locatedness. The politics that emerge from this fieldwork of lived relations are not yet fully realized – but they provide exciting possibilities for embodiment theorists and activists as they undermine binary structures without giving up a sense of direction and intentionality.

The world engages us, embraces us, is part of us. Immersion, and messy edges, are part of this phenomenological experience of the world. Abstract knowledge and individual experience become part of the same trajectory, points on the same scale. In the reading of cyberwork that follows, the disabled person's experience of difference and its communication is presented with an emphasis on a surface-interiority, a seduction of images as membranes. These membranes are not seen as distanced images opposing the self, but as co-extensive with the self, as part of the flesh of the world. The particular audience address of cyberwork, where physical action is required to activate and participate in the work, echoes for me the tactile/visual sense of Merleau-Ponty, this sensorium that opens up to touch rather than division.

Caressing the screen

Contact 17 are a Germany-based group of disabled and non-disabled performers, who, like many contemporary artists, have started to explore the net as a new delivery medium and aesthetic environment for art work. The web and e-lists have opened up important avenues for members of diasporas, certain minority groups, and people with restricted access to conventional social spaces.[11] Disabled people have early on grasped the enriching possibilities of the Internet, and communication services, e-lists, e-groups and technology help-groups have been around for a significant amount of time. In our shared social environments, access needs are still often unmet: stairs, noisy and busy street scenes, vehicular access or public transport continue to be problematic for many disabled people, and set up barriers to shared public events. Disability artists have explored a range of ways of overcoming these problems: disability art is often featured in festivals, sometimes with organized transport, where a range of artists present their work in a concentrated amount of time, allowing people to experience disability art in one short, intense burst. Another avenue is disability art representation on the Internet.[12] GoAccess was created in this framework: bringing disability performance and corporeal realities of non-normate bodies to computer users in their homes.[13]

When you first open www.goAccess.de, you need to work, move, act in order to find your way in. The initial screen contains text chasing across the monitor, and a user is required to capture one symbol (>>>) in order to click herself into the next webworld. This interface mode sets the scene for the kind of interaction this piece demands: it is not passive, but requires activity and involvement of the audience in order to function. Referencing a live scene, the audience becomes part of the piece, and, again similar to a live performance, things change in each repetition. It is only in the nagging uncertainty of how to proceed, where to click, chasing the symbol, that the action of engaging with the mouse becomes perceptible. As Drew Leder reminds us, reading Merleau-Ponty but giving particular attention to the issue of reflexivity, 'the body itself is not a point but an organized field in which certain organs and abilities come to prominence while others recede' (Leder, 1990: 24). For Leder, the corporeal aspect to perception 'disappears' into a form of neutral background – the body becomes transparent in its use. When pain is experienced, when states alter, or when a new skill is to be learned, a person monitors movements, is aware of physicality. Thus, when learning a new body skill:

Figure 12 Contact 17/GoAccess publicity postcard. (Reproduced by courtesy of the artist)

> The problematic nature of these novel gestures tends to provoke explicit body awareness. . . . Yet the successful acquisition of a new ability coincides with a phenomenological effacement of all this.
>
> (Leder: 1990: 31)

Using a mouse has aspects of this oscillation of attention and disappearance: it is only when something doesn't work smoothly according to one's learned expectations that the action of moving a mouse in order to see a new screen becomes foregrounded. In the GoAccess screen, the coordination of eye and hand movement in a chase is relatively unusual, and retrieves the disappearance of the body in visual engagement, making the enworlded nature of vision appear on one's sense screen.

The language of the site further reinforces this live, theatrical mode of engagement, this requirement of interactivity and presence. The screen describes in German the piece about to be entered: 'A Room and a Performance amidst the Net (im Netz) in 4 Acts and an Epilog (Nachspann – the German word references cinematic credits rather than theatrical engagement)'.[14] Apart from the cinematic reference of 'Nachspann' the reference points here are spatial (room) and durational (performance), not visual or aural.

The viewer is warned that she is about to 'enter' an experience, not receive conventionalized web-information. The viewer reads: Please take your time. This is not a homepage – 'Dies ist keine Heimatseite'. Interactivity in the form of a two-way dialogue is referenced by a call to leave messages and questions in a guestbook.

As one of these viewers, a mouse click delivers me into a scrolling multitude, an assault of script running from bottom to top across my screen. The script runs too fast, my eyes cannot hold it. As I try to point my mouse, phrases are highlighted, and hold still for my eyes. These passages, mined from media texts and performance scripts, prepare me for a world of technology, an unstable body, a new world, a new time:

> 'I want to be connected'
> 'Er wartet auf Euch. Er ist eine Ubung, oder ein unvermeidliches Experiment'
> 'He's/ It's waiting for you. He is/It is an exercise, or a necessary experiment' (a Deleuze quote)
> 'Ich weiss nicht, was ein Korper vermag' (I don't know what a body can do)
> 'Beginnen wir von neuem' (let's begin anew)

Sound embraces me as I am trying to make out the rules of engagement of this world. Mechanical/electronic sounds looped and beeping create a sensation of a computer world: I hear amplified modem clicks, the crackle of telephone lines, and a strong rhythm created by echoing metal.

As I sit and explore the avenues of interactivity open to me, I can find an option not in the texts and their meaning but in the spaces in between. Silhouettes are erased out of the scrolling texts, shadows that are not quite there. These bodies cut out of the text are in movement poses: stand-ins for presence, frozen aspects of a performance that might have happened elsewhere. As I click on these interstitial bodies, various things can happen: I might be delivered to a superimposed text panel which provides a context to the quotes floating across the screen (the passages I can access include texts by Gilles Deleuze and by Jerome Bell). At other times, I hear a voice speaking to me – 'hallo?' At some point, my click arrests the scrolling text, and thickens the page, as the texts accumulate without scrolling, heaping up a mass of text which becomes the solid gray of a spider's web, until the page dissolves under the weight of the arrest, and I am transported onto the next page. Rules are once again there to be discovered. The silhouettes are now freed of their confinement within the shadow texts, and two women's backs sit black on white in a rectangle. As my mouse nears them, they react: they contract and expand, move sideways and upwards, evading or playing with my electronic presence in their vicinity. Cause and effect are not clear: the bodies twitch in rhythm to the electronic beat playing – is it my mouse, or an internal rhythm, that moves these women? Every time I play this game, the results differ: I might end up at a blank white screen, the two silhouettes blinking out of existence, frustrating my desire to make them move, to interact with them. Other times, they hover and shimmer as I click on them, or retreat into the background. They turn around, upside-down, or merge into a strange, unknowable creature. Sometimes, a figure elongates and stands upright like a ballerina, sometimes she rests across the bottom of the screen like a queen. One throws the other one out of the frame. One inches back slowly, coaxed by my cursor – or by a director movie script? Sometimes, the bodies stay in two-dimensional space as they move around their axes, but at other times, they gain depth, and the black-and-white image presents me with volumes moving three-dimensionally. At the end of my play with these figures, a hand appears on my cursor movement. Like the visual trick of the face and the vase, the silhouette mutates into a black hole in the screen, though which a photographed hand appears, seemingly beckoning to me.

In my play with its rooms and pages, uncertainty and curiosity are the guiding themes of this page. New Media work and its promise of interactivity here always reflects back on me, making me aware of my desire to control, to discover, to engender movement and meaning. This act of GoAccess does allow for forms of indirect interactivity, but it does so on its own terms: time goes by, this is not a fast and easy play that delivers its rules and mechanisms transparently. By thus veiling its activity, the page forces me to see the elements on screen, and on the soundtrack, not merely as clickable controls, purely there to get me from A to B. Instead, I am thrown back to the thickness of these images: I have time to ponder what they are, how they were made, what the situation before the camera was, why these silhouettes move the way they do.

This thickness of meaning encounters the thickness of my access to the work: my mouse isn't invisible to me, naturalized into the apparatus of engagement offered by conventional web-browsing. Instead, my bodily engagement in the act of knowing, the physical act of making-meaning is made visible and tangible. Act one, the hastening texts, didn't allow audience contemplation. Text, the conventional meaning-making tool of the Internet, receded into materiality (the gray web of text debris). In Act two, what does invite immersion are remnants of bodies, placeholders of presences that have left unclear markers to their activity, their spatiality, and their rules. Their abstract movement interacts with my actual movements, creating sensing echoes across different realms of fantasy. This thickness of humanity, of physical possibility, opens into Act three, where a revelation points to a mastertrope of unknowability and unclear boundaries: physical disability, and the relationships of physicality, technology and control.

Clicking on the beckoning hand of Act two gives me the illusion of control – the hand enlarges, fills the rectangle that recedes and leaves a black screen in which it hangs like a strange fruit. Voices start to speak to me:

'hallo'
'Sind Sie ein korperlicher Mensch?' (Are you a bodily human?)
'Wo ist ihr Atem jetzt?' (Where is your breath now?)
'Mit welchem Teil ihres Korpers verbinden sie sich am liebsten?' (With which part of your body do you preferably connect with?)
'Wollen sie ihren Korper so annehmen, wie er ist?' (Do you want to accept your body as it is?)

'Glauben Sie, dass der Korper veraltert its?' (Do you believe that the body is obsolete?)

All these voices offer me different viewpoints on my body – viewpoints in space, near and far, viewpoints in terms of agency – questions that assume that the body is under voluntary direction, or that a body can be separated from a self.[15] The web has traditionally been associated with disembodiment – a link that is reinforced by the mass of material that researches identity on the net, and the manipulation of individual identity in web-based communication.[16] The questions presented here open up a gap between embodiment (for instance, the body as locus of the involuntary act of breathing) and control (by asking where the breath is, this involuntary action becomes present to the viewer and emerges into con-sciousness). In the same way, asking whether you accept your body as it is references an illusion of control (as if you could decide to disavow your body). These issues of body under control, under conscious agency take on a specific urgency and charge as a form of embodied difference begins to assert its presence. While these strange questions address me as voices and as writing on the screen, a mysterious, undulating sound creates a continuous sound-carpet, and the filmic hand begins to move in a strange dance. Once again, my presence can change the scene: a mouse-click stops the video, arrests the dancing hand.

The two bodies on the previous screen looked individualized and strange, 'not normal', but this strangeness went largely unmarked, since their mediation as visuals allowed for distortion – their move from abstraction to presence, in and out of two- and three-dimensionality, swallowed any other form of pre-technological difference. In this short looped clip of the hand, though, bodily difference becomes referenced. The film-clip is not abstract, black-and-white, but a video shot of a hand circling a lower arm, fingers flexing, moving. It becomes increasingly likely (but not knowable) that the hand photographed here belongs to a disabled body, moving within the range associated with people with spastic impairments. The issues of body choice and control echo differently as the possibility of difference nudges the images, and opens up a gap in the aesthetic field that goes beyond the materiality of representation (the distorted body images that could be explained by their mode of representation, by some PhotoShop action or some twist of the camera's lens). A person experiencing cerebral palsy[17] can exactly not fully control the voluntary actions of her body, or, with some people who experience spastic movement, it isn't always transparent how and where a specific command, action, thought, will find its effect in the body; in arms, legs, and muscle-movement. Certain parallels and metaphors present themselves to me: just as my mouse-click doesn't always have predictable results, so spastic movement can be richly different, or frustratingly vague – watching the other throws back upon me my desires, my feelings, my reading. But this metaphor emerges only in my thought-ful interaction with the screen, paying attention to the modes of engagement open to me, and to my thoughts and feelings during the process. It isn't spelt out, demonstrated or made 'clear'. Disability remains unknown, is touched but not encompassed, individual experience remains unpredictable, like the interface of the site. This experience of difference isn't 'foreign' and distanced, but touches on my own embodiment and my engagement with the world through the vague web-controls. A category of 'flesh of the world' opens up, as Merleau-Ponty's 'laps' of difference and sameness press up against one another.

Instead of flattening out difference into known language categories, I am physically paying attention to my engagement, learning rules of being-in-the-world that move me out of my normal, everyday engagement into one that witnesses difference, even if that difference isn't spelled out as belonging to any one specific body out there. A cyberbody engagement is fantasized, phenomenologically experienced, in the encounter between physicalities in the space of the web. I have to give up control, or the illusion of it, if I want to experience this precarious moment. The object of the phenomenological encounter, shrouded behind fantasies, is looking back at me.

The last screen of the presentation opens itself up to me sometimes, but not always: occasionally, it withholds its secret, and leaves me with a new image of the hand, static, not reacting to my various attempts to initiate a reaction. When I do succeed in opening the last act, I am rewarded. A range of senses are addressed in a rich display: speed, voyeurism, narrational drive are all addressed by the spectacle that makes up the final act of GoAccess. In this act, my gaze meets a performance, stitched together, sutured, like an old-fashioned thumb-cinema where images flicking into one another create the illusion of movement. Here, a strip of individual photographs of body parts roll past my gaze, like a slowed down, fragmented film strip. At first, these images are relatively clear, but as the strip rolls on, changes happen: the camera lens or post-production distorts the body on the other side of the camera. Is the body strange, or the gaze that fixes it? The technology that captures it? Is this hand foreshortened by biology, or by the perspective of the visualization apparatus, the lens or the digital processing? Towards the end of the clip, the body shots give up even less under scrutiny: they capture motion, and the bodies are blurred, caught in time, undecidable. These bodies present only their trace to me – but in such a way that the absence of truth, capture or depth is witnessed by me. I know that these images are a skin, a something connected to the flesh of the world, to a shared physicality, and I mourn my inability to touch this flesh, or arrest it, either caress or do violence to it.

I can try to hold on to the strip, stop it, reverse it, engage my desire to see clearly – but all that happens when I touch this body through the mouse is stasis. A marker appears, with a number, disrupting the immediacy of her body/my body. This marker acts as a trace of the apparatus of vision: the film strip, the digital image, the movie clip. But if I decide to let the other control run freely, I get rewarded with a token of presence. I hear a voice. This voice is different from the many voices which spoke to me so far. This voice is hard to make out, unclear, grainy. Roland Barthes discussed the 'grain of the voice' as that which exceeds the semiotic meaning of language, that which inserts the bodily, the physical, into the act of communication. While there is a problem with delegating the body yet again into the realm of mere 'matter', supposedly insensible and 'natural' canvas to our social endeavors, his vibrant metaphor springs immediately to my mind as I listen to this woman's voice. I can't make her out, but words appear on screen, translating the sounds for me, haltingly, in rhythm with the sounds. One by one, then grouped together. This act of repetition aligns my ear with the diction of this woman, and I am beginning to hear the meaning in her voice, not just the effects of her impaired speech apparatus. She starts to convey her meaning to me, and it isn't just the conventionalized meaning of her body. Having been forced by repetition to pay attention, to listen, to touch through the grain of her voice, I begin to see the message. The words spell out this text:

> Mein Korper baumelt frei von oben. Nichts, woran der Blick haften bleibt. Durchsichtig. (My body dangles freely from above. Nothing to capture the gaze. Transparent)

The images on the strip have presented the bodies against a black backdrop. The human flesh with its brilliant hues isn't anchored on a floor, against a wall. The movement speaks of speed, maybe of contact improvization with its precarious balances, its risky encounters and trusts. Maybe the live performance behind the performance of encounter enacted by the site allowed for that measure of freedom – just as the fact that she isn't fully present to me doesn't allow me to capture her fully, to categorize her, to see her once and decide to look away. The apparatus of the website, the mode of address, makes me pay attention, and see complexity.

In the analysis above, the emphasis was on the interacting I, on the audience of one viewing the webpiece on her monitor. The actions and reactions of the receiver, reader, spectator, and witness were ultimately under investigation; the thick, layered access to the world of the web acts became the point of analysis. In new media art, the apparatus of vision becomes physicalized in ways that it hasn't been for over a century (not since you had to move the scope by hand, or thumb the pages of a thumb-cinema to see the image jump): the mode of spectating, the labor involved in vision becomes apparent as you try to move the mouse and negotiate the monitor as a spatial field.

Performing the mapped body

On the website *Navigating the Body: A Visibility Project*, Canada-based web-designer Susan Harman displays a meditation on pain and identity as an art installation. On these pages, she works with the writings, images and performances of Donimo, Karen Frederickson and Rose Williams, three women with fibromyalgia. She describes her project: 'My objective for *Navigating the Body* is to try to give voice to the unspoken and express the invisible through art.'

Navigating the Body addresses issues of surface and depth, location and curiosity, performance, mediation and the living body – digital photography and video are the main media used to translate the experience of inner states into visible states.

These media are encountered in a consciously performative framing. An inter-coiling of bodies, the interweaving of self and other, imparts traces of living, of flesh, of performativity to the images.

As a spectator/witness of these webcollages, one needs to move physically through the display – few webpages fit into the browser window, even on a large monitor. The pages load slowly (an issue Harman acknowledges – 'This is an art installation . . . be patient.') The spectator becomes aware of the construction of the images, as they load bit by bit, in a collage, at different locations on the page. These images do not show the glossy, smooth surface of a 'window onto a world', they present themselves as time-based media and non-transparent articulations of experience. No whole body framed by realist convention is offered to the surfer, but a surface to glide over, and to read for cues in a multitude of clamoring voices. The knowledge presented in these pages indeed needs navigating, not merely absorbing.

Locating the Source is the first page of Donimo's cycle in the website. The page is collaged out of x-ray images of a spine, layered with a face with eyes defiantly staring out of the image. These images are de-naturalized with layers that are reminiscent of body tissue, marble or maybe thin tree-trunks – blue and red veins run over the manipulated photographs. At the temporal end of the journey over the image (in the Western readers' eyes, wandered to over time by the labor of the mouse-holding hand), the right hand bottom corner, is a photo of a woman.

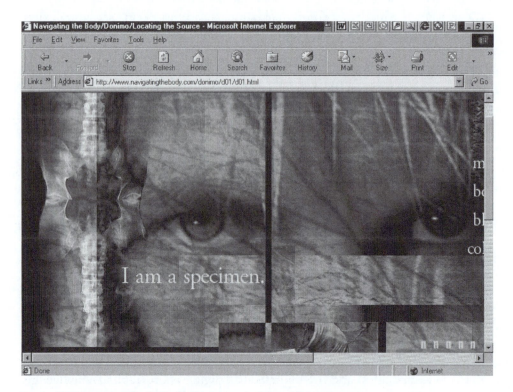

Figure 13 Navigating the Body (web-capture), Susan Harman

She is lying on what looks like a medical scanner, and her body is depicted in the conventions of x-ray photography, but in violent yellow and blue instead of black and white. To me, the image connotes violence and anger. Into these images, words are integrated: the first (towards the left hand top corner of the image) are 'I am a specimen'. Blocks of 'needles' stab graphically into the images, and lists of intrusions (x-rays, myograms, bone scans, blood tests, colonoscopy) and surveyors (physiotherapists, chiropractors, orthopedic surgeons, rheumatologists, lawyers) are given white on black. The image does not show a docile subject, or a performance of symptomatology, but instead points to the politics and mechanisms of making visible. Vision as a touching, invading, penetrating stare is made explicit not only in the images, but also in the trajectory of physical search. The website presents the viewer with a survey that the viewer has to engage in. The spectator/ surfer is implicated in the desire to know by her surveillance of the image, and by the accusatory stare of the eyes dominating the page. At the same time, perceiving the medical, body-in-pieces images reference the temporal nature of living. Leder writes about the effects of encounters, even visual encounters, as a dialogue with an emergent sensation of death-in-life:

> My own corpse is experienced in an anticipatory fashion, residing implicitly within my living body. Exhaustion reminds me of the sheer weight of my limbs; an X ray reveals my skeleton to vision; accidents remind me of my exquisite vulnerability . . . These reminders of death constitute a force of dys-appearance, recalling me to my embodied state. The corpse is always approaching from within.
>
> (Leder, 1990: 144)

Encountering the body in pieces scratches uncomfortably at the skin obscuring the embodied involvement in the world. By moving my mouse over these images, the temporally distanced but potentially present violence to (my own) body bubbles up, creates a potential for a fantasized empathy with the other behind the screen.

This violence of the medical stare, and the subject's stare back, breaks in the next webpage, *Lost Passions*. The overall feel of this page is melancholia, and the viewer is invited into a subjective experience. This page can be contained in one browser-window: 'boxing in' is its literal theme. External violence shifts to internal experience, and the effect is not located on the surface of the body, but in the interaction between representation and the living body.

The image shows the owner of the eyes (we assume, Donimo) in three different positions arranged on the page in a three-dimensional sharp-edged object, a long, thin box. The box is filled with images of clouds at night, with a moon shining. At three points of the box, a thumbnail image of Donimo shows her sitting in a garden, in movement. The movements consist of a hand banging against an invisible wall, a head moving against it, and her whole body, legs and arms, flaying as she sits on a rectangular mirror amidst grass, with all her struggling movements contained in the imaginary edges of a virtual box outlined by the 'real' photographed mirror. The text arranged around the box-object tells us: 'I live in a box', and lists outdoor pursuits that Donimo can no longer participate in – 'how can I *forget them?*'.

The image and the videos set up a contrast between nature and the artificial box-shaped object, and a relationship between interiority and self-image in the mirror and the invisible boundaries. The moving body has a strong impact after various web-pages of still images and text: the quality of living corporealizes the woman's experience without invalidating her sorrow, or her previous anger. It is clear that no image or collage alone can capture the intricacies of living – the physical revolt against the box, which can be read as an assault on one's pain threshold, are also full of life and verve, lush against the background of greenery. At the same time, an interesting merging of vision/touch is referenced by the 'imaginary' mirror-box edges: we see the boundaries her movement articulates, and we catch a glimpse of the kinaesthetic containment, boundary-setting effect of pain on one's movement. The fantasy of virtual vision merges with echoes of a form of embodiment dominated by rules of engagement with the outer world.

The two images *Locating the Source* and *Lost Passions* together are a complex engagement with desires, visions, textures, self-image and medical visualization, emotion and motion. The juxtaposition of digital imagery and 'home-video' shots of a living, moving body of a woman combine to create messages that neither theatrical representation nor still images alone could have achieved. As the website invites its user on a journey through its imagery, with various more videos interacting with text and still images, the multi-layered effect of meaning set in motion by a vision/touch interaction becomes ever stronger. Neither surfaces, depths or fantasy visualizations of bodies, nor personal texts hold finite meaning, but dance together and invite the websurfer to engage with different embodiments without delivering certainty.

Final touches

The fantasized yet personally experienced meetings between spectator/actor and performer/image in these mediated performances, GoAccess and *Navigating*, are fleeting and precarious. Something happens, but the momentary seductions pass into the background of an image-saturated media world. I want to read an erotics of encounter in the attention I give to my physical being-in-the-world as I engage in the kinetics of the mouse chase or the 'fort-da' touch of my awareness of intrusion into Donimo's world. I want to read a touching of flesh, the flesh of a world of which I am only a part, a world I am immersed in, and that unites the surfaces of my eyes, my fingertips, and the skin of the performers far out of reach.

My reading practices create meetings that aren't clearly locatable in terms of individual agency, or loci of action. A search for touch, intimacy and immersion drives the works I discussed in their interleaving with my readerly longing. As disabled performers continue to search for ways to undermine certainties about bodies and ways of being, edging into the cyberian nets becomes a valid way of investigating knowledges. The information world is the new locus for the generation of (un)certainty, the data archive, the local of the Visual Human Project (see for instance Waldby, 2000 and Cartwright, 1998). It is here that global information is generated and shared. Stretching its modes of address to include references of different forms of embodiment can be a new political frontier. In all projects, attention oscillates between intersubjectivity as ground for our empathic readings, and the awareness of individual embodiment in our attention to our ways of being in the world. These two poles of being on the outer and inner edge of our 'body schema' can combine to keep options open, keep a sense of wonder at differences alive. From here, I want to travel back to the everyday world of disabled people, and to local, specific, embodied interventions into the techniques of modernity. In the epilog, I want to discuss how some of the traces of the unknown mined in these chapters find their way into community practice.

Toward the unknown body

Stillness, silence, and space in mental health settings

> Since 1970, my practice and resources as a dancer and choreographer have shifted from physical to perceptual challenges.
>
> (Deborah Hay, 1988: 22)

As a disabled performance artist who has spent many years exploring physical and dance theater, I have attempted to find new and collaborative ways of creating performances with disabled people, including people who are living with pain, people living with cancer, and older people. In this work, the need to evade, play with, or subvert the meanings of bodies – whether gendered, disabled, racial, or class-based – has been paramount. Initially, my practice focused on creating stage performances inspired by Brecht, Artaud, Boal, and the aesthetics of performance art. More recently, however, the community performance work[1] executed by my company, The Olimpias Performance Research Projects, has become increasingly process-based. My collaborators and I now conceive of it as an ongoing intervention rather than as a progression toward a traditional stage performance.

What has brought about this change in practice? I have been involved with people in mental health settings such as social clubs and day care workshops, as well as with people who identify as 'mental health system survivors', working outside medical settings in more self-determined frameworks. These experiences have led me to experience the same shift noted by Hay, forcing the question of 'perceptual challenges' to the forefront of my practice and leading me to re-examine my own emphasis on visual representation and the divide between stage and auditorium. Work in these settings is dominated by the fact that all participants have been medically diagnosed as mentally ill, and have experienced the effects of the mental health system. A limited range of images is available to the general public about people with mental health differences – images that range from the homicidal maniac to those involving self-neglect and screaming fits. People who are labeled mentally ill and who use the mental health system's resources encounter the effects of these public images in sometimes not so subtle ways: day care homes are attacked and despoiled, planning applications for new centers are blocked by people who fear for their safety. This socially expressed hatred and fear can easily be internalized by people who have been diagnosed by the mental health system.

In the light of this work with people diagnosed as mentally ill, Hay's statement inspired me to ask a series of questions. What does it mean to work with perceptual challenges? If we can find ways to challenge perception, the way we experience the world, are these then not also ways to challenge representation and the processes through which we make meaning out of what we *see*? How can challenges to audiences' perceptions inform a performance practice that does not offer clear-cut images but rather subverts representational certainties? In particular, how can changes in perception help shape a performance aesthetic that can be useful for people whose bodies have been violently read for clues to their 'abnormal' minds?

This chapter charts how the concept of perceptual challenge has spurred our group to explore new forms of community artwork that chime with the search for unknowability and the play with borders which I discussed as the horizon of the disability arts performances in this book. Contemporary theorists such as Brian Massumi (2002) have called for a re-evaluation of sensation and affect as political tools – it is this journey that the work described here is engaged in. This chapter shares our creative process in order to show how traditional frames for performance and theories of bodies and space can inform each other in a quest to create new political art. Specifically, I am synthesizing a theory of the body in space developed by Rudolf Laban with a theory of being-in-time-and-space advanced by Henri Bergson in order to articulate the theoretical framework that drives our work.

Much of the work I describe here has been originally developed with one specific group in the Welsh valleys, an economically depressed area in the United Kingdom. The members of this group were all clients of Mental Health Day Care Services. In Britain, people diagnosed with moderate to severe mental illness (including schizophrenia, voice hearing, and depression) can be referred by medical practitioners to Day Care Services. Part of the responsibility of these services is to organize events or sessions for their clients (e.g., rambling, bingo, yoga, swimming, tea groups). At the Day Care Services where I worked with them, all clients could choose up to three events a week to attend and they were able to change their preferences whenever they wish. Day Care Services provided transport for clients (many of whom cannot use public transport by themselves). From 1997 to 2000, I collaborated with Day Care Services on this project, along with Tan Dance and Swansea University Adult Outreach Department. About ten people were meeting once a week for two hours, first in a social care environment (a residential center), and then outside formal care institutions in a local community arts center. Day Care Services regarded our group as successful since we were running with viable numbers and had a dedicated core group, who had been working together from the start, even though we experienced occasional intermissions due to hospital admissions. After the first two years, we worked without an attending social worker.[2]

The vision fueling the collaboration was that of an artistic rather than a medical or therapeutic intervention.[3] We were not primarily engaged in the kind of drama work that is often termed 'socially driven', which uses role play, autobiographical writing, and other techniques to foster self-expression and social and political awareness. While these emancipatory elements were at work in our weekly meetings, our prime impetus was toward experiencing movement not as a mimetic vehicle but as an expression in and of itself. The project worked with the idea that movement is both expression and source of life: a communicable form of being in the world. Our work in the mental health sessions was driven partially by the agenda of movement therapy, which places its main focus on the experience of movement by the individual; its therapeutic drive is to help the individual toward a full experience of human movement. Additionally, and at their core, our sessions had an *artistic* impetus that involved sharing the work, bringing the individual expression into the social arena, providing alternative visions of mental illness for society.

A major outcome of this work, which continued over four years, was a video installation called *Traces*. This chapter chronicles the path, both conceptually and practically, that we took in order to create *Traces*. My hope is that the synthesis of theory and practice that led to *Traces* provides a case-study for other artists using performance to explore the boundaries of time, space, and perception.

Straitjackets of representation

Within our culture, people with severe mental health problems are excluded from self-representation. The cultural histories of hysteria, depression, and schizophrenia are histories of silencing, muting the 'other'. The artwork of people institutionalized within mental health systems has often been perceived within the framework of 'therapy'. This therapeutic frame has meant that this work may be read as a way 'into the patient' – as a way to understand her experiences, often as a more or less transparent tool in the diagnostic process. A representation of self outside the clinical categories is made impossible by the discourses that govern the idea of the 'free self'. Instead, the theme of madness subsumes self-expression, or governs it. Moreover, just as forms of therapy have become subjects of art discourse, many artists themselves have become case studies for different forms of treatment of 'mad' people. Antonin Artaud and Sylvia Plath, for example, have become associated with different forms of electroshock therapy. Mary Barnes has become the 'hypersane' pet-artist whom R.D. Laing claimed as recovering through her work, even while he used her as a romanticized lens for perceiving the malaise of the 'normal' world.[4]

At the same time, performance work with people diagnosed with mental health problems has to deal with a history of bodily stagings, of recognized and (potentially rehearsed) performances. The readability of 'hysteria' and 'fits' fascinated the psychoanalysts Charcot, Freud, and Breuer. As Elaine Showalter notes, they photographed or analyzed hysteric women in turn-of-the-century French 'madhouses' and found that the strange physical contortions and paralyses of these women's bodies could be read and labeled as stage symptoms of mental states and brought back to normality by the talking cure.[5] More contemporary performances of 'madness' include Hannibal Lecter's animalistic sniffing in *The Silence of the Lambs* (1990), and the sudden and explosive destructive fits of other film madmen in *The Shining* (1980) and *Session 9* (2001). The demented homicidal maniac has become a recognizable set piece in horror and thriller films.[6]

By working with people in mental health settings, I soon realized the existence of a connection between the physical and the representational, their deep implication in each other. Many of my performers' physical experiences seemed to mirror their representational silencing or distortion in the media. Some were people who found no space for themselves, their bodies, their movements in their social and physical environments. They were excluded from living alone, getting an apartment, leading a life free from constant contact with medical practitioners or rigorous timetables of pills and injections. Their bodies could be invaded, as the law allows them to be drugged against their will. Many had been temporarily hospitalized. This lack of physical and mental privacy had undermined many people's ability to be confident in their use of space. The representational and social aspects of madness had affected the sense of embodiment of people diagnosed with mental health difficulties.

My experience in these settings showed that potentially, as a result of these exclusions, 'centering exercises' – as every performance class knows them – could be difficult. I came to see that it is not just drug-induced spasticity and rigid body-tensions that prevented the performers from claiming the space – that is, owning the portion of a room inhabited by their bodies. Some had fundamental difficulties asserting their physical space: standing still, breathing deeply, or allowing their voices to resonate. With this inability to take space, simple actions such as reaching and touching became problematic.

As a result, validating our spatial experience became an important aspect of our work. We had to rethink spatial and temporal aspects of embodiment, and politicize them. In other words, we had to find ways to assert the simple acts of breathing and being as interventions into the social sphere. By working on the sense of embodiment at its most fundamental levels, we were at the same time working on the images and practices that limited our experience in the first place. Breathing exercises, creating an awareness of the body's inner space through visualization, feeling our muscles relax, reacting to the influx of breath: these acts became not warm-ups but the actual core event. When later during our sessions we physically walked through the room while imagining ourselves clad in exquisite clothes or waltzing through shimmering halls, this theatrical experience was designed to lead us back into our inner space experience, to strengthen our focus on the perception of movement rather than providing training to be channeled into a performance event.

Based upon these realizations, we began to use the following process in our sessions. They started and ended with meditative exercises in which we explored movement in stillness. Thus, I might lead the group through a relaxation sequence, asking them to count their breaths or see their breath run through their bodies, into their feet and hands. By slowly working their way through their bodies, always connecting the exploration back to the filling of breath and relaxing of limbs, the group members could experience themselves as taking space – able to be filled by breath, able to 'see' and 'feel' their bodies as spatial forms. While they were in a state of deep relaxation, I ran them through a visualization. These visualizations did not aim to explore psychological issues: there were no portals, doors, or other mechanisms to get the participants to explore some inner 'truths' about themselves. Instead, all of my visualizations were aimed at sensory and movement experiences.[7] These experiences included sailing among clouds, in outer space, through oceans, over deserts, or floating in streams and meadows. I tried to create a sensation of being corporeally engaged in an experience by using strongly kinesthetic vocabulary such as 'gliding', 'rushing', 'hovering'. I also carefully avoided giving a lot of visual information (I hardly ever mentioned the colors of landscapes) but, rather, placed more importance on sensations such as 'you can feel the sun on your hands' or 'smell the fresh air'. This was important in order to ensure that participants could feel safe – they were never left alone to cope with new situations in their dream world (a device often used in conventional visualization). This relatively continuous input was seen as particularly helpful by those performers who were voice-hearers (a condition often cited as a symptom of schizophrenia); they felt they needed the continual connection to my voice, with concrete instructions, in order to combat the competing commands or emotional pleas they often heard.[8]

This facilitation of different corporeal experiences and intense focus on the sensation of corporeality in space were designed to foster what I want to call 'body-ownership': an awareness of one's own body in space, and the pleasures and possibilities of this embodiment. Thus, after the dream journeys, we briefly exchanged information about the experience – not in order to 'probe deeper' but in order to share how everybody saw different colors or encounters different 'movement partners' such as fish or weaving plants. Everybody owned a unique corporeal memory of the visited spaces. In the more conventional movement work that we created together, we also found ways of maintaining individual input. This was highly valued by the participants. (One member said in an evaluation session, 'I am proud because we are not copying each other, we do our own movement.') We often used storytelling devices to create new physical experiences and open up our movement imagination. In these sessions, we sat in a circle and started up a story, with everybody adding to it, either by witnessing others' contributions or adding a word or a longer passage, depending on people's vocality and willingness to participate. After the story was created, we explored it physically: first mimetically, then more freely. The impetus for the story was shared, but the execution was individual. We echoed other people's movement through our own physicality, but made each movement our own.

It is important to stress that the experience of the dream spaces was whole; just as a dream can regulate body temperature and accelerate a person's heart rate, these dream journeys were experienced by the participants as whole sensory experiences, not merely as 'films' of purely visual information or as 'radio plays' in which my voice provided the sole sensory input. I found that some participants became so proficient in the use of meditative techniques that they could sometimes use them to control their voices in everyday situations and overcome restlessness.

In these movement sessions, the political impetus consisted not of claiming roles in traditional theatrical formats but rather of claiming inner space. Work that happens at this initial level can eventually change the participants' sense of themselves and, through this, power relations and representations in the larger social sphere. This appropriation and habitation of inner space is a way toward being wholly in the shared, social space.

Placing emphasis on this interior work for its own sake does not, however, preclude public sharing. Our work in this group involved a journey that culminated in the public sharing of our video installation, *Traces*. This journey also helped the development of a theory that, in conjunction with the practice, suggests a method for moving from private group work toward public sharing, as well as for understanding the transformative effect such sharing can have on an audience.

Seeing elsewhere

In silence and stillness, the borderline between performer and spectator becomes problematic, as does the borderline between the 'everyday' and the performed. The flexibility of these border areas has informed some performance art practices in the last decades, and it is to these that I looked for inspiration. Hay writes, 'My goal as a dance performer is complete stillness. I give myself another 20–25 years. By then, I imagine audiences with a similar regard for the beauty of their perceptions' (Hay, 1988: 23). Through this pursuit of stillness, Hay's dances concern themselves more with multiple cellular experiences unfolding simultaneously in the body, perceived both by the dancer and the spectator, who join each other as rapt audience of the living body. Susan Leigh Foster elaborates on the implications of cellular experience in Hay's work:

> The dancer maintains a vigilant awareness of all areas of the body, registering any reluctance to move, invigorating any insensitive area with new energy. . . .
>
> Hay and her dancers are simply the sum total of the body's cells, each of which participates fully in the moment of the dance. . . . As witnesses to this process, dancers and audience together can affirm their harmonious placement as part of the world's ongoing movement.

(Foster, 1986: 11–14)

Similarly, John Cage's silent concert 4' 3" (1952) consists of 4 minutes and 33 seconds of silence. Within an auditorium, this silence quickly becomes something filled and meaningful: members of the audience moving in their seats, clearing their throats, one's own heartbeat, one's breath – all these aural effects make each performance a distinctive, interactive event. The collaborative perceptual effort of spectators and performers replaces the muscular activity of a performer presenting to a passive house.

In the presence of Hay's stillness or Cage's silence, concentration on the mode of perception becomes possible. The spectator's attention is focused on the manifestations of encounters and intensities that create coherences across, inside, and within bodies. The spectator's body is no longer removed from the performer's body; both are aggregates of cellular living, patterns, and placements (in Hay's case), or spaces filled with sounds and movements (in Cage's case). This kind of work can subvert the differences between people as members of social groups by focusing on the individualized specificity of embodied living. The participant's attention is turned inward into the variety of feelings and movements at work in her own body, as well as to the performances that emerge when close attention is paid to the movements of many bodies in one space.

Hay and Cage spur a rethinking of images, bodies, and interventions through the *activity* of performance. Based upon their examples, I believe that activating different ways of experiencing oneself as embodied and paying attention to the specificity of corporeal feeling can break down the ossified representational structures that keep performers and spectators apart.

Space and bodies

Attention to the physicality of perception in body work is at the heart of Laban's writings on movement and dance. His sometimes enigmatic writings on movement point toward a similar understanding of the continuity between mental effort and physical expression. In creating and theorizing my work in the community, I have found his work helps me think about perception and emotion as spatial phenomena. His writing allows me to apply the innovations of Hay and Cage to the movement work I facilitate in mental health settings.

In writings initially formulated in the 1920s, Laban puts forward a vision in which movement in space becomes the fundamental principle of life, a wild vision that links German idealism and Pythagorean geometry to contemporaneous theories of physics:

> Today we are perhaps still too accustomed to understanding objects as separate entities, standing in stabilized poses side by side in an empty space. Externally, it may appear so, but in reality continuous exchange and movement are taking place. Not for a moment do they come to a complete standstill, since matter itself is a compound of vibrations.

(Laban, 1966: 4)

In this work, Laban articulates an 'energetics' of life in order to develop a vision of movement as redemptive tool, a means to overcome the rigidity of modern life. Laban locates emotion, individuality, and space-sense in movement, fore-shadowing Hay's dance of molecules. Like Hay, Laban posits a fluid relationship between 'outer' and 'inner' dance. Perceptual attention to 'orientation' of move-ment allows Laban-based movement analysis to describe movement from its intention, not necessarily its physical extension. Movement and dance express the mobile nature of living:

> Dance is the transition into a world in which the illusory, static appearances of life are transformed into clear spatial dynamism. Awareness of this spatial world and its exploration open up a horizon of unexpected breadth. From the simplest motion to the artistic creation of dancing, the flowing stream of movement expresses dynamic space, the basis of all existence.
>
> (Laban, 1966: 93–94)

In order to practically explore this vision of movement as an opening into an other world, Laban-based movement work uses exercises to locate the body in space. It explores the extension of the body in its 'kinesphere' – the spatial scope of the body's reach, its potential location. Laban also provides a vocabulary to analyze physical movement in what he calls its 'dynamosphere' – the dynamics, effort, or 'color' of the movement. In the visualization journeys that I describe above, action verbs such as gliding, pushing, hovering, or rolling capture such dynamics and facilitate an awareness of the potentials of the body in space.

In my work, I have been able to use Laban's movement vocabularies as a scaffold to construct varieties of physical expression. The spheres are maps that can be located and explored in the participants' own bodies, and through them the performers can feel their own extension in their environment. But in order to perform, we first have to explore the spheres introspectively: physically rela-tively still, silent, non-hysterical, we start to create 'mental' spaces to move in. This means we pay attention to the volume of our bodies. For instance, when we are engaged in visualizations of breath filling our bodies, we focus on the body's extension backward and forward. When we are standing up, we focus on the body's location in the pull of gravity and the muscles' force. Like Hay, we have to train ourselves to attend to the motility of our bodies through an increasing awareness of minute movement possibilities.

But, as Laban intimates, the mind and the body are constituted as a continuity, and we have found that 'mental mapping' of spaces and movements affects our physicality. Thus, after we meditate and move through our bodies' volume, extension, and place in (relative) stillness, our steps grow bolder as we externalize movements later in the sessions. After a visualization of the body in running water or the ocean, and the specific effects on movement and spatiality communicated by these spaces, we might work on a movement sequence that focuses on water. We might improvize by channeling imaginary water over our bodies, careful not to spill a drop, and to 'hand' that water over to a fellow performer who can continue the movement with her whole body. It is astonishing to see that, even after a long meditation sequence on the floor, these movements are not stiff but fluid, the performers' joints and muscles warmed-up. The inner movement directly affects their physical bodies and allows them to fully engage with the tasks.

In the materialist framework that can be glimpsed in Laban's writing, the scope of the movement is subservient to the intention behind it. It does not necessarily matter if one extends an arm, finger, or chin in order to place oneself into a spatial form and experience (for instance, steepness or flatness, or the specific combination of time and weight in the dynamics of pressing or dabbing).[9] My creative work within mental health contexts explores these potentials by taking the movement to its smallest, invisible, concentrated extreme.

Openings

A general problem with working toward an aesthetic that tries to find spaces for the unknowable is that the 'other' too quickly becomes fixed into otherness. In the case of my work within mental health contexts, it is too easy to allow the spectator to see the performers as 'mad' and to see the traces of that 'madness' evidenced on their bodies. The diagnostic gaze reduces the presence of bodies to texts that need to be read and categorized. While Laban's analysis already allows me an antidote to this problem, I also have sought an account of sharing that allows me to conceptualize generative 'unknowing' and value uncertainty as a way of allowing openness toward difference and the possibility of change. I have found a basis for this aesthetic strategy in work by Henri Bergson.

Bergson theorizes the importance of perceiving movement. Movement changes the world in its temporal dimension (what he calls 'the Whole'); it opens up the lived experience to the new. According to Bergson, we perceive our world and time-change through fixed snapshots of 'systems' (elements in a specific relation to each other). We see change occurring from one moment to the next by seeing the change within the systems. But our time perception is always bound to the elements changing; we do not witness directly the phenomenon of 'duration' – that is, time passing in its pure state, where it is not bound to these everchanging snapshots. However, we can *partake* in duration through the movement of systems (including perceiving one's body and those of others) in time. To perceive time movement is to perceive one's own being in time – the fact that one is implicated in everything. Waiting means bearing witness to the possibility of change, which is the nature of the Whole. Bergson uses the example of a spoonful of sugar dissolving in a glass of water. By witnessing such a transformation, we can sense the echo of being in the world: what it means to be part of the Whole.[10]

The Whole is also the space of difference – a difference not yet fixed into the binaries of same and other. That space of not-yet-known difference is the 'Open'. Gilles Deleuze paraphrases Bergson this way:

> If the whole is not giveable, it is because it is the Open, and because its nature
> is to change constantly, or to give rise to something new, in short, to endure.
>
> (Deleuze, 1992: 9)

To witness movement is to witness that there is a changing, open Whole – more
than just a system changing itself. Accordingly, Bergson's definition of living
foregrounds time perception and openness to change and difference: 'Wherever
anything lives, there is, open somewhere, a register in which time is being
inscribed' (Deleuze, 1992: 10). Life is lived in relation to duration, and the witnessing of life affords a bridge between spectator and object, via the 'third term',
change, without collapsing the object into the same (that is, without making
the spectator and the object the same).

With my community group, I realized that, if we could create a performance
in which change is present but not clearly categorizable into the 'other', we could
hope to create a performative type of witnessing. In this kind of alternative performance, with its specific demands on the audience's perception of the performers,
the unclearly, imperceptibly moving and breathing bodies withholding their inner
experience would be *alive* – that is, not fixed into difference. Something would
be moving, and the fact that it would not be clear *what* is moving and *how* would
draw attention to the not-quite-stillness of the performers, and the spectators'
desire to see and to witness. The inner movements of both performers and
spectators would be foregrounded. The 'closed system' of the spectators' worldview
might just open up to the implications of difference, the glimpse of duration in
the encounter with the 'other'. For the performer, the one who put herself forward
as object to be witnessed, this conception of our moving in time would mean that
her being becomes the point at which the 'given' (social reality) transforms into
'becoming' (the opening toward potential change).

Traces

As we started to think about sharing our work, validating it outside our own
community, a performance of our moving bodies in a traditional stage format
neither seemed appropriate nor was desired by the performers. For many in the
group, the ability to remember and engage physically with tasks varied greatly from
week to week, and they generally felt nervous at the thought of embarrassing
themselves and losing their concentration. The performers were happy to share
mediated images of themselves and invite photographers and video artists into
our sessions but were adamant about not performing in conventional settings.
Other strategies of presentation needed to be found. I now had to think about a
workable way of creating the active/passive performance dynamic that Hay and
Cage explored – a way that could be brought back into the communities of my
performers. The way needed not to rely on the performers' presence but nevertheless had to foreground spatial presence and challenge the audience perceptually,
getting them to engage not just with the image but with the presence of the

performers. We found an answer in a video installation – a format that allows immersion in shared space while at the same time maintaining distance, a format that is relatively easy to transport and yet does not rely on traditional performance environments.

Traces was developed over a period of two years. We invited photographers and video artists to document our meditative work together and to capture our intensity and concentration. Ownership was important: at every visit, each participant was asked specifically whether she wanted her image to be taken on that day. Before any images left the privacy of our workspace, they were put forward for inspection, and the performers could decide to withdraw them. Together with video artist Margaret Sharrow, we created video footage of the still movements of the performers, which became the raw material for the installation. The emphasis was not on representing the spatial experience of the performers but on changing the spatial experience of the spectators, who would enter the installation as performers in their own right. Mobility was important: *Traces* was designed to be shown in many different places, including community centers, libraries, and other non-conventional performance venues.

The setup varies slightly from venue to venue, but ideally *Traces* consists of two large monitors and one video projector set up either in a small, intimate room or a dark theater or gallery space. The context is explained on a notice outside the room that makes clear both the geographical nearness of the work (developed in the same geographic area of the Welsh valleys as the community hall) and the mental health setting. This is an area of sensitivity, given the social stigma of mental health issues. Through discussion with the participants, we decided to describe the work as being created by 'users of the mental health system and other members of the community'. It was vital to us that no single member be definitely fixed as 'mentally ill' by spectators. Members were also given the option to have their names appear in the exhibition leaflet. Most, indeed, chose to name themselves.

Spectators are invited to come in and sit down on comfortable, velvety cushions. A note on the door advises them: 'This is a place of calm. Please enter, one to three at a time.' This note sets up a performance contract and expectation, and the doorway provides a transition. The spectators enter and find a space for themselves within the arrangement of screens and monitors. In order to see the images, the spectators need to come into the center of the monitors and screens. The neutral spectator positions – of sitting on a chair in a theater or standing and wandering in a gallery – are not readily available. This means that spectators have to make a decision about where they want to be in the space and how far they want to participate. On the screens are close-ups of the performers, lying on the floor, with their faces and bodies concentrated on a visually absent experience. The video images have been edited onto three tapes, between four and nine minutes long, which cycle against each other so that no arrangement is the same. The shots fix on heads, upper bodies, and hands, or travel down lying bodies. The images have been shot so traces of the photographer's body remain – in the movement of the

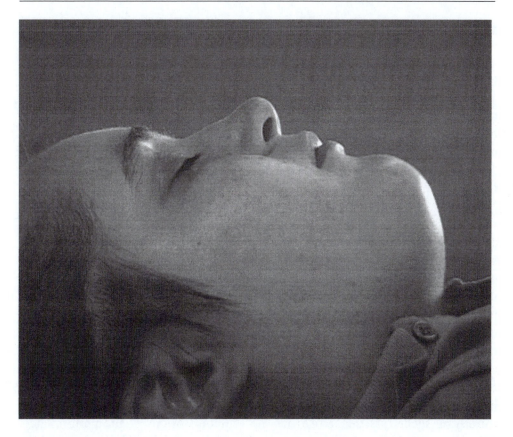

Figure 14 Traces, video-still, photographer Margaret Sharrow. (Reproduced by courtesy of
        The Olimpias)

hand-held camera, in the rhythm of panning and cuts.[11] On an accompanying
soundtrack, a voice calls out a choreographed relaxation sequence and dream-
journey cues (working through different physical experiences, as described earlier),
allowing the spectators to slip into the experience themselves, if they choose to.[12]
This soundtrack also allows a non-visual mode of access to the work.

The aesthetics of *Traces* rely on the interaction between the spectators'
engagement as witnesses and the potential for movement unfolding before them.
The silence of the still bodies invites an intense scrutiny. But this desire to see
never wholly delivers its object into the full purview of the spectators. Too much
is unseen, unknown. The silent bodies on the screens are not the silenced
hysterical women of Charcot's photographs, who are fully read and 'known'
through their physicality and the display of bodily symptoms. Rather, the multiple
screen event fosters the intense presence of the performers' bodies, while withholding such a 'truth'. Instead of 'live' stage presence, *Traces* chooses the virtual
encounter of spectating body and either not there or overwhelmingly present
performers in the onscreen close-ups, crowded together into a small room. By
presenting their faces changing not through clear movements and gestures
but through nearly imperceptible stillness, *Traces* seeks to recreate the wonder of

witnessing. It aims to create a spectator who can give full attention to the traces of living.

As an aesthetic strategy, *Traces* refuses the 'normal' images of people with mental health differences: hysterical displays of bodies out of control, fits, excess, and 'being outside one's body'. Nor does *Traces* explore 'positive images': it does not attempt to normalize experiences that are 'different'. In *Traces*, what you see is what you get – concentrated faces, breathing bodies, close-ups of tiny movements. The participants and their bodies remain unknowable. Closure is denied. The spectator is not given access to the truth about these people's experiences and thoughts. The silence of the non-hysteric body offers the sanctuary in which we can experiment with the meaning of physicality.

Traces requires the activation of and engagement with an 'other' perception, a perception trained onto the minute, the silent, the still – a perception that is a movement itself, a movement between the visible and invisible. The performance of *Traces* emerges when spectators watch the still faces surrounding them in the installation cubicle, following their unfolding in space through visual, aural, and imaginative clues. Even at the moment of presentation, in the virtual space of the installation, this performance is already gone and becoming: it is a performance that refuses to arrest people whose bodies have historically been read for symptoms of inner states. The symptom (the movement) never emerges fully but remains enshrouded in its potentiality. We hope that the bodies on the screen remain liminal, their full spatial extensions present as ghostings. Only activation by the witnessing spectators, separate from the temporal origin of the performance indexed by the camera's image, can create a new performance of encounters, flows, and spaces. Laban's and Bergson's worlds present a critique of the differentiation between the physical and the mental: movement is what drives both and lets each partake in the other so that they are continuous. The visible is only one aspect of the unfolding dimensions of moving. Openness characterizes this vision of moving people. This openness is the horizon of *Traces*'s political agenda: to move against the fixed images of mad people, of people captured in semiotic frames where the body's movement is read as (hysterical or excessive) negativity. By pointing again and again to the unknown behind the images, to silence, to the open, and by allowing our perception to explore the potentials of connection and unknowability, *Traces* hopes to address differences, shaping new horizons for performances.

This study emphasized this quest for openings and sharings that open up to unknowability, a quest that tried to vision a form of social discourse that is not fixed and closed. I read generative uncertainty at the heart of Jo Spence's photos that give the lie to capture, as the driving force in Greg Walloch's staged confessions, I read it in Aaron Williamson's play between the body and the work, and in Contact 17's play with surfaces. It is in this agenda, this reaching out towards what is not here yet, that my writing ends, and I look towards new configurations of theory and practice in the world.

Notes

Performance and disability: An introduction

1 Since the analyses of performance art as an art genre from the 1970s onwards, many scholars and critics have attempted to define the constellation of reactive aesthetics that underlie this form, which developed out of desires to implode and explode the categories of the art world, and to bring together political action and aesthetic labor. The term 'performance' is complicated by its currency in many traditions: sociology, anthropology, and linguistics among others. Performance studies, then, is a walk on the borders of fields, questioning disciplinarity and secure knowledges. In sociology, from the 1950s onwards, researchers such as Erving Goffman (for instance, 1959) have used 'performance' and 'roleplay' to understand social interaction, and the way we make sense of ourselves as agents in the social world. In anthropology, Victor Turner is associated with the discipline's move towards an interdisciplinary base. Turner's work speaks about the power of the 'liminal' to play with and invert structures, ultimately in the service of strengthening social bonds (for instance, 1969). Richard Schechner has created the most influential meetings of the social sciences and theater studies: he brings together understandings of performing on the social stage with performing in aesthetic contexts (1977, 1985). John Austin, Mikhail Bakhtin or Jacques Derrida are the names most often associated with an attention to the performance of language, and the effects of the tension between the conceptual character of language and its instantiation. As performance studies becomes sedimented as a field of study in its own right, various studies have charted the theoretical and methodological background – see Carlson, 1996, Schechner, 2002.

2 'Modernity' and 'the modern' have many meanings, not necessarily overlapping, and many are activated in the readings in this book: a modern world is characterized by alienation, by mobility, by the loss of certainties. Modern life is a life dominated by visuality, by mass media, by the structuring effects of images overriding older certainties of dogma. Modern society is a society of strife, unequal access to resources, transitory social relations, race, gender, and other binaries both constructed and deconstructed, utopia and distopia. As Benjamin shows, at some point, or maybe even at its conception, this society flips over into the post-modern moment: the relation between image and world becomes even more unstable, signifiers flow freely and refuse to anchor down, reality becomes unstable, the world boils down to a morass of numbers and a network of metaphors. Within critical theory, historical models for these periods/ways of thinking abound, as do rationales and explanatory frameworks. This book grows out of the soil provided by these theorists, and works most closely with Foucault's project of undoing disciplinary 'truths', showing our knowledges as local, historical practices.

3 Benjamin is fully aware of the price that is sometimes paid by the flaneur and his fellows (invariably it's a male flaneur – Benjamin's figures provide interesting spaces for

thought, but not blueprints for social struggle). Writing about psychopathology, Anthony Vidler cites Benjamin's awareness of the mental assault that the new vision of the city can provide:

> Writing of the Place du Maroc in Belleville, Benjamin noted this strange power of names and spaces to construct, as if with hashish, a complex and shifting image beyond that of their material existence.

(1994: 26)

He goes on to show how Benjamin's flaneur can become the vagabond amnesiac caught in these fantastical spaces.

4 Many identity politics artists have used similar strategies – the feminist, black, and gay struggles for visibility and space dominate so far the (short) history of performance art. Many of these artists use body-based actions as ways of materializing their difference in our cultural environment, inside the gallery and stage, but outside, too (see, for instance, Hart and Phelan, 1993; Betterton, 1996; Schneider, 1997). Disabled performers are building on these heritages.

5 In this book, I am using the terminology of 'disabled artist' paired with 'people with specific impairments' – this use shows a sensibility born out of British disability culture. In this context, the term 'disabled' is embraced as a sign of a shared cultural and structural oppression (structurally similar to the term 'black' in British usage). Individual differences and medically labeled conditions, when mentioned at all, are called 'impairments'. In contrast, in the US context, for instance, other sensibilities rule: here, a 'people first, disability second' politics leads to formulations such as 'people with disabilities', 'people with visual disabilities' etc., and the term 'impairment' is avoided. The two ways of speaking about disability are incompatible, so I made the decision to employ British usage. What should be celebrated, though, is that together these different codes show the impact disability politics and liberation movements can have on our language. For a discussion of the differences between 'disabled person' and 'person with disabilities', see for instance Oliver, 1990.

6 Peggy Phelan investigates a melancholia of non-recognition at the heart of the drive to performance – the attempt to see the self recognized in the gaze of the other. The origin of this melancholia is the gap between knowledge and being, between the declaration, the name, the label, and the fullness that cannot be shared:

> Identity cannot, then, reside in the name you can say or the body you can see – your own or your mother's. Identity emerges in the failure of the body to express being fully and the failure of the signifier to convey meaning exactly. Identity is perceptible only through a relation to an other – which is to say, it is a form of both resisting and claiming the other, declaring the boundary where the self diverges from and merges with the other. In that declaration of identity and identification, there is always loss, the loss of non-being the other and yet remaining dependent on that other for self-seeing, self-being.

(Phelan, 1993: 13)

7 This is the language of de Certeau, a writer who values the everyday in its potential for minor intervention into the structures of power (1988).

8 Legally, disability has a range of different definitions in different countries. In the US, the American With Disabilities Act (1990) centers 'limitation' as a core aspect of its definition: 'disability is a physical or mental impairment that substantially limits one or more major life activities'. Predictably, the openness of both 'limit' and 'life activity' give rise to much discussion. Other countries followed the US's ADA law with their own versions: Australia created a law in 1992, and, in the UK, the Disability Discrimination Act was instituted in 1995. This DDA states that a 'person has a disability for the purposes of this Act if he has a physical or mental impairment which

has a substantial and long-term adverse effect on his ability to carry out normal day-to-day activities'. A German law defines 'Schwerbehinderte', major disability, by reference to norms or rules:

> Behinderung im Sinne des Schwerbehindertengesetzes (§ 3 SchwbG) ist die Auswirkung einer nicht nur vorübergehenden Funktionsbeeinträchtigung, die auf einem regelwidrigen körperlichen, geistigen oder seelischen Zustand beruht. Regelwidrig ist der Zustand, der von dem für das Lebensalter typischen abweicht.

> Disability in relation to the major disability law is the effect of a non-transitory functional restriction that rests on a non-normed bodily, mental or psychological way of being. Non-normed (against the rule, in the literal translation) is a way of being that deviates from that typical for the specific life stage.
>
> (Own translation)

Within disability rights organizations in different countries, definitions are developed that do not focus on loss or negative difference associated with the individual body, but instead with disabling barriers erected by social factors. In the UK, this model is called the 'social model', and it distinguishes between the impairment, a value-free difference, and the disability, which occurs at the meeting of impairment and social world (this dividing apart of different aspects of the disabled definition is a common strategy – see also the United Nations Definition, widely favored by activists, and Wendell's critique of its terms, 1996: 13–19). Academics associated with this line of thinking include Hunt, 1966, Finkelstein, 1980, Oliver, 1990. For a discussion of the controversies surrounding the social model and its universalizing tendencies, see Barnes, 1996, Marks, 1999, Corker and Shakespeare, 2002. In the USA, similar debates have focused on ethnic group membership (see Note 15). For a study on the relationship between disability constructions and meanings in interaction, in the classroom, see Robin Smith (2001).

9   James Wilson and Cynthia Lewiecki-Wilson write that this issue of

> exclusion and lack of agency forms the basis of legal discourse about disability. For example, *Black's Law Dictionary*, the professional standard, defines disability as 'the want of legal capacity for the full capability to perform an act'.
>
> (Wilson and Lewiecki-Wilson, 2001: 4,
> quoting *Black's Law Dictionary*, 1990: 461)

For other discussions of this totalizing effect of the disability label and its effect of shutting down the agency of a person, see also Fine and Asch, 1988: 12. For a discussion of the intersection between politics of disability and queerness in performance work, see Sandahl (2003).

10 Many discussions of the effect of the 'disability label' refer back to the theorization of stigmatizisation by Goffman (1963). The management of different constructions of self and their effect on one's emotional and psychological status relate in interesting ways to the concept of double consciousness, as developed by W.D. de Bois, as a feature of black consciousness.

11 This issue is at the heart of Butler, 1993. The intersection between passivity and activity in the discursive construction of disabled bodies, and 'being' in opposition to a more active 'performing' will be discussed in Chapter 3.

12 For a reading, for instance, of the specifics of the 'tragedy' meaning of disability in popular representation and its implications for the disability arts movement in the UK, see Hevey, 1993. For an in-depth discussion of disability as metaphor, see Mitchell and Snyder, 1997. For the use of disability in film and popular culture, see Norden, 1994; Klobas, 1988; Longmore, 1987; Pointon and Davies, 1997, Darke, 2003.

13 The history of binary gender allocation and the spaces open for biological difference

are discussed in depth by Anne Fausto-Sterling, 2000. At every point in history, people have been born who do not fit a binary scheme of man/woman, and each historic society found different mechanisms to deal with the resultant category confusion. Fausto-Sterling shows how modern Europe and America cling to a rigid gender binary. See also Shildrick and Price (1998).

14 For a differentiated history of attitudes to people categorized as 'mad', their changing position and visibility in the social fabric as new ways of reading 'madness' became prevalent, see Foucault (1973). Other writers, such as Martha Edwards (1997), chart different definitions of disability and different discursive positions, i.e. different ways of making sense of disability in history and in different cultures.

15 Disability culture, its definitions, shape and *raison d'être* is much discussed: the term stems from an understanding of disability as a minority culture issue rather than as a medical phenomenon. In the UK, founding parents of the disability arts initiatives, conceived in terms of 'culture', included Vic Finkelstein, Anne Rae and Sian Vasey. Finkelstein saw that 'disability culture' was a problematic term in relation to disabled people's history of segregation and enforced difference, but he saw a value for

> disabled people presenting a clear and unashamed self-identity . . . [it is] essential for us to create our own public image, based upon free acceptance of our distinctive group identity. Such a cultural identity will play a vital role in helping us develop the confidence necessary for us to create the organisations which we need to promote the social change that we all want.
>
> (1987 speech given at the launch of the London Disability Arts Forum, quoted in Campbell and Oliver, 1996: 111)

For the development of and issues relating to the 'minority group model' in the US, see for instance, Hahn (1987) and Shapiro (1993). How the tensions and developments of an evolving understanding of disability as a way of life (to cite Raymond Williams's definition of 'culture', 1961) work themselves out in a Germany's literature, see Hamilton (1997). A subsection of the discussion of a 'minority culture' has centered on Deaf issues. For a critical discussion of the relationship between nation, Deaf culture and disability issues, see Davis, 1999.

16 The collection by Wilson and Lewiecki-Wilson (2001) assembles a range of voices on these uneasy issues between individuality and social group, language and experience, and rhetorical intervention into stable discourses.

17 Susan Wendell (1996) provides a complex reading of the multitudes of psychological mechanisms that make up a 'disability experience' in her discussion of disability from a feminist perspective – a perspective trained in recognizing structural imbalances, tensions between public and private, and the mythic overstructure of biology. It is this perspective that also influences my work.

18 This moving on of knowledge through the poles of textuality and embodiment, semiotic and phenomenological knowledge, is focused on by Csordas, when he speaks of them as 'corresponding methodological fields' and 'dialectical partners' (1994: 12). Within the disability studies field, a very interesting study addressing issues of valuing difference can be found in James Overboe's work (1999). Overboe finds a place outside the category:

> After I overcame the uncertainty and the fear of being 'different for itself' (to use Deleuze's term) with no category with which to anchor my existence or no place to belong, I felt a sense of freedom because I was released from the restrictions of the ability/disability categories.
>
> (1999: 27)

Making this experience socially visible, extending beyond the boundaries of the individual, is the labor that still needs to be done.

19 Studies of disability as a theme or metaphor in various performance context are rich
    and are becoming more numerous. For collections that deal with the themes, see Fahy
    and King (2002), and Auslander and Sandahl (forthcoming). Journal issues on the
    topic of disability and performance include an *American Theater* special section edited
    by Carrie Sandahl (2001), an issue of the *Michigan Quarterly Review*, edited by Marcy
    Epstein and Susan Crutchfield (1998), and a special double edition of the *Contemporary
    Theater Review*, 2001, No. 3+4, edited by Petra Kuppers. See also Sandahl, 2003 and
    1999; Albright, 1997, and studies of individual performances such as Strickling, 2002.
    A fascinating chapter of disability performance that is not dealt with in these pages is
    Deaf performance work: Sign Language Theater, which is emerging into artistic
    maturity. For further information, see O'Reilly (2001) and Kochhar-Lindgren (2002).
    Also not discussed in this study are the specific and fascinating implications of visual
    impairment-based arts for the oscillatory epistemological politics I develop in these
    pages. See, for instance, the work of the dance group Touchdown, the development
    of audio-description as aesthetic event, sculpture/installation work and different
    experiences of space, or, often within disability culture's cabaret format, dramatic work
    surrounding the Helen Keller myth. For a highly useful study of integrated dance work
    that employs an art rather than a therapy frame, and gives plenty of practical advice,
    see Adam Benjamin (2002). This study provides significant historical information about
    the formation of integrated dance groups – an important chapter in disability arts.
20 This study is not a 'history' of disabled performers: while the large story has been one
    of exclusion, many disabled voices have woven themselves into the history of art,
    although often their difference has been invisibilized. Others have been important in
    the development of contemporary art practices: Chapter 1 discusses Jo Spence who,
    together with other artists such as Christopher Knowles (a collaborator of Robert
    Wilson), Bob Flanagan, or model Aimee Mullins in her appearance in Matthew
    Barney's Cremaster series, have left their mark on the modern art canon. Many artists
    have powerfully dealt with their changing status, using their already acquired social
    visibility to speak strongly about disability experiences – dancer Homer Avila,
    performer Christopher Reeves, visual artist Hannah Wilke, theater artist Joe Chaikin
    are some of these voices that have found their way on different paths into the disabled
    community.
21 There are other traditions in contemporary performance practice that have become
    important and useful to many disabled performers, in particular work developing out
    of the practices of the Theater for the Oppressed by Boal, 1985 (in relation to disability
    issues, see for instance, Hammer, 2001, and Mitchell, 2001), and, in dance, work that
    stems out of the Contact Improvisation scene. The development of sophisticated
    community based performance models have been important in the development of
    inter-arts models, and in the developing critique of creative industries and institutions
    (for historical perspectives, see van Erven, 1988; for contemporary international
    developments, see Haedicke and Nellhaus, 2001; van Erven, 2001; for public art
    approaches, see Lacy, 1995 and Weintraub, 1996; for issues of 'Outsider Art', see
    Zolberg and Cherbo, 1997). As the disability studies community grows and writes its
    histories, more sites of disability performance emerge: for instance, a historical
    perspective on The Amputettes, a gender-bending dance troupe of veteran amputees
    in Forest Glen, Maryland, USA, in 1945, is provided by Serlin, 2003.

I Practices of reading difference

1 This function of 'loading' otherness is a familiar device in the representation of
   disability: from a position in the normalized center, disability is often aligned with a
   gendered, racial or class-based other (see, for instance, Pernick, 1997, on the conflation
   of disability and 'blackness' in two pro-eugenic US feature films of the 1910s and 1920s,

or Gilman, 1982: 2–6, on the darker skin color of images of 'mad' people, linked with the medical explanation of 'dark' humors as well as wider connotational aspects of 'wildness').

2 Quotation from commentary section, 2002 DVD of OZ.

3 'Disability' is the term to use, for social legibility, even though it always carries its secondariness to 'ablility' – short of devising sub-languages that subvert the differential of the dominant codes, both center and periphery are forced to use the master's language. An awareness of these mechanisms leads to the formation of codes in disability circles: 'crips' has a currency as a self-referent for use amongst disabled people. Similar to other non-dominant groups, disabled people have developed 'signifin' practices' (see Gates, 1988).

4 The 'branch' of phenomenology most influential to my work comes from Maurice Merleau-Ponty (1962, 1968) and his exigetes (for instance, Grosz, 1994, Leder, 1990, and Jones, 1998). Other traditions emerge from Hussel (1970, 1982, 1991), Heidegger (1996), Sartre (1992), de Beauvoir (1973) and others.

5 'We can say that, with regard to the determination of the objectives represented within it, every literary work is in principle incomplete and always in need of further supplementation; in terms of the text, however, this supplementation can never be completed' (Ingarden, 1973: 251).

6 See also Davis's discussion of Spence's photowork, 1997: 63/4.

7 Within art discourses, Spence's work has been positioned both within feminist and class-based political work: her own writings have strongly stressed the class issues in her work. In more recent work on the body, her photos have resurfaced as examples of the grotesque body at work, or as appropriations of the female nude as oppositional discourse (e.g. Nead, 1992; Meskimmon, 1996).

8 Tracy Warr in her writing on body art sees how it is caught in a historical moment where the immediate is receding in the larger cultural field:

> The increasing absence of 'embodiment' caused by technology – global communications including the telephone, television, satellites and the internet – all make it easier to conceive of other people as distant, and therefore irrelevant, Other. Mediation through technology does stifle the impact of the empathetic body – war on TV news, for instance – but the efficaciousness of the human presence should not be romanticized. Whilst soldiers and politicians are often physically distant from the victims of their actions, torturers torture close up, using other techniques to distance their victims to non-human status.
>
> (Warr, 1996: 7)

I am not sure whether we are yet to give up on immediacy in the times of 'new' technologies: at various points in this study, I am reading phenomenological potential in 'mediated' forms. See also Jones, 1997, and her analysis of 'technophenomenology'.

9 This is a different conception of the body as mask than the one offered by Mike Featherstone in his work on age. He sees a 'mask of aging' as a set of cultural images which depict the 'outer body' of older, potentially disabled people as 'misrepresenting and imprisoning the inner self' (Featherstone, 1995: 227). I read Spence's play with the photographed 'narratives' of female aging as aiming at the fact that she is the body, but that that body is always excessive to the reader's reading of it.

10 A similar moment, a female body denying its meaning to the gaze by drawing the desire to know into the mouth-cave, is explored by Peggy Phelan (1993). In her reading of Robert Mapplethorpe's photograph of the painter Alice Neel, Alice Neel (1984), the open mouth of the dying artist mirrors the open lens of the photographer who died of AIDS. The reflection of the self in the other is the witness of the vanishing of self: the desire to know Alice Neel reveals itself as the frustrated desire to see the self. In her Lacanian reading, Phelan reads performance art for the unmarked, the unseen.

> Unable to reverse her own gaze (the eyes obstinately look only *outside* the self), the subject is forced to detour through the other to see herself. In order to get the other to reflect her, she has to look for/at the other.
>
> (Phelan, 1993: 23)

Phelan's readings probe for the vanishing point of the gaze: for the moment when the self which is searching for itself is faced with its own unmarkedness.

11 Roland Barthes' jouissance seems to take this position 'outside' the system, only to be put to use within it – it is a moment of freedom that reflects back on the condition of unfreedom and provides an escapist pleasure. The shackles of subjectivity are thrown off for an unstable moment, but the moment leads to – nothing.

> The 'grain' is the body in the voice as it sings, the hand as it writes, the limb as it performs. If I perceive the 'grain' in a piece of music and accord this 'grain' a theoretical value (the emergence of the text in the work), I inevitably set up a new scheme of evaluation which will certainly be individual – I am determined to listen to my relations with the body of the man or woman singing or playing and that relation is erotic – but in no way 'subjective' (it is not the psychological 'subject' in me who is listening; the climactic pleasure hoped for is not going to reinforce – to express – that subject but, on the contrary, to lose it). The evaluation will be made outside any law, outplaying not only the law of culture but equally that of anticulture, developing beyond the subject all the value hidden behind 'I like' or 'I don't like'.
>
> (Barthes, 1977: 188)

This is Barthes' assertion of a non-culture space, non-subject space, but it is firmly fixed in the binary of body/language, signifier/signified, presence (of the subject)/absence (of the subject). As a moment of non-communication, non-culture, non-sharing, the moment *is* a moment in the constitution of the psychological subject – it is the subject-imagination of the struggle at the heart of subjectivity-formation. I want to see this disruption as more constitutional, questioning the function of making meaning, of language, itself. Barthes' dissolution of the subject in jouissance, or in the moment of free signifier play ('meaning in its potential voluptuousness'), the significance, provides the binary polar to culture/language with its construction of the subject. The construction of subjectivity/culture as '*one* form of life' (my emphasis) is not part of Barthes' system of meaning-making. His achievement is his attempt to delineate the contour of the unspeakable by navigating its boundaries, but he does not attempt to shift these boundaries by pointing to the fact that they are not 'naturally' cultural. I want to find a way of working the grain of the voice and the body not just as an adjunct, negative pleasure enriching subjectivity in culture, but as a political pleasure that actively challenges binary constructions.

12 An analogue might be found in Deleuze and Guattari's work in which they deal with different usage of space, time and bodies. 'Deep semantic structures' stem from semiotic/structuralist analysis, and a poststructuralist analysis sees these not as givens, but as determined by dominant ideology (e.g. the binary of male/female; black/white). A complete rethinking of space would dislodge binaries (as spatial concepts) and allow for a rethinking of communication at different meeting points – the 'lines of flight' that escape the 'striated space' – see also the discussion of the smooth and the striated in Chapter 4. Deleuze and Guattari

> dissolve all stable 'reals' – the subject, its objects, the placid and granite extension of spaces – and rearticulate them in a modified universe of rapidity, movement, speeds and slownesses, reversible distances, atomized particles, transient coalitions, and escaping aggregates. Their theory relies on space without relying upon its usual coordinates of depth, distance, volume, and direction.
>
> (K. Kirby: 1996, p. 112)

They recombine the subject without losing sight of the 'state'. Materiality and discourse align in their concept of agency.

13 It is this movement potential, this undecidability of living matter, that Brian Massumi points to as the ground for a different form of political materialism: 'When a body is in motion, it does not coincide with itself. . . . In motion, the body is in an immediate, unfolding relation to its own nonpresent potential to vary' (2002: 4). Attention to movement and sensation, to affect and living, can disrupt the certainties of categories, can open up glimpses into different futures.

14 There is a further level at play in my reading of the photo: the potential contradiction between the kinetic experience of the pose and the representational signification. Ruth Douglas (1995) points to the double meaning that memory of kinetic experience can have on dance. In this case, the grasping of a teddybear, head bowed and body contained, reminds me of a secure, safe state. Visually, though, the pose of containment, minimalizing the body's exposed surfaces and shielding the center, together with the references to the child, create a powerless, negative image.

15 I find this complex evocation of life and death in the photography of bodies also in Hannah Wilke's photo work, when she opposes her own body with that of her mother, a survivor of breast cancer, in the late 1970s, and later, when she charts her own journey with lymphoma, in the early 1990s. Another interesting instantiation of these issues can be found in Kiki Smith's work. In a recent exhibition of women and surrealism (San Francisco Museum of Modern Art, see Chadwick, 1998), Smith displayed a photo of her head (probably her reflection in a mirror), as if her skin had been removed, flattened out and laid out on a board: a distorted, flat image in which back and front are visible at the same time, and issues of wholeness and distruption are queried in the large, floating, blue-tinted display. As a self-portrait, the image queries the closed-ness of the sign, the ultimate meaning of a picture of a cadaver able to present herself. A similar evocation of life and death, connection and separation, life presence and preserved death is at work in David Wojnarowicz's *Untitled* (1982–91), where photos of bloodied bodies are displayed in light boxes (thus they are not just visible, but projected, in flux), connected by 'umbilical' cables (see discussion in Mirzoeff, 1995: 27). Again, the body is torn apart and held together at the same time. Robert Sember discusses Wojnarowicz's work in relation to 'infected vision' – a vision that allows again to side-step the 'natural' (of time) and to see the workings of structure (1998). Mary Kelly's photography work evokes the live-ness of the body, and its passing through time, without the body's presence in the photograph. Apter (1995) reads Kelly's photograph of leather clothes, displayed floatingly (like Smith's photos in lightboxes) on plexiglas as signs of 'skin as chronotype' (67): so far removed from the female body that humour, sensuality, pleasure and irony can come into play.

16 More artists and community activists are now creating work around imagery, media dissemination, health education and community practice in relation to breast cancer. For a discussion of these issues, see for instance Solomon (1992), and Cartwright (2000).

17 *Cultural Sniping* is the title of one of Spence's posthumously published books (1995), where she describes and contextualizes her photographic interventions, and 'Cultural Sniper' is the name of a vibrant 1990 photo which shows her with balaclava, bared teeth and smeared in paint, ready to launch a stone from a sling at the viewer.

2 Freaks, stages, and medical theaters

1 The freakshow has found wide critical attention, with writers such as Leslie Fiedler (1978), Robert Bodgan (1988), John McKenzie (1993), Rosemarie Garland Thomson (1996, 1997, 1999) and Andrea Stulman Dennett (1997) discussing the relationship between the freakshow's display and the social organization in the wider social world.

Issues of race, class, gender, disability and other forms of difference are heightened and made hysterical in the freak display. Colonial spectacle, moral and hygiene issues, the organization of industrial society: all these themes can be illuminated through the acts half-hidden on the city's margin.

2 On Coney Island, Fraser was actually offered a job (and took it up for a while, a year later), to perform at one of the few still existing freakshow spectacles. He references the offer in the 'Sealboy' program notes (and confirmed it to me in an interview): 'Sideshows by the Seashore' on Coney Island, existing in the same spot that David Rosen's 'Wonderland' sideshow used to occupy, offered Fraser a job there when he was interviewing the owner about Sealo. The conditions were 10 hours a day, 6 days a week, 11 dollars an hour.

3 All information from Mat Fraser's 'Sealboy' program notes, 2001.

4 Graeae is a professional disability theater group in London, UK, founded in 1980. The history of their inception, the notion of making non-disabled people listen to, and be touched by, disabled people as 'real' people, is charted in Richard Tomlinson's *Disability, Theater and Education* (1982), an important document of the history of disability performance. Many important disabled performers have come up through the workshops and education offered by Graeae, and actors associated with the group include Nabil Shaban, a familiar face to British TV audiences who starred in productions such as *Wittgenstein* (dir. Derek Jarman, 1993), and Kate O'Reilly, a deaf playwright (see O'Reilly, 2001). Workshopping, professional theater education as well as theater-in-education approaches constitute an important part of Graeae's impact. Some of their working processes are documented in Hammer, 2001.

5 Teratology as a term was coined by Isidore Geoffroy Saint-Hilaire in 1822, as part of the movement to medicalize birth defects, and to let science draw freaks up and away from the popular environment (see Garland Thomson, 1997: 75).

6 It is predictable that this search for certainty never finds its goal, always remains stuck in the muddiness of indistinct distinctions. As 'an institution historically capitalizing on contaminated binarizations' (McKenzie, 1993: 107), the freakshow undermines the genre of humanity, showing it as a genre, allowing the other to emerge where only (impossible) one-ness can assuage the troubling knowledge that there is difference. It is the hysterical search for fixed boundaries in a world that unravels certainty that gives freakshows their frisson.

7 This breakdown of certainties enacted and emblematized in the freakshow has meant that it has become a familiar locus for the investigation of identity. Within theater history, Carson McCuller's play *The Member of the Wedding* (1950) is one example of this use of the freakshow as metaphorical playground of identity search. For a discussion of the play in relation to freakshow literature, see Thomas Fahy, 2002.

8 Of course, new places have sprung up for this kind of engagement, places often mediated through TV: Jerry Springer and his offsprings, and the World Wrestling Federation/Entertainment programmes recreate some of the audience engagements of the old freakshow, with its permission of (verbal) interaction. In particular the WWF/WWE shows actively encourage the audience to read the bodies of the contestants, only marginally helped by the talkers' patter (often hard to understand in the live event). Mazer points to the morality play at the heart of wrestling as a performance, as well as to the transgressive, carnivalesque potential inherent in its play with license, with violence, with death (1998: 27), a point made also by Fiske, who reads transgressive potential in the fan engagement with wrestling (1987). Kennedy (2001) posits that sports allow for an alignment with fellow spectators that theater does not offer. Similar to the old freakshow, sports events give license for the creation of moral clarities, to a delineation of 'us' versus 'them'. Also, the affectual investment in the event taking place at the same time allows for the excess noted by Fiske and Mazer, and the 'unmanly', problematically gendered behavior of football fans embracing and weeping

noted by Kennedy (2001) and Buford (1991). The issue of stratification and liminality at work in the audience address of the freakshow can be further explored in relation to Victorian sensibilites, but what is also of interest here is the issue of spectatorial violence in relation to performance. Lucy Davis (2000) has read spectatorial violence in the context of a site-specific installation in Singapore as an indication of discomfort with unfamiliar spaces, and as a response to affectual liminality. During the installation, various art works were destroyed by passers-by, images were peeled off tables, items were stolen. She proposes this spectatorship as an effect of the location, of the nature of site-specificity: 'In a state where surveillance stretches from elevator cameras to washrooms, spaces that are not yet governed by strict codes of practice seem to be the spaces where violence emerges' (125) – public art can be seen by definition to be liminal, outside the gallery, not quite of the street. In relation to the Introduction's notion of the turtle walker, interesting intersections might emerge in further investigation of the relationship between physical involvement, violence and public art.

9   This move from the freakshow to the medical theater is played out in Bernard Pomerance's *The Elephant Man* (1979). For a discussion of the doctor/patient/object issues at work in the play, see Shapiro (2002).

10 Different countries have different histories and rationales for the demise of the freakshow, and the specific constellation of counter-freakshow voices and their arguments. In the US context, scholars have put forward different narratives of the change-over from freakshow to the medical theater (Garland Thomson, 1996, 1997), or linking the demise of the show to moral outrage (Bogdan, 1988). Later on in Sealboy, Berent will react angrily to 'do-gooders' who want to do him out of a job, by protesting against the exploitation of disabled people.

11 The carnivalesque aspects of the practices in the Bologna anatomy theater are discussed by Ferrari (1987).

12 Bob Flanagan is well discussed in performance literature: Amelia Jones discusses him and French performance artist Orlan, who uses surgery in her performance work. Jones discusses the phenomenology of pain at work in his performances: his material draws our gaze and attention through its flamboyant display of pain, but keeps us at bay because of the unknowable nature of someone else's pain (1998: 230). His work is also discussed by Kauffman, 1998, in relation to other body-art projects, and a lot of material by and about him is collected in Juno and Vale (2000), as well as in his own writing, in particular his pain-journal (2000). Other writers who discuss pain and body art include Olalquiaga (1999), O'Dell (1998) and Hart (1998). In disability studies, Rosemarie Garland Thomson has paid attention to Flanagan's use of sexuality as a means to stave off the rhetorics of sentimentality (2001), see also Sandahl (2000).

13 This sense of performance as a ritual engagement with illness is at the heart of a number of performances, including the work by Gretchen Case, discussed in Case, 2001.

14 This historical practice of exhibiting hysteria patients in the medical theater has been commented on extensively by Showalter, 1987; Beizer, 1994; Phelan, 1996; Bronfen, 1998; McCarren, 1998; Schutzman, 1999 and many others. See also Kuppers, 2004.

15 For an in-depth discussion of the politics of gay and disabled identities played out in solo performances, including an analysis of Walloch's work, see Sandahl, 2003.

16 An excerpt from *White Disabled Talent*, by Greg Walloch, quoted with permission of the author, see also discussion in Sandahl (2003: 48).

17 Another example of this genre is a performance sketch developed by the St. Louis based DisAbility Project's Stuart Falk, a wheelchair-using long-standing member of this community theater group. In his sit-up performance rant, he uses the genre of the holiday story to distort the power-relations between himself and the medical system:

> So I just flew back in from vacation and man are my arms tired!. Ahh . . . Club Med
> – St. John's white sand beaches, lazy breezes, reggae mon, beautiful women –

Alright, so it wasn't the Caribbean. But I couldn't really go on vacation with a urinary tract infection. It was actually Club Med . . . icine. And it wasn't St. John's the island. It was St. John's Mercy Medical Center . . . It starts out exotically enough. I just call my favorite travel agent, at 911. Then, suddenly, I'm transferred into a gurney and I find myself in the back of a warm van with a woman in uniform. She says, 'What's your name', and begins touching me in different places. 'How does this feel'? 'Here?' 'Now, do you have insurance?' (Script outline as basis of improvisation, developed by Stuart Falk, Ann Fox and Joan Lipkin, quoted from interviews with Joan Lipkin, Artistic Director of the DisAbility project.)

For further information about the DisAbility Project, see Lipkin and Fox, 2001 and 2002.

18 It is this ambivalence, this uncertainty in how to read the proliferating sexualities, the child's pleasures, one's implication in the gaze, that Sandahl reads in her analysis of this scene (2003: 48).

19 For a discussion of this image as location, situated above Freud's sofa, see Read (2001).

20 See for instance Elaine Showalter, 1987: 149ff., Stephen Heath's discussion of hysteria's cultural transition of a disturbance in visuality to one that is cured by Freud's talking cure (1982: 33–49), Judith Mayne's discussion of the hysteric and the primitive (1990: 219–221), Barbara Creed's analysis of the womb as object of horror (the womb being associated with the site of hysteria), (1993), Rebecca Schneider's discussion of performance artists such as Karen Finley quoting from women's history (1997: 115–116), and the discussions of visual fantasies of women in Victorian culture in Bram Dijkstra (1986), who discusses topoi such as the *Nymph with the Broken Back*, the *Cult of Invalidism*, *Clinging Vines*, etc., many of which are at work in the representations and cultural imagery of hysteria. Janet Beizer discusses 'ventriloquized bodies', where the construction and maintenance of hysteria is a gendered struggle over the site of speech – she sees Charcot's engaged in the creation of a scenario where women's bodies signify through 'inarticulate body language, which must be dubbed by a male narrator' (1994: 9).

21 Often literally: up until the 1970s, the 'ugly laws' were in force in certain parts of the US, decreeing that people with 'unsightly' difference were banned from public places.

22 Garland Thomson makes these references apropos Cheryl Marie Wade's poetry of disability experiences, and focuses on the gendered violence that is amplified when the woman is disabled (see also Garland Thomson, 1999).

23 How to read Bakhtin and contemporary culture has been an issue of fascination to cultural critics. Jan Christian Metzler (2000) discusses disabled fashion models, imaginatively clad by Alexander McQueen for a special feature of *Dazed and Confused* (for a discussion of Fraser as one of these models, see Kuppers, 2002). Metzler moves towards a reading where the contemporary media scene becomes the carnivalesque culture of Bakhtin's conception (77).

24 A point also made in relation to the grotesque body by Mary Russo: 'The grotesque body of carnival festivity was not distanced or objectified in relation to an audience. Audiences and performers were the interchangeable parts of an incomplete but imaginary wholeness. The grotesque body was exuberantly and democratically open and inclusive of all possibilities' (Russo, 1994: 78).

25 Lennard Davis focuses on this relation of the grotesque body to a 'disturbance to the visual field'. The grotesque body is not an embodied subject, not a 'set of characteristics through which a fully constituted subject views the world' (Davis, 1995: 151).

3 Deconstructing images: Performing disability

1 Adam Benjamin (2001) gives much needed historical background to the creation of this innovative performance group and their path to professional integrated dance work. With these kinds of publications, we can begin to construct our own history of disability arts.

2 Butler's theories of performativity do not easily accommodate themselves to being aligned with performace in theatrical frameworks (see Diamond, 1997: 46–47, also Diamond, 1996). Butler rejects theatrical performance as performativity since theater implies a shaping consciousness, a pre-theatrical. As I will move on to show, the problematic that disarticulates 'acting' and 'being/bodily existence' in the theater performance is very much at stake in disability performance.

3 The concept of performativity is often attacked on these grounds, and critiques of Judith Butler as the foremost proponent of this thinking in the area of gender have included attacks on the idea of 'gender as garment'. In her introduction to *Bodies that Matter*, 1993, Butler seeks to clarify the deeper structure of gender, as something that precedes subjective agency.

4 See for instance, Bordo (1993), who introduces her study with a poem by Delmore Schwartz, and a reading of that poem's use of a bear as body metaphor, a metaphor that can be extended to align with cultural attitudes to the body as the other to the mind:

> The bear who is the body is clumsy, gross, disgusting, a lumbering fool who trips me up in all my efforts to express myself clearly, to communicate love. Stupidly, unconsciously, dominated by appetite, he continually misrepresents my 'spirit's motive'.
>
> (Bordo, 1993: 2/3)

5 Albright also analyzes the film, and comes to a different appreciation than I: she sees the large gap in mobility between different dancers involved in the film, and posits that the alignment of wheelchair with the negative connotations of disability is not broken (1997: 81). I concede her point, but I am pointing in my reading to moments in the film where the natural is undercut by the amalgamation of visual and kinesthetic clues.

4 Outsider energies

1 One of the strongest depictions of this myth's connection with gendered energies can be found in Martha Graham's dance *Errand into the Maze* (1947). In her recasting of the Greek myth, Graham tells the story from the perspective of the female character (Ariadne), and the issue at stake in the encounter between bull-man and woman is power – 'what terrifies her is the man's sexual attraction and the knowledge that yielding to it will put her into a subordinate position. The loss of her own power represents an ultimate humiliation to her' (Siegel, 1981: 202). But the power-structures embodied in the choreography and the dancing bodies themselves negates any one reading of the flow of domination. With Graham's hallmark expressive body-language, the tension of psychological encounters turn in on themselves: '[the bull-man] seems absurdly muscle-bound, confined almost by his own dominance' (Adair, 1992: 134).

2 The subject described here, the searching subject who wants to encounter the gaze back on itself, is the lost Hegelian subject, divorced from itself by the mechanisms of knowledge itself, by the dis-unity of object and subject of knowledge. The nature of the 'I' bounds off the plenitude of full experience.

3 Other familiar characters from the disability drama canon can be seen in a similar light, as borderline figures, haunting the border countries of humanity – creating myths out of Kaspar Hauser (in dramas such as *Kaspar*, Peter Handke, 1968, *Kaspariania* by Eugenio Barba, 1967, *The Mutation Show* by Joseph Chaikin, 1971, and films by Werner Herzog,

1975), and the *Elephant Man* (in dramatic form by Bernard Pomerance, 1979, in the cinema by David Lynch, 1980).

4 Information gleaned from program notes, website and interviews with festival programers.

5 Within an art context, writers such as Gablik (1992) and Lomas call for a re-evaluation of the relationship between indivdiual agency and the 'community' – understanding the self as an embedded entity, a leaky conglomeration within a larger framework. Lomas (1998) is writing about community dance with people with learning disabilities in the frameworks created by Jabadeo, a community dance resource company in the UK. She sees the acts of improvizing and creating in a community as political methodologies, reminding us of reservoirs beyond exhausted individualism, and their potential for renewing social energies.

6 Calling Artaud to this chapter's project is appropriate beyond the argumentation for a non-human theater – Artaud himself has been read as a posterchild for the mad genius, the disabled person closer to the 'truth' of the universe due to his sufferings. Artaud experienced mental distress and was institutionalized for long periods. Sometimes, this has been read not as a negative comment on the coherence of his thought, but as a validation of his unique perspective, something that stands him apart from the mere 'theater'. For instance, Artaud's friend, theater maker (and collaborator on Artaud's *To Have Done with the Judgement of God*) Roger Blin writes:

> Every time some young guy rolls around on the ground uttering shrieks they call him the son of Artaud. He looks at himself in the mirror, he tells himself: 'I'm pale, I'm son of Artaud', add a little dry-ice and we're off! I've always dismissed that kind of thing, though I recognise that the work of the Living Theater or that of Growtowski is important. Growtowski stole a great deal from Artaud more or less directly. But without Artaud's terrible experience, all that can be nothing more than mimickery.
>
> (Blin, 1986: 69, trans. Batty)

Authenticity is the issue in this passage: and Artaud's authenticity is guaranteed by his 'terrible experience'. Other critics have seen Artaud's difficult writing in relation to the investment that Artaud had in his theories: as something that wasn't articulable in writing, but that remained intricately connected to the body. Susan Sontag's influential reading of his work comments on this density as a denial of abstraction:

> It demands a special stamina, a special sensitivity, and a special tact to read Artaud properly. It is not a question of giving one's assent to Artaud – that would be shallow – or even of neutrally 'understanding' him and his relevance. What is there to assent to? How could anyone assent to Artaud's ideas unless one was already in the demonic state of siege that he was in? Those ideas were emitted under the intolerable pressure of his own situation. Not only is Artaud's position not tenable; it is not a 'position' at all . . . What Artaud has left behind is work that cancels itself, thought that outbids itself, recommendations that cannot be enacted . . . To detach his thought as a portable intellectual commodity is just what that thought explicitly prohibits. It is an event rather than an object.
>
> (Sontag, 1976: lvi)

It is this same observation of the indivisible nature of flesh and word that governs Derrida's reading of Artaud, and that aligns itself with Derrida's formulation of deconstruction, with its always already deferred match of signifier and signified.

> Artaud attempted to destroy a history, the history of the dualist metaphysics . . . the duality of the body and the soul which supports, secretly of course, the duality of

speech and existence, of the text and the body, etc. The metaphysics of the commentary which authorized 'commentaries' because it *already* governed the works commented on. Nontheatrical works, in the sense understood by Artaud, works that are already deported commentaries. Beating his flesh in order to reawaken it at the eve prior to the deportation, Artaud attempted to forbid that his speech be spirited [*souffle*] from his body.

(Derrida: 1978: 175)

It is here that Artaud's theater of cruelty is most aligned with Lingis's shark – the collapse of language in the face of absolute presence. The human is quiet in the presence of that which brings to the forefront an experience of non-divisibility, of self-presence.

7 It is through the unleashing of this theater storm that the human actor does/does not insert agency into the non-human forces. Jane Goodall talks about Artaud's work as a revolt against the impossibility of action:

> Artaud's whole oeuvre could be read as a furious rejection of the prospect of being swept along in the currents of a drama in which the forces are all fatal or metaphysical, and the human is possessed of no counter-charge through which to effect a catastrophe.

(Goodall, 1996: 2)

She characterizes the play of Artaud as a game, as a ritual of strategy, of restless action, of energetic discharge:

> Artaud's project has been characterized in various ways, but one of the characterizations I like best, is the summary view that he was a gambler. Certainly, he was nothing if not reckless, but gambling is something more than recklessness. It is driven by a fascination with winning and losing, and with strategy. You can gamble against an opponent, or against chance itself. Artaud combined these approaches, by casting fatality *as* his opponent. He was prepared to stake everything, perpetually, and was always on the look-out for ways of raising the stakes.

(Goodall, 1996: 3)

And the opponent in this theater of gamble is the origin of sense itself, as Gallop calls it with Artaud's radiopoem, the *Judgement of God* (part of which is cited at the beginning of this chapter):

> You have to have done with the judgement of God, because God's judgement is screwed. He's screwed things up in the making of the world. He's screwed us into being. That image keeps coming up in the writing, and it's a very sexual image: god has screwed created being, and continues to screw it, all the time, and in the process of screwing creation, he's screwed the senses, they're actually twisted.

(Goodall, 1996: 10)

This sense of a mistrust in the nature of things, and the nature of sense and sense-impression, then, is at the heart of Artaud's project. A de-centring of sensibility is necessary to see beyond the veil of the screwed, to see the sexual action of screwing in the act, of catching the meaning-making machine in its turns.

8 Critiques of Artaud's impossible theater and his style, 'positively Delphic in its poetic obscurity' (Innes, 1981: 6) abound in theater studies. He had significant influence on the development of Western avant-garde theater, but 'he left no concrete technique behind him, indicated no method. He left visions, metaphors.' (Grotowski, 'He Wasn't Entirely Himself', 1969: 86)

9 See also Mike Pearson and Lyn Levett's work, in particular with Welsh theater group Brith Gof. Pearson describes his work with Mike and Lyn, who has cerebral palsy, as an exercise in physicality, presence and change. (Pearson and Levett, 2001, Pearson, 1998)

10 Steven Connor reads a relationship between the radio play by Artaud which opened this chapter, and Williamson's body/voice:

> In the radio performance of Artaud, and in performances which simulate the eyeless exposure of the voice, such as Beckett's *Not I*, or the contorted, abstract sound-ballets of the contemporary deaf performer Aaron Williamson, in which the shouts, groans and crepitations of the performer act out the struggles of an earless voice to establish a relation to itself, the voice is forced to make its own body out of its privation.
>
> (Connor, 2001: 91)

Swinging in here is the negativity of a 'earless voice' in need of an Other to recognize it – but it is equally fruitful to think of Williamson's body/voice as a more playful engagement with the ground of language, and the language/matter of signification. The self to be recognized is always out of reach – the struggle is transposed from a muscular activity to the sensibility of the viewer trying to read affect in physicality. For another brief reading of Williamson and Artaud, see Dyer, 1993.

11 Deleuze and Guattari's knowledge project is a fibrillation of knowledge categories, but the price they pay for their language on the edges of bodies and words is a loss of immediate political impact. Thus, their use of 'medical' terms as metaphors evacuates a sense of lived experience, and has led to much critique. As Elizabeth Grosz states:

> In both *Anti-Oedipus* and *A Thousand Plateaus*, Deleuze and Guattari invest in a romantic elevation of psychoses, schizophrenia, becoming, which on one hand ignores the very real torment of suffering individuals and, on the other hand, positions it as an unlivable ideals for others.
>
> (1994: 163)

5 Encountering paralysis: Disability, trauma, and narrative

1 Performance art as an art form stems from a period where the division between mind and body were forcefully challenged, and the political implications of any divisionary strategy were explored by feminists, black artists and other groups whose political oppression rests on an alignment with the 'lower', the 'natural', the 'unrestrained' and 'primitive'.

2 Roland Barthes discusses the construction of a discourse of 'truth' which includes the camera and its archiving of moments of time:

> the development of specific genres like the realist novel, the private diary, documentary literature, news items, historical museums, exhibitions of old objects and especially in the massive development of photography, whose sole distinctive trait (by comparison with drawing) is precisely that it signifies that the event represented has *really* taken place.
>
> (Barthes, 1981: 18)

But the problem with the photo as archive is its split from the reality documented, its problematic status as placeholder – it is unable to attest to the liveness of the moment 'before the camera', as Barthes discusses in *Camera Lucida*. When talking about his mother's photo, he as viewer is left outside, apart, 'in it nothing can be refused or transformed' (1982: 91), it keeps the viewer at bay by its 'unendurable plenitude' (1982: 90). As Tagg (1995: 297) writes:

> The presence it discloses is entirely finished – complete and gone – and no displacement to a register of cultural meaning can allay or give voice to the 'suffering' Barthes now experiences 'entirely on the level of the image's finitude'.
>
> (Barthes, 1982: 90)

As we will see in this chapter, the evidentiary character of cinematography can crumble as it refuses to be archived, refuses to be aligned with a 'register of cultural meaning', such as the structure of a linear story-development.

3 For a history of these stereotypical uses of disability as a narrative marker in film, see Norden, 1994, also Note 4 in Introduction

4 Disability as a narrative device in theater is discussed by various critics who have commented on Victorian melodrama's use of visible difference, including disabled people, as 'speaking bodies', able to communicate complex issues without words (Mulvey, 1989; Gledhill, 1987). The theater historical background to these practices is a dearth of words: in the eighteenth and nineteenth centuries, only a limited number of houses in England and France had 'royal patents', allowing them to have spoken dialogue. This injunction, together with a strong tradition of non-verbal performance practices, provided a rich field for the proliferation of disability as metaphor (Gledhill, 1987: 17–19; Stoddard Holmes, 2001). The 'short-hand' of disability could carry large affective weights: for the melodrama scholar Brooks, disability, specifically, 'represent[ed] extreme moral and emotional conditions: as well as mutes, there are blind men, paralytics, invalids of various sorts whose very physical presence evokes the extremism and hyperbole of ethical conflict and manichaeistic struggle' (1976: 57). Disability studies scholars such as Martha Stoddard Holmes draw attention to the value of reading the narrative strategies of Victorian melodrama together with the wider social embedment of disability and its specifics. Stoddard Holmes writes about the 1850 play *The Blind Wife*, attributed to John Wilkins: 'Blind people, the play affirms, are particularly distanced from sexual relationships because they are ontologically poised between body and spirit, heaven and earth, the living and the dead' (2001: 14); and she goes on to show how this liminality, in particular sexual undecidedness, characterizes social discourse surrounding the blind woman.

5 In a more complex twist, trauma can also make a productive intervention into a person's life: the compulsive nature of trauma's retelling can set off stories and creativity, allowing people to position themselves in our culture through the act of telling (Frank, 1995).

6 This use of disability as a *mise-en-labyme* for film as a narrative medium is explored by other encounters of critics and filmmakers, as well: see, for instance, Caroline Molina (1997), reading Jane Campion's *The Piano* (1994).

7 This play between making and marking evokes Walter Benjamin's correlation between storytelling and pottery: a story 'bears the marks of the storyteller much as the earthen vessel bears the marks of the potter's hand' (Benjamin, 1968: 92).

8 As is the making problematic of narrative – see E. Ann Kaplan's (1999) use of different structuring devices (dialogue, parallelism) to represent a temporal experience of telling and analyzing. The making and unmaking of narrative, the refusal to begin and the necessity to plunge are references in her performative analysis of analyzing trauma in therapy.

9 The same moment can also be read within the economy of representing another unrepresentable moment: pain. Elaine Scarry (1994) investigates the hysteria of pain representations, the impossibility of the image referencing its signified, in her analysis of advertising for pain killers. The techniques of cinematic representation and narrativity are brought into play to point to the absent 'body truth'.

10 The instance of the photo again echoes Barthes' too full photo in *Camera Lucida*: a photo that doesn't anchor the subject in certainty, but that marks the passing of time: the photo 'possess an evidentiary force', even if 'its testimony bears not on the object but on time' (Barthes, 1982: 88-89). Behind it all, in Barthes, is his mother. A moment that was, but whose fullness is only perceivable in its absence, chimes through the witnessing photo.

6 New technologies of embodiment: Cyborgs and websurfers

1 For an introduction to disability and its position in Merleau-Ponty's work, see Iwakuma (2002). Iwakuma pays attention to the sensuous nature of addenda:

> When a lover of a person in a wheelchair touches the chair, s/he shivers as if the flesh of the person were caressed. In a sense, the person was touched: the lover touched the wheelchair as an extension of the person. (2002: 78)

2 This story stems from E.T.A. Hoffmann's *The Sandman*, and has been recycled into ballets such as *Coppelia*, and the opera *Hoffmann's Tales*. In critical theory, the story has currency through Freud's interpretation of it in *The Uncanny* – the prosthetic body becomes the original 'unheimliche' body.

3 For a personal discussion of these complex devotee and amputee issues, see for instance the film *My One Legged Dream Lover*, dirs Penny Fowler-Smith and Christine Olsen, Australia 1999.

4 For a description of performance practices at this interface of biology and technology, see Wilson (2002), 157ff.

5 Janet Murray (1997: 97–125) comments in detail on this immersive quality, its attributes and effects on narrative and sensation. In her highly influential book *Hamlet on the Holodeck*, she analyzes the immersive as a participatory form, and participants in it as learners of a theatrical form of embodiment – a real/non-real form of engagement. Other critics such as Sue Ellen Case (1996a) and Stone (1995) question the effects of the move into the electronic on performance, on the 'live', and on the fantasies that sustain this new media encounter. The history of the move towards and away from different screens, and their effects on bodily engagement, is also discussed by Manovich (2001): 103–111.

6 It is important to be aware of the metaphoricity of these 'attributes' of the web: they are not ontological essences of the medium, but fantasies that sustain public imagination around the Internet. Just as freedom is a metaphor for the web, so surveillance and invasion become increasingly significant keywords in relation to discourses that describe corporations tracking our web-communications, planting cookies, monitoring usage and harvesting more and more intrusive demographical data. Critics such as Katherine Hayles (1996) draw attention to the mechanisms and effects of these fantasies: she investigates the disjuncture between information and body, and analyzes texts where this forgotten link resurfaces.

7 One aspect of critiques of phenomenology is also important in this respect: its potential emphasis on a self-knowing, self-reflective intentional subject. The forms of embodiment discussed here allow for the unconscious, and for a layered depth-model of the psyche in its temporary and spatial development. It aligns itself more with Merleau-Ponty's than with Husserl's phenomenology. It is this form of phenomenological inquiry that also fuels contemporary approaches such as Sobchack (1992), Marks (2000) and Moore (2000).

8 For a discussion of these approaches, see for instance Moser, 1996; Smith and Dean, 1997; Birringer, 1998: 124ff., and Wilson, 2002: 729ff. In relation to disability issues, the performance piece 'Virtual Dervish: Virtual Bodies' is particularly interesting, since one of the creators, Diane Gromala, related the VR environment and its 'unfamiliar sensations and cognitive disruptions to [her] strategies of dealing with chronic pain, that is, for a reconfigured and enhanced experience of [her] body, a 're-embodiment' (quote from *Riding the Meridian*, hypertext).

9 For a fascinating example of this kind of performance, see Suzan Kozel's dance installation *Telematic Dreaming* (1994): the 'natural' body is absented for the audience, as the dancer's virtual body (she terms it telepresence) is projected onto a bed and interacts with spectators in a ghostly dance. The interaction happens in real time, but the space created by the projection is wholly technological.

10 While Merleau-Ponty in particular, and phenomenology in general, is again becoming an exciting field for critical theorists, the issue of politics remains a problematic area. Phenomenologists are charged with not paying attention to difference, and being unable to account for structural issues of power-relations (Weiss, 1999, Bourdieu and Wacquant: 1992, Ostrow, 1990). The struggle surrounding these issues has given rise to works such as Young, 1990a; Grosz, 1994; Battersby, 1998, and, in the field of art and performance studies, Jones, 1998. Another area of generative tension are the connections between Foucault and Merleau-Ponty – see Crossley, 1994; Coole, 2001. For an historical overview, see the readings collected in Moran and Mooney (2002).

11 Investigations into creating political work on the new medium are ongoing. For instance, Cameron Bailey discusses the problematics of articulating race issues on the 'disembodied' medium of the web (1996).

12 See for instance the gallery and links section maintained by the National Disability Arts Forum in the UK, www.ndaf.org, or the National Arts and Disability Center in the US, www.nadc.ucla.edu. Beyond its enabling factors, new media communications have also proven problematic in some disability areas – e-communities can again efface differences, fostering the sense of the ideal, disembodied cybersurfer. They can be an excuse for poor environmental access and social integration. Another point of criticism is the emphasis on visual communication on the Internet today, often not accessible to people with visual impairments,

13 James Overboe (1999) addresses some of the writing surrounding disability as metaphor in cyber-writing, in particular Baudrillard's writing on disabled people as 'expert(s) in the motor or sensorial domain. . . . They may precede us on the path towards mutation and dehumanization' (Baudrillard, 1988). Overboe is concerned that disability as an embodied experience will be once again subsumed into metaphor. The work here shows how disabled artists explore the aesthetics of the web for their own purposes, negating the boundaries between image and body. But at the same time, it is important to hold on to the sense of cultural minority, and political oppression, invisibility and negation that makes these tactics of representation necessary.

14 All translations are author's own.

15 The quotes also reference perspectives on the body in culture, with soundbytes that echo Stelarc's concern with the obsolete body, and a phrase from a marriage ceremony that echoes Austin's discussion of speech acts.

16 'Where do you want to go today?' was the advertising slogan of a major computer manufacturer in the late 1990s. Mobility, and physical presence independent from the physical body were presented as part of the tropes that govern the image of the web. The idea of websurfing connotes the same complex of images, and references Gibson's Neuromancer and other cyberwriting: a disembodied, fast body electric that travels along the neural paths of a new cyberworld.

17 The term 'experiencing cerebral palsy' once again points to the problematics of naming – as Overboe explains, 'I realize that the term "cerebral palsy" is a restrictive category itself, but presently I do not have a language that adequately describes my experience' (1999: 27). In the writing on these pages, I need to hold on to the malleable and changing nature of language: new terms will emerge.

Epilog: Toward the unknown body: Stillness, silence, and space in mental health settings

1 The term 'community theater' has a British resonance (other terms, in other cultural contexts, are amateur theater, activist theater, political theater, community based performance, etc.). In this national context, the term is charged with a political project, and a utopian vision. Ann Jellicoe sees its mission as the facilitation of self-discovery and strengthening:

Communities need community events to continually refresh them. Community drama can be a celebration of community; discovering the nature of a community, articulating it *to* that community. (1987)

In the British context, the notion of finding a voice is central, writing or performing one's own story, sometimes with professional artists as translators. For a discussion of the work-practices of this model of work, see Somers, 2001. Theater practitioners in this tradition include the French director Armand Gatti, who writes about the aesthetic challenges of these approaches:

the theater must enable people who have been deprived of a chance to express themselves to do so. We said: we have to get out of the ghetto of the theater world and away from the language of commercial production. We had to try to develop a multiplied language that resembled the language of the street. (1994: 112)

The Olimpias stand in this tradition of recognizing the value of communities as places of political action, of seeing local and owned stories as central, and of developing an aesthetic appropriate to community work.

2 Given the social stigma of mental health problems, the attendant curiosity about symptoms, diagnosis, and effects, and the project's preoccupation with unknowability and ownership, this chapter will not mention any names, mental diagnoses or physical impairments, or relate highly specific, individual instances of the group's work. Terminology is also important to note here: in this chapter, I am using terms such as 'mental health system users', 'mental health settings', and 'mental health differences'. In other projects, The Olimpias have worked within mental health system survivors groups, who clearly embraced the more challenging and confrontational term of 'survivors', with its implications of institutional violence. This term was not used by many of the people working on the *Traces* project, although some of those willing to speak about these issues also saw institutional and social oppression as part of their disability experience. The terms try to convey an awareness of the complex language politics surrounding mental health, of the issues at stake in naming, and in laying claim to a name. For an insight into these problematics, see Church, 1995.

3 This chapter does not chart the challenges associated with working as an artist in medically defined areas. For everything that did work, many things didn't. One group in Swansea eventually folded since it proved impossible to impress upon the daily workers that the sessions needed concentration opportunities; we were very often disrupted by tea wagons and care workers coming in and going out. A mental health nurse forebade one of his clients to attend the sessions because of the dream journeys involved; his argument focused on the client's need to distinguish reality from fantasy. The individual involved wanted to come; once I made clear to the nurse that the content of the journeys were specifically movement-based and that the sessions involved a safe rehearsal space for these borderline experiences and their negotiation, the client eventually rejoined the group. Ultimately, the distinction between therapy and artwork cannot really be maintained (and is only included here in the sense of distinguishing our work from that initiated by the 'medical establishment'). The work remains open for people to take many things away from it – self-esteem, safe places for self-expression, etc. The group members report on many different positive outcomes of our work together. 'We've all been there together in the mental health hospital ward, etc.'; 'We get our frustrations and anger out in some movement, and can be free to relax and listen to other movements'; 'I feel alive when I get home on Tuesdays'; 'When we create something, I am talking to the family about it, and it gets me out of myself'; 'I don't feel so empty now.' (These comments were made in an evaluation session in which I asked members whether there was anything they would like to tell people who read this chapter.)

4 This romantic image of the mad artist is problematic. At the 1977 premiere of David Edgar's play about her experiences, *Mary Barnes*, Barnes told reporters that she still experienced depression and periods of withdrawal (Showalter, 1987: 286). Today, the depiction of the drug Prozac as a lifestyle accessory has initiated new discussions about the relationship between art, consumerism, and health. In the public health service of an economically depressed part of the UK, the main form of treatment available to the people I work with is drugs and a variety of activities offered to them through daycare services (rambling, yoga, writing, card playing, crafts, etc.). Given the differences in medical treatment of mental conditions throughout the last two centuries, the images of 'mad' people in the mainstream remain relatively constant. The hysterical woman and the homicidal man are still with us.

5 For examples of how these historical scenarios can inform queries in performance studies, see the discussion in Chapter 3.

6 This connection between seeing and recognizing madness is also made by Sander Gilman in his highly influential studies (1982, see also 1988), which speak about the ways that madness is represented along a continuum of visual otherness. Michel Foucault analyzes the history of the clinical gaze, a structure of knowledge that allows clinicians to turn their seeing (voir) into knowledge (savoir) (1994). These certainties, anchored in the 'transparency' of seeing, need unanchoring if one wants to challenge mental health representation.

7 My dream-journey calling and the preceding relaxation sequences were informed by my training in autogenic (self-hypnosis) methods and Gerda Alexander's eutony – two techniques that involve biofeedback. Both are healing methods that allow people to live more fully and aware. Here, again, we are on the borderline between therapy and art. These healing *forms* were *used* in our artmaking; they were not specifically aimed at the symptoms of the people with whom I was working. For more information on somatic practices such as eutony, see Johnson, 1995.

8 As time went by, it was possible to offer more and more 'free space' – longer periods where people could explore their physicality in the dream-spaces created. Participants reported that the work in the sessions was able to give them ownership of thoughts as well. Some felt better able to acknowledge the presence of voices in their heads, and thereby to continue with whatever they were doing when the voices started up, without putting all of their energy into either listening to or shutting out the voices. It is important to stress, though, that the work was quite clearly focused on physical experience and sensory perception, and not on feelings or sharing oneself through language. The group respected privacy and the 'unknown' condition of the other.

9 It is this open aspect of Laban's work that drew me to his writings. When I worked in different settings – for instance, when working toward a stage performance as a wheelchair or crutch-using movement artist – I had to search to find a sharable format that allows for precision of spatial orientation and dynamic quality without full physical determination of limb position. Laban's vocabulary of movement analysis can be fully accessible to people with many different impairments.

10 This witnessing of time allows Bergson access to the ground of being. In his work on Bergson, Deleuze writes:

> Bergsonism has often been reduced to the following idea: duration is subjective, and constitutes our internal life. And it is true that Bergson had to express himself in this way, at least at the outset. But, increasingly, he came to say something quite different: the only subjectivity is time, non-chronological time grasped in its foundation, and it is we who are internal to time, not the other way around.
>
> (Deleuze, 1989: 82–83)

It is this locating of the self in an other that isn't undefined, but that provides the ground for narrativity and identity itself, and that is beyond the boundaries of the self that is fascinating to me. Time becomes the ground of intelligibility, but not by referencing lack (as in psychoanalytic traditions) nor by positing the body as a pre-linguistic mass of pre-differentiation. Bodily life becomes part of the machine that produces meaning.

11　In previous publications about *Traces*, I chose not to illustrate the writing with photographs since such photographs would be only remnants, verging too close to images of hysteric women *or* strange men. But a range of visual practices were excited by *Traces*: Photographer/dancer Jenny Cameron work-shadowed my sessions in the community and created enhanced images out of the photos she took at the sessions. Multicolored, hazy, and beautiful, these images captured the dignity of the performers' concentration and spatial presence in their own bodies. When these images were brought back to the performers, many were stunned and moved. They had never seen themselves represented as beautiful and worth looking at. The deep presence evident in the photos is overwhelming. Through the active choice of the participants, these photos have been exhibited and appeared in community magazines. These beautiful photos, though, are different from *Traces*. They are not informed by the tension between stillness and change that drives the installation. The photo I am using in this chapter is a still from the *Traces* videos.

12　Spectators were invited to leave comments in a book provided. Some commented on the challenge that the installation posed to them. If they went with the relaxation sequence (lying down and closing their eyes), they couldn't see the images. They had to make decisions and reflect on them. Others commented on the differences that opened up in their attention to the minute, to the close-up of living. One commentator wrote that her own concentration was interrupted by the twitching eyelid of one performer on screen, and that she found her reaction to this 'irritant' thought-provoking. Some spectators left notes saying that they had witnessed the installation more than once; others commented on the length of time they had spent in it. A worker at one of the arts centers wrote, 'One day, all workplaces will have a room like this.' This comment stands in interesting juxtaposition to society's exclusionary attitude toward mental health problems.

Bibliography

Aalten, Anne (1997) 'Performing the body, creating culture', in Kathy Davis (ed.), *Embodied Practices: Feminist Perspectives on the Body*, London, Thousand Oaks, New Delhi: Sage: 41–58.

Adair, Christy (1992) *Woman and Dance: Sylphs and Sirens*, Houndsmill, Basingstoke: Macmillan.

Albright, Ann Cooper (1997) *Choreographing Difference: The Body and Identity in Contemporary Dance*, Hanover and London: Wesleyan University Press.

Altick, Richard D. (1978) *The Shows of London*, Cambridge, MA: Belknap Press of Harvard University Press.

Apter, Emily (1995) 'Out of the closet. Mary Kelly's corpus (1984–85)', *Art Journal*, Spring, 66–70.

Artaud, Antonin (1993) *The Theater and its Double*, Montreuil, London, New York: Calder.

—— (1988) *To Have Done with the Judgement of God*, a radio play (1947), in Susan Sontag (ed.), *Antonin Artaud: Selected Writings*, Berkeley: University of California Press: 570–571.

Bachelard, Gaston (1994, orig. 1958) *The Poetics of Space*, trans. Maria Jolas, Boston: Beacon Press.

Bailey, Cameron (1996) 'Virtual skin: Articulating race in cyberspace', in Mary Ann Mosel with Douglas MacLeon (eds), *Immersed in Technology. Art and Virtual Environments*, Cambridge, London: MIT Press: 29–49.

Bakhtin, Mikhail (1968) *Rabelais and his World*, trans. H. Iswolsky, Cambridge, MA: MIT Press.

Barnes, Colin (1996) 'Theories of disability, and the origins of the oppression of disabled people in Western society', in Len Barton (ed.), *Disability and Society. Emerging Issues and Insights*, London: Addison Wesley Longman: 43–60.

Barthes, Roland (1982) *Camera Lucida: Reflections on Photography*, trans. Richard Howard, London: Cape.

—— (1981) 'The discourse of history', trans. Stephen Bann, *Comparative Criticism: A Yearbook, No. 3*, E. Shaffer (ed.), Cambridge: Cambridge University Press: 7–20.

—— (1977) *Image, Music, Text*, trans. Stephen Heath, London: Fontana Press.

Battersby, Christine (1998) *The Phenomenal Woman: Feminist Metaphysics and the Patterns of Identity*, London and New York: Routledge.

Baudrillard, Jean (1988) *The Ecstasy of Communication*, trans. Bernard Schultze and Caroline Schultze, New York: Semiotext(e).

Beauvoir, Simone de (1973) *The Second Sex*, trans. H.M. Parshley, New York: Vintage Books.

Beizer, Janet (1994) *Ventriloquized Bodies: Narratives of Hysteria in Nineteenth-Century France*, Ithaca and London: Cornell University Press.

Benjamin, Adam (2001) *Making an Entrance: Theory and Practice for Disabled and Non-Disabled Dancers*, London and New York: Routledge.

—— (1995) 'Unfound movement', *Dance Theater Journal*, 12, 1: 44–47.

Benjamin, Walter (1976) *Charles Baudelaire: A Lyric Poet in the Era of High Capitalism*, London: Verso.

—— (1968) 'The storyteller: Reflections on the works of Nikolai Leskov', *Illuminations*, trans. Harry Zone, New York: Schocken: 83–110.

Bergson, Henri (1988) *Creative Evolution*, trans. Arthur Mitchell, New York: Dover.

Betterton, Rosemary (1996) *An Intimate Distance. Women, Artists and the Body*, New York and London: Routledge.

Birringer, Johannes (1998) *Media and Performance: Along the Border*, Baltimore and London: Johns Hopkins University Press.

Black's Law Dictionary (1990) 6th edn, St Paul: West.

Blin, Roger (1986) *Souvenirs et propos*, Paris: Gallimard.

Boal, Augusto (1985) *Theater of the Oppressed*, trans. Charles A. and Maria-Odilia Leal McBride, New York: Theater Communications Group.

Bogdan, Robert (1988) *Freak Show: Presenting Human Oddities for Amusement and Profit*, Chicago: University of Chicago Press.

Bordo, Susan (1993) *Unbearable Weight: Feminism, Western Culture, and the Body*, Berkeley, Los Angeles, London: University of California Press.

Bourdieu, Pierre (1984) *Distinction: A Social Critique of the Judgement of Taste*, London: Routledge and Kegan Paul.

Bourdieu, Pierre and Wacquant, Loïc (1992) *An Invitation to Reflexive Sociology*, Chicago: University of Chicago Press.

Brecht, Bertolt (1984) *Brecht on Theater: The Development of an Aesthetic*, John Willet (ed.), New York: Hill and Young.

Bronfen, Elisabeth (1998) *The Knotted Subject: Hysteria and its Discontents*, Princeton, NJ: Princeton University Press.

Brooks, M. (1976) *The Melodramatic Imagination*, New Haven: Yale University Press.

Buford, Bill (1991) *Among the Thugs*, London: Secker and Warburg.

Burt, Ramsay (1995) *The Male Dancer: Bodies, Spectacle, Sexualities*, London and New York: Routledge.

Butler, Judith (1993) *Bodies that Matter: On the Discursive Limits of Sex*, New York and London: Routledge.

—— (1991) *Gender Trouble*, New York and London: Routledge.

Campbell, Jane and Oliver, Mike (1996) *Disability Politics: Understanding our Past, Changing our Future*, New York and London: Routledge.

Carlson, Marvin (1996) *Performance: A Critical Introduction*, London and New York: Routledge.

Cartwright, Lisa (2000) 'Community and the public body in breast cancer media activities', in Janine Marchessault and Kim Sawchuk (eds), *Wild Science: Reading Feminism, Medicine and the Media*, London and New York: Routledge: 120–138.

—— (1998) 'A cultural anatomy of the visible human project', in Paula Treichler, Lisa Cartwright and Constance Penley (eds), *The Visible Woman: Imaging Technologies, Gender, and Science*, New York and London: New York University Press.

—— (1995) *Screening the Body: Tracing Medicine's Visual Culture*, Minneapolis, London: University of Minneapolis Press.

Caruth, Cathy (1996) *Unclaimed Experience: Trauma, Narrative, and History*, Baltimore and London: Johns Hopkins University Press.

Case, Gretchen (2001) 'X-rays and Catholic schoolgirls: Performing medical and personal history', *Contemporary Theater Review*, Vol. 11, No. 3+4: 149–158.

Case, Sue-Ellen (1996) *Split Britches: Lesbian Practice/Feminist Performance*, London and New York: Routledge.

—— (1996a) *The Domain-Matrix. Performing Lesbian at the End of Print Culture*, Bloomington and Indianapolis: Indiana University Press.

Certeau, Michel de (1988) *The Practice of Everyday Life*, Berkeley, Los Angeles, London: University of California Press.

Chadwick, Whitney (ed.) (1998) *Mirror Images: Women, Surrealism, and Self-Representation*, Cambridge, MA and London: MIT Press.

Church, Kathryn (1995) *Forbidden Narratives: Critical Autobiography as Social Science*, London and New York: Routledge.

Cixous, Hélène (1984) 'Aller à la mer', trans. Barbara Kerslake, *Modern Drama*, 27: 546–548.

Cohen Bull, Cynthia J. (1997) 'Sense, meaning and perception in three dance cultures', in Desmond, J. (ed.), *Meaning in Motion*, Durham and London: Duke University Press.

Connor, Steven (2001) 'Violence, ventriloquism and the vocalic body', in *Psychoanalysis and Performance*, Patrick Campbell and Adrian Kear (eds), London and New York: Routledge: 75–93.

Conquergood, Dwight (1985) 'Performing as a moral act: Ethical dimensions of the ethnography of performance', *Literature in Performance*, Vol. 5, 1–13.

Coole, Diana (2001) 'Thinking politically with Merleau-Ponty', *Radical Philosophy*, 108, 17–28.

Corker, Mairian and Shakespeare, Tom (eds) (2002) *Disability/Postmodernity. Embodying Disability Theory*, London and New York: Continuum.

Cowl, C. (1997) 'Small fish', *Animated*, Autumn, 16–17.

Creed, Barbara (1993) *The Monstrous-Feminine. Film, Feminism, Psychoanalysis*, London, New York: Routledge.

Croce, Arlene (1994/5) 'Discussing the undiscussable', *The New Yorker*, 26 Dec.– 2 Jan: 54–60.

Crossley, Nick (1994) *The Politics of Subjectivity: Between Foucault and Merleau-Ponty*, Aldershot: Avebury.

Csordas, T.J. (1994) 'Introduction: The body as representation and being-in-the-world', in T.J. Csordas (ed.), *Embodiment and Experience: The Existential Ground of Culture and Self*, Cambridge: Cambridge University Press: 1–27.

Curtis, Bruce and Ptashek, Alan (1988) 'Exposed to gravity', *Contact Quarterly*, 13, 3: 18–24.

Darke, Paul (ed.) (2003) *White Sticks, Wheels and Crutches: Disability in the Moving Image Catalogue*, London: British Film Institute.

Davis, Lennard J. (1999) 'Nation, class, and physical minorities', in Timothy B. Powell (ed.), *Beyond the Binary: Reconstructing Cultural Identity in a Multicultural Context*, New Brunswick, NJ, and London: Rutgers University Press: 17–38.

—— (1997) 'Nude Venuses, Medusa's body and phantom limbs: Visuality and disability', in David T. Mitchell and Sharon L. Snyder (eds), *The Body and Physical Difference: Discourses of Disability*, Ann Arbor: University of Michigan Press: 51–70.

—— (1995) *Enforcing Normalcy: Disability, Deafness, and the Body*, London: Verso.

Davis, Lucy (2000) 'Natural born vandals (or the desire for real interactions with real people)', *Focas. Forum on Contemporary Art and Society*, No. 1: 123–134.

Deleuze, Gilles (1992) *Cinema 1: The Movement Image*, trans. Hugh Tomlinson and Barbara Habberjam, London: Athlone Press.

—— (1989) *Cinema 2: The Time Image*, tran. Hugh Tomlinson and Robert Galeta, London: Athlone Press.

Deleuze, Gilles and Guattari, Felix (1988) *A Thousand Plateaus*, trans. Brian Massumi, Minneapolis: University of Minnesota Press.

—— (1977) *Anti-Oedipus*, trans. Robert Hurley, Mark Seem and Helen R. Lane, New York: Viking Press.

Dempster, E. (1988) 'Women writing the body: Let's watch a little how she dances', in Susan Sheridan (ed.), *Grafts: Feminist Cultural Criticism*, London: Verso, republished (1999) in Angela Carter (ed.), *The Routledge Dance Studies Reader*, London, New York: Routledge.

Dennett, Andrea Stulman (1997) *Weird and Wonderful: The Dime Museum in America*, New York: New York University Press.

Derrida, Jacques (1992) *Acts of Literature*, Derek Attridge (ed.), New York and London: Routledge.

—— (1978) *Writing and Difference*, London: Routledge and Kegan Paul.

Derrida, Jacques and McDonald, Christie V. (1995) 'Choreographies', in Ellen W. Goellner and Jacqueline Shea Murphey (eds), *Bodies of the Text: Dance as Theory, Literature as Dance*, New Brunswick, NJ: Rutgers University Press: 141–156.

Diamond, Elin (1997) *Unmaking Mimesis*, New York and London: Routledge.

—— (1996) 'Brechtian theory/feminist theory: Toward a gestic feminist criticism', in Carol Martin (ed.), *A Sourcebook for Feminist Theater and Performance: On and Beyond the Stage*, New York and London: Routledge: 120–135.

Dijkstra, Bram (1986) *Idols of Perversity: Fantasies of Feminine Evil in Fin-de-Siècle Culture*, New York, Oxford: Oxford University Press.

Dolan, Jill (1993) *Presence and Desire: Essays on Gender, Sexuality, Performance*, Ann Arbor: Michigan University Press.

Douglas, Ruth (1995) 'An exploration of relationships of the visual and kinetic experience of dance as a performing art', *Dance 95. Move into the Future: Proceedings*, Bretton Hall, Leeds: 27–30.

Duffy, Mary (1989) 'Cutting the ties that bind', *Feminist Art News*, 2, 10, 6–7.

Dyer, Richard (1993) 'The anatomy of utterance. The poetry and performance of Aaron Williamson', Simon Dwyer (ed.), *Rapid Eye*, London: Annihilation Press: 112–116.

—— (1986) *Heavenly Bodies: Film Stars and Society*, New York: St Martin's Press.

Eco, Umberto (1977) 'Semiotics of theatrical performance', *The Drama Review*, 21, 107–117.

Edwards, Martha (1997) 'Constructions of physical disability in the ancient Greek world: The community concept', in David T. Mitchell and Sharon L. Snyder, *The Body and Physical Difference*, Ann Arbor: Michigan University Press: 35–50.

Ellsworth, Angela (2001) 'Performing illness: Crisis, collaboration and resistance', *Contemporary Theater Review*, Vol. 11, No. 3+4: 137–148.

Epstein, Marcy and Crutchfield, Susan (1998) Introduction, *Michigan Quarterly Review*, 36: 185–195.

Evans, Jessica (1988) 'The iron cage of visibility', *Ten.8*, 29: 48–51.

Fahy, Thomas (2002) '"Some unheard-of thing": Freaks, families, and coming of age in the member of the wedding', in Thomas Fahy and Kimball King (eds), *Peering Behind the Curtain. Disability, Illness, and the Extraordinary Body in Contemporary Theater*, New York and London: Routledge: 68–83.

Fahy, Thomas and King, Kimball (eds) (2002) *Peering Behind the Curtain. Disability, Illness, and the Extraordinary Body in Contemporary Theater*, New York and London: Routledge.

Fausto-Sterling, Anne (2000) *Sexing the Body. Gender Politics and the Construction of Sexuality*, New York: Basic Books.

Featherstone, Mike (1995) 'Post-bodies, aging and virtual reality', in Mike Featherstone and Andrew Warnick (eds), *Images of Aging: Cultural Representations of Later Life*, London and New York: Routledge: 227–244.

Fenemore, Anna (2001) 'The Pigeon Project: a study of the potential for embodied praxis in performance spectating', unpublished PhD thesis.

Ferrari, Giovanna (1987) 'Public anatomy lessons and the carnival: The anatomy theater of Bologna', *Past and Present*, 117: 50–106.

Fiedler, Leslie (1978) *Freaks: Myths and Images of the Secret Self*, New York: Simon and Schuster.

Fine, Michelle and Asch, Adrienne (eds) (1988) *Women with Disabilities: Essays in Psychology, Culture, and Politics*, Philadelphia: Temple University Press.

Finkelstein, Vic (1980) *Attitudes and Disabled People: Issues for Discussion*, New York: World Rehabilitation Fund.

Fiske, John (1987) *Television Culture*, London, New York: Routledge.

Flanagan, Bob (2000) *The Pain Journal*, Los Angeles: Semiotext(e).

Foster, Susan L. (1995) 'Harder, faster, longer, higher – a post-modern inquiry into the ballerina's making', in *Bordertensions: Dance and Discourse*, Proceedings of the Fifth Study of Dance Conference, University of Surrey, UK: Department of Dance Studies: 109–114.

—— (1986) *Reading Dancing: Bodies and Subjects in Contemporary American Dance*, Berkeley, Los Angeles, London: University of California Press.

Foucault, Michel (1994) *The Birth of the Clinic. An Archeology of Medical Perception*, New York: Vintage Books.

—— (1980) 'Two lectures', in C. Gordon (ed.), *Power/Knowledge: Selected Interviews and other Writings 1972–1977 by Michel Foucault*, New York: Pantheon: 78–108.

—— (1979) *Discipline and Punish: The Birth of the Prison*, trans. Alan Sheridan, New York: Vintage.

—— (1978) *The History of Sexuality*, New York: Pantheon.

—— (1973) *Madness and Civilisation. A History of Insanity in the Age of Reason*, New York: Vintage Books.

Frank, Arthur (1995) *The Wounded Storyteller*, Chicago: University of Chicago Press.

Franko, Mark (1993) *Dance as Text: Ideologies of the Baroque Body*, Cambridge: Cambridge University Press.

Fraser, Mat (2001) 'Sealboy: Freak', unpublished manuscript, quoted with permission of author.

Freud, Sigmund (1953) 'The Uncanny', in *The Standard Edition of the Complete Psychological Works of Sigmund Freud*, trans. J. Strachey, Vol. XVII, London: Hogarth: 219–252.

—— (1948) *Collected Papers*, London: Hogarth.

Fries, Kenny ((ed.) (1997) *Staring Back: The Disability Experience in America*, New York: Penguin, 1997.

Fulcher, G. (1996) 'Beyond normalisation but not utopia', in Len Barton (ed.), *Disability and Society: Emerging Issues and Insights*, London and New York: Longman: 167–190.

Gablik, Suzi (1992) *The Re-Enchantment of Art*, London, New York: Thames and Hudson.

Garland Thomson, Rosemarie (ed.) (2001) 'Seeing the disabled: Visual rhetorics of disability in popular photography', in Paul Longmore and Lauri Umansky (ed.), *The New Disability History. American Perspectives*, New York and London: New York University Press: 335–374.

—— (1999) 'Narratives of deviance and delight: Staring at Julia Pastrana, the "Extraordinary Lady"', in *Beyond the Binary. Reconstructing Cultural Identity in a Multicultural Context* (ed. Timothy B. Powell), New Brunswick, NJ, and London: Rutgers University Press: 81–104.

—— (1997) *Extraordinary Bodies: Figuring Physical Disability in American Culture and Literature*, New York: Columbia University Press.

—— (1996) *Freakery: Cultural Spectacles of the Extraordinary Body*, New York and London: New York University Press.

Gates, H.L. (1988) *The Signifying Monkey*, Oxford: Oxford University Press.

Gatti, Armand, interviewed by Helene Chatelain (1994) 'Seventeen ideograms and the search for the wandering world', *New Theater Quarterly*, 38 (10), 107–121.

Gilchrist, Roberta (1994) 'Medieval bodies in the material world: Gender, stigmata and the body', in Sarah Kay and Miri Rubin (eds), *Framing Medieval Bodies*, Manchester: University of Manchester Press: 43–61.

Gilman, Sander (1988) *Disease and Representation: Images of Illness from Madness to AIDS*, Ithaca and London: Cornell University Press.

—— (1985) *Difference and Pathology: Stereotypes of Sexuality*, New York: Cornell University Press.

—— (1982) *Seeing the Insane*, Lincoln and London: University of Nebraska Press.

Gilman, Sander, King, Helen, Porter, Roy, Roussbow, G.S. and Showatter, Elaine (1993) *Hysteria Beyond Freud*, Berkeley: University of California Press.

Gledhill, Christine (1987) 'The melodramatic field: An investigation', in Christine Gledhill (ed.), *Home is where the Heart is: Studies in Melodrama and the Woman's Film*, London: British Film Institute: 5–39.

Goffman, Erving (1963) *Stigma. Notes on the Management of Spoiled Identity*, New York: Simon and Schuster.

—— (1959) *The Presentation of Self in Everyday Life*, Garden City: Doubleday.

Gonzalez-Crussi, F. (1995) *Suspended Animation: Six Essays on the Preservation of Bodily Parts*, San Diego, New York, London: Harvest Original.

Goodall, Jane (1996) 'Cosmological mischief: Artaud and the play of power', *Electronic Document, Proceedings, PastMasters: Antonin Artaud*, Center for Performance Research, Aberwystwyth, Wales.

Gromala, Diane (1999) 'Re-embodiment. Dancing with the virtual derwish: Virtual bodies', *Riding the Meridian*, 1:2 (webjournal: http://www.heelstone.com/meridian).

Grosz, Elizabeth (1994) *Volatile Bodies. Toward a Corporeal Feminism*, Bloomington and Indianapolis: Indiana University Press.

Grotowski, Jerzy (1969) *Towards a Poor Theater*, London: Methuen.

Gunning, Tom (1990) 'The cinema of attractions: Early film, its spectators and the avant-garde', in Thomas Elsaesser (ed.), *Early Cinema: Space, Frame, Narrative*, London: British Film Institute: 56–62.

Haedicke, Susan and Nellhans, Tobin (2001) *Performing Democracy: International Perspectives on Urban Community-Based Performance*, Ann Arbor: University of Michigan Press.

Hahn, Harlan (1987) 'Civil rights for disabled Americans: The foundation of a political agenda', in Alan Gartner and Tom Joe (eds), *Images of the Disabled, Disabling Images*, New York, Westport, London: Praeger: 181–203.

—— (1988) 'Can disability be beautiful?' *Social Policy*, 18: 26–32.

Halford, Victoria and Beard, Steve (2001) '"To die for": Ritual clowning, disability and monstrosity in 90s performance art', *Contemporary Theater Review*, Vol. 11, No. 3+4: 163–170.

Hamilton, Elizabeth (1997) 'From social welfare to civil rights: The representation of disability in twentieth-century German literature', in David T. Mitchell and Sharon L. Snyder (eds), *The Body and Physical Difference: Discourses of Disability*, Ann Arbor: University of Michigan Press: 223–239.

Hammer, Kate (2001) '"Doing Disability": Remembering a forum theater-in-education case study', *Contemporary Theater Review*, Vol. 11, No. 3+4, 61–79.

Harpham, Geoffrey Galt (1982) *On the Grotesque: Strategies of Contradiction in Art and Literature*, Princeton: Princeton University Press.

Hart, Lynda (1998) *Between the Body and the Flesh: Performing Sadomasochism*, New York: Columbia University Press.

Hart, Lynda and Phelan, Peggy (eds) (1993) *Acting Out: Feminist Performances*, Ann Arbour: Michigan University Press.

Hay, Deborah (1988) 'Remaining Positionless', *Contact Quarterly*, 13, 2: 22–23.

Hayles, Katherine (1996) 'Embodied virtuality: Or how to put bodies back into the picture', in Mary Ann Mosel, with Douglas MacLeon (eds), *Immersed in Technology. Art and Virtual Environments*, Cambridge, London: MIT Press: 1–28.

Heath, Stephen (1982) *The Sexual Fix*, London and Basingstoke: Macmillan.

Heidegger, Martin (1996) *Being and Time*, trans. J. Stambaugh. Albany, NY: State University of New York Press.

Henderson, B. (1983) 'Tense, mood and voice in film', *Film Quarterly*, Fall: 4–17.

Hevey, David (1993) 'The tragedy principle: Strategies for change in the representation of disabled people,' in John Swain, Vic Finkelstein, Sally French and Mike Oliver (eds), *Disabling Barriers – Enabling Environments*, London, Thousand Oaks, New Delhi: Sage: 116–121.

—— (1992) *The Creatures that Time Forgot: Photography and Disability Imagery*, London and New York: Routledge.

Hickel, K. Walter (2001) 'Medicine, bureaucracy, and social welfare', in Paul K. Longmore and Lauri Umanksy (eds), *The New Disability History. American Perspective*, New York and London: New York University Press.

Hunt, Paul (1966) 'A critical condition', in *Stigma: The Experience of Disability*, London: Geoffrey Chapman.

Husserl, Edmund (1991) *Ideas Pertaining to a Pure Phenomenology and a Phenomenological Philosophy*, Second Book, trans. R. Rojcewicz and A. Schuwer, Dordrecht and Boston: Kluwer Academic.

—— (1982) *Ideas Pertaining to a Pure Phenomenology and a Phenomenological Philosophy*. First book, trans. F. Kersten, Dordrecht and Boston: Kluwer Academic.

—— (1970) *The Crisis of European Sciences and Transcendental Phenomenology*, trans. D. Carr, Evanston: Northwestern University Press.

Ingarden, Roman (1973) *Cognition of the Literary Work of Art*, Evanston: Northwestern University Press.

Innes, Christopher (1981) *Holy Theater. Ritual and the Avant Garde*, Cambridge, London, New York: Cambridge University Press.

Iwakuma, Miho (2002) 'The body as embodiment: An investigation of the body by Merleau-Ponty', in Mairian Corker and Tom Shakespeare (eds), *Disability/Postmodernity. Embodying Disability Theory*, London and New York: Continuum: 76–87.

Jameson, Frederic (1988) 'Postmodernism and consumer society', in *Postmodernism and its Discontents*, E.A. Kaplan (ed.), London: Verso: 13–29.

Jellicoe, Ann (1987) *Community Plays and How to Make Them*, London: Methuen.

Johnson, Don Hanlon (1995) *Bone, Breath and Gesture. Practices of Embodiment*, Berkeley, San Fransciso: North Atlantic Books.

Jones, Amelia (1998) *Body Art. Performing the Subject*, Minneapolis and London: University of Minnesota Press.

Juno, Andrea and Vale, V. (2000) *Bob Flanagan: Supermasochist*, New York: RE/Search Publications.

Kaplan, E.A. (1999) 'Performing traumatic dialogue: On the border of fiction and autobiography', *Women and Performance*, 10 (1–2), 33–58.

Kauffman, Linda (1998) *Bad Girls and Sick Boys: Fantasies in Contemporary Art and Culture*, Berkeley, Los Angeles, London: University of California Press.

Kennedy, Dennis (2001) 'Sports and shows: Spectators in contemporary culture', *Theater Research International*, Vol. 26, No. 3: 277–284.

Kirby, Kathleen M. (1996) *Indifferent Boundaries: Spatial Concepts of Human Subjectivity*, New York, London: The Guilford Press.

Kirby, Vicki (1997) *Telling Flesh: The Substance of the Corporeal*, London and New York: Routledge.

Kirkland, G. (1986) *Dancing on my Grave*, Harmondsworth, Middlesex: Penguin.

Klobas, Laurie E. (1988) *Disability Drama in Television and Film*, Jefferson, North Carolina: MacFarland.

Kochhar-Lindgren, Kanta (2002) 'Between two worlds: The emerging aesthetic of the National Theater of the Deaf', in Thomas Fahy and Kimball King (eds), *Peering Behind the Curtain. Disability, Illness, and the Extraordinary Body in Contemporary Theater*, New York and London: Routledge: 3–15.

Kuppers, Petra (2004) 'Bodies, hysteria, pain: Staging the invisible', in Carrie Sandahl and Phil Auslander (eds), *Bodies in Commotion*, Ann Arbor: University of Michigan Press.

—— (2002) 'Image politics without the real: Simulacra, dandyism and disability fashion', in Mairian Corker and Tom Shakespeare (eds), *Disability/Postmodernity. Embodying Disability Theory*, London and New York: Continuum: 184–197.

—— (1998) 'Vanishing in your face: Embodiment and representation in lesbian dance performance', *Journal of Lesbian Studies*, 2/3: 47–63.

Kuryluk, Ewa (1987) *Salome and Judas in the Cave of Sex: The Grotesque: Origins, Iconography, Techniques*, Evanston, Illinois: Northwestern University Press.

Kwon, Miwon (2000) 'One place after another: Notes on site specificity', in Erika Suderburg (ed.), *Space, Site, Intervention: Situating Installation Art*, Minneapolis: University of Minnesota Press: 38–63.

Laban, Rudolf (1966) *Choreutics*, Lisa Ullmann (ed.), London: Macdonald and Evans.

Lacy, Suzanne (ed.) (1995) *Mapping the Terrain*, New Genre Public Art, Seattle: Bay Press.

Leder, Drew (1990) *The Absent Body*, Chicago: University of Chicago Press.

Lehmann, Haus-Thics (1999) *Posdramatisches Theater*, Frankfurt a. Main: Verlag der Autoren.

Lingis, Alphonso (1983) *Excesses: Eros and Culture*, Albany: State University of New York Press.

Linton, Simi (1998) *Claiming Disability. Knowledge and Identity*, New York and London: New York University Press.

Lipkin, Joan and Fox, Ann (2002) 'Res(Crip)ting feminist theater through disability theater: Selections from the disability project', *NWSA Journal*, Vol. 14, No. 3: 77–98.

—— (2001) 'The dis-ability project: Towards an aesthetic of access', *Contemporary Theater Review*, Vol. 11, No. 3+4: 119–136.

Levy, Pierre (1997) Cyberculture: Rapport au Conseil de l'Europe dans le cadre du projet 'Nouvelles technologies: cooperation culturelle et communication', Paris: Editions Odile Jacob.

Lomas, Christine (1998) 'Art and the community: Breaking the aesthetic of disempowerment', in J. Shapiro, *Dance, Power, and Difference: Critical and Feminist Perspectives on Dance Education*, Champaign, IL: Human Kinetics: 148–169.

Longmore, Paul K. (1997) 'Conspicuous contribution and American cultural dilemmas: Telethon rituals of cleansing and renewal', in David T. Mitchell and Sharon L. Snyder (eds), *The Body and Physical Difference: Discourses of Disability*, Ann Arbor: University of Michigan Press: 134–158.

—— (1987) 'Screening stereotypes: Images of disabled people in television and motion pictures', in *Images of the Disabled, Disabling Images*, Alan Gartner and Tom Joe (eds), New York: Praeger: 65–78.

Longmore, Paul K. and Umansky, Lauri (2001) *The New Disability History: American Perspectives*, New York: New York University Press.

Mairs, Nancy (1996) *Waist-High in the World: A Life Among the Nondisabled*, Boston: Beacon Press.

Manovich, Lev (2001) *The Language of New Media*, Cambridge: MIT Press.

Marks, Deborah (1999) *Disability: Controversial Debates and Psychosocial Perspectives*, London and New York: Routledge.

Marks, Laura (2000) *The Skin of the Film: Intercultural Cinema, Embodiment and the Senses*, Durham: Duke University Press.

Martin, Carol (1996) 'High critics/low art', in Gay Morris (ed.), *Moving Worlds. Re-Writing Dance*, London, New York: Routledge: 320–333.

Massumi, Brian (2002) *Parables for the Virtual. Movement, Affect, Sensation*, Durham and London: Duke University Press.

Mayne, Judith (1990) *The Woman at the Keyhole. Feminism and Women's Cinema*, Bloomington and Indianapolis: University of Indiana Press.

Mazer, Sharon (1998) *Professional Wrestling: Sport and Spectacle*, Jackson: University of Mississippi Press.

McCarren, Felicia (1998) *Dance Pathologies: Performance, Poetics, Medicine*, Stanford, California: Stanford University Press.

McKenzie, Jon (1993) 'Tabloid theory and the remains of science', *Lusitania*, 1 (4): 101–112.

Merleau-Ponty, Maurice (1968) *The Visible and the Invisible*, trans. A. Lingis, Evanston: Northwestern University Press.

—— (1964) *The Primacy of Perception*, trans. James Edie, Evanston: Northwestern University Press.

—— (1964b) *Signs*, trans. R. McCleary, Evanston: Northwestern University Press.

—— (1962) *Phenomenology of Perception*, trans. C. Smith. London: Routledge.

Meskimmon, Marsha (1996) 'The Monstrous and the Grotesque, *Make* 72: 6–11.

Metzler, Jan Christian (2000) 'Model(l) – Körper – Karneval. Zur Inszenierung behinderter Models als diskursives Ereignis', *KuluRRevolution*, No. 40: 67–79.

Meyerhold, Wsewolod E. (1969) *Meyerhold on Theater*, trans. and ed. Edward Braun, New York: Hill and Wang.

Mirzoeff, Nicholas (1995) *BodyScape: Art, Modernity and the Ideal Figure*, London and New York: Routledge.

Mitchell, David T. and Snyder, Sharon L. (2000) *Narrative Prosthesis. Disability and the Dependencies of Discourse*, Ann Arbor: University of Michigan Press.

—— (1997) 'Introduction: Disability studies and the double bind of representation', in David T. Mitchell and Sharon L. Snyder (eds), *The Body and Physical Difference: Discourses of Disability*, Ann Arbor: University of Michigan Press: 1–31.

—— (eds) (1997) *The Body and Physical Difference: Discourses of Disability*, Ann Arbor: University of Michigan Press.

Mitchell, Richard W. (2001) 'Creating theater on society's margin', *Contemporary Theater Review*, Vol. 11, No. 3+4: 93–104.

Molina, Caroline (1997) 'Muteness and mutilation: The aesthetics of disability in Jane Campion's *The Piano*', in David T. Mitchell and Sharon L. Snyder (eds), *The Body and Physical Difference: Discourses of Disability*, Ann Arbor: University of Michigan Press: 267–282.

Moore, Rachel (2000) *Savage Theory: Cinema as Modern Magic*, Durham: Duke University Press.

Moran, Dermot and Mooney, Timothy (2002) *The Phenomenology Reader*, London and New York: Routledge.

Moser, Mary Ann, with MacLeon, Douglas (eds) (1996) *Immersed in Technology. Art and Virtual Environments*, Cambridge, London: MIT Press.

Mulvey, Laura (1989) *Visual and Other Pleasures*, Bloomington: Indiana University Press.

Murray, Janet H. (1997) *Hamlet on the Holodeck: The Future of Narrative in Cyberspace*, Cambridge: MIT Press.

Nead, Lynda (1992) *The Female Nude: Art, Obscenity and Sexuality*, London and New York: Routledge.

Norden, Martin (1994) *The Cinema of Isolation: A History of Physical Disability in the Movies*, New Brunswick, NJ: Rutgers University Press.

O'Dell, Kathy (1998) *Contract with the Skin. Masochism, Performance Art and the 1970s*, Minneapolis, London: University of Minnesota Press.

Olalquiaga, Celeste (1999) 'Pain practices and the reconfiguration of physical experience', in Bill Burns, Cathy Busby and Kim Sawchuk, *When Pain Strikes*, Minneapolis, London: University of Minnesota Press: 255–266.

Oliver, Michael (1990) *The Politics of Disablement: A Sociological Approach*, New York: St Martin's Press.

O'Reilly, Kate (2001) 'What words look like in the air: The multivocal performance of common ground dance theater', in *Contemporary Theater Review*, Vol. 11, No. 3+4, 41–47.

Ostrow, James (1990) *Social Sensibility: A Study of Habit and Experience*, Albany: State University of New York.

Overboe, James (1999) 'Difference in itself: Validating disabled people's lived experience', *Body and Society*, 5 (4): 17–29.

Paxton, Steve (1992) 'Three days', *Contact Quarterly*, 17, Winter: 14.

Pearson, Mike (1998) 'My balls/Your chin', *Performance Research*, 3, 2: 35–41.

Pearson, Mike and Levett, Lyn (2001) 'Devices and desires', *Contemporary Theater Review*, 11, 3+4: 81–92.

Pernick, Martin S. (1997) 'Defining the defective: Eugenics, aesthetics, and mass culture in early-twentieth-century America', in David T. Mitchell and Sharon L. Snyder (eds), *The Body and Physical Difference: Discourses of Disability*, Ann Arbor: University of Michigan Press: 89–110.

Phelan, Peggy (1997) *Mourning Sex: Performing Public Memories*, London and New York: Routledge.

—— (1996) 'Dance and the history of hysteria', in *Corporealities: Dance, Knowledge, Culture and Power*, Susan Leigh Foster (ed.), London, New York: Routledge: 90–105.

—— (1993) *Unmarked: The Politics of Performance*, New York and London: Routledge.

Pointon, Ann with Davies, Chris (eds) (1997) *Framed: Interrogating Disability in the Media*, London: British Film Institute.

Pomerance, Bernard (1979) *The Elephant Man*, New York: Grove Press.

Powell, Timothy B. (ed.) (1999) *Beyond the Binary: Reconstructing Cultural Identity in a Multicultural Context*, New Brunswick, NJ: Rutgers University Press.

Read, Alan (2001) 'The placebo of performance: Psychoanalysis in its place, in *Psychoanalysis and Performance*, Patrick Campbell and Adrian Kear (eds), London and New York: Routledge: 147–165.

—— (1993) *Theater in Everyday Life: An Ethics of Performance*, London and New York: Routledge.

Russo, Mary (1994) *The Female Grotesque: Risk, Excess and Modernity*, New York and London: Routledge.

Sanchez-Colberg, Ana (1996) 'Altered states and subliminal spaces: Charting the road towards a physical theater', *Performance Research*, 1, 2: 40–56.

Sandahl, Carrie (2003) 'Queering the crip or cripping the queer?: Intersections of queer and crip identities in solo autobiographical performance', *GLQ*, 9, 1–2: 25–56.

—— (2001) 'Performing metaphors: Aids, disability, and technology', *Contemporary Theater Review*, 11, 3+4: 49–60.

—— (2000) 'Bob Flanagan: Taking it Like a Man', *Journal of Dramatic Theory and Criticism*, 15: 1.

—— (1999) 'Ahhh freak out! Metaphors of disability and femaleness in performance', *Theater Topics*, 9, 1: 11–30.

Sartre, Jean Paul (1992) *Being and Nothingness: A Phenomenological Essay on Ontology*, trans. H. Barnes. New York: Washington Square.

Scarry, Elaine (1994) *Resisting Representation*, New York, Oxford: Oxford University Press.

—— (1985) *The Body in Pain. The Making and Unmaking of the World*, Oxford: Oxford University Press.

Schechner, Richard (2002) *Performance Studies: An Introduction*, New York, London: Routledge.

—— (1985) *Between Theater and Anthropology*, Philadelphia: University of Pennsylvania Press.

—— (1977) *Essays on Performance Theory 1970–1976*, New York: Drama Book Specialists.

Schilder, Paul (1950, orig. 1935) *The Image and Appearance of the Human Body: Studies in the Constructive Energies of the Psyche*, New York: International University Press.

Schneider, Rebecca (1997) *The Explicit Body in Performance*, London and New York: Routledge.

Schutzman, Mady (1999) *The Real Thing: Performance, Hysteria and Advertising*, Hanover and London: Wesleyan University Press.

Sedgwick, Eve Kosofsky (1994) *Tendencies*, London, New York: Routledge.

Sember, Robert (1998) 'Seeing death: The photography of David Wojnarowicz', in Peggy Phelan and Jill Lane (eds), *The Ends of Performance*, New York: New York University Press: 31–51.

Serlin, David (2003) 'Crippling masculinities: Queerness and disability in military culture, 1800–1945', *GLQ*, 9 1–2: 149–179.

Shannon, Bill (2000) 'Interview/Video Section', Juliet Robson and Kate Stoddart (eds), *Vital. Exposing New Views*, CD-ROM, Nottingham: Intermedia Film and Video.

Shapiro, Johanna (2002) 'Young doctors come to see the Elephant Man', Thomas Fahy and Kimball King (eds), *Disability, Illness, and the Extraordinary Body in Contemporary Theater*, London, New York: Routledge: 84–91.

Shapiro, Joseph (1993) *No Pity: People with Disabilities Forging a New Civil Rights Movement*, New York: Random House.

Shildrick, Margrit and Price, Janet (eds) (1998) *Vital Signs. Feminist Reconfigurations of the Bio/logical Body*, Edinburgh: Edinburgh University Press.

—— (1996) 'Breaking the boundaries of the broken body', *Body and Society*, 2, 4: 93–113.

Showalter, Elaine (1987) *The Female Malady: Women, Madness and English Culture 1830–1980*, London: Virago.

Siegel, Marcia (1981) *The Shapes of Change*, New York: Avon Books.

Silverman, K. (1988) *The Acoustic Mirror: The Female Voice in Psychoanalysis and Cinema*, Bloomington and Indianapolis: Indiana University Press.

Smith, Hazel and Dean, Roger (1997) *Improvisation, Hypermedia and the Arts since 1945*, Amsterdam: Harwood.

Smith, Robin M. (2001) 'View from the ivory tower: Academics constructing disability', in Linda Rogers and Beth Blue Swadener (eds), *Semiotics and Dis/Ability: Interrogating Categories of Difference*, Albany: State University of New York Press: 55–74.

Smyth, Ailbhe (1998) 'Loving the bones: Medi(t)ating my bodies', in Margit Shildrick and Janet Price (eds), *Vital Signs. Feminist Reconfigurations of the Bio/logical Body*, Edinburgh: Edinburgh University Press: 18–29.

Sobchack, Vivan C. (1992) *The Address of the Eye: A Phenomenology of Film Experience*, Princeton: Princeton University Press.

Solomon, Alisa (1992) 'The politics of breast cancer', *Camera Obscura*, 28: 157–177.

Somers, John (2001) 'Discovering seminal stories: Community theater as cultural memory', in Susan Headicke and Tobin Nellhaus (eds), *Performing Democracy: International Perspectives on Urban Community-Based Performance*, Ann Arbor: University of Michigan Press: 166–180.

Sontag, Susan (1976) *Selected Writings of Antonin Artaud*. Introduction. New York: Farrar, Straus and Giroux.

Spence, Jo and Solomon, Joan (1995) 'What can a woman do with a camera'? *Photography for Women*, London: Scarlet Press.

Spence, Jo (1995) *Cultural Sniping: The Art of Transgression*, London and New York: Routledge.

—— (1986) *Putting Myself in the Picture: A Political, Personal and Photographic Autobiography*, London: Camden Press.

Stacey, Jackie (1997) *Teratologies: A Cultural Study of Cancer*, London and New York: Routledge.

Stam, R., Burgoyne, R. and Flitterman-Lewis, S. (1992) *New Vocabularies in Film Semiotics: Structuralism, Post-Structuralism and Beyond*, London, New York: Routledge.

Stoddard Holmes, Martha (2001) 'Performing affliction: Physical disabilities in Victorian melodrama', *Contemporary Theater Review*, Vol. 11, No. 3+4: 5–24.

Stone, Allucquere Rosanne (1995) *The War of Desire and Technology at the Close of the Mechanical Age*, Cambridge: MIT Press.

Strickling, Chris Anne (2002) 'Actual lifes: Cripples in the house', *Theater Topics*, 12 (2): 143–162.

Studlar, Gaynor (1996) *This Mad Masquerade: Masculinity and Stardom in the Jazz Age*, New York: Columbia University Press.

Swain, J., Finkelstein, V., French, S. and Oliver, M. (1993) *Disabling Barriers – Enabling Environments*, London, Thousand Oaks, New Delhi: Sage.

Tagg, John (1995) 'The pencil of history', in Patrice Petro (ed.), *Fugitive Images: From Photography to Video*, Bloomington: Indiana University Press: 285–303.

Thomas, Helen (1993) 'An-other voice: Young women dancing and talking', in H. Thomas (ed.), *Dance, Gender and Culture*, Houndsmill, Basingstoke: Macmillan.

Todorov, T. (1977) *The Poetics of Prose*, Ithaca, New York: Cornell University Press.

Tomlinson, Richard (1982) *Disability, Theater and Education*, London: Souvenir Press.

Turner, Victor (1982) *From Ritual to Theater*, New York: Performing Arts Journal Publications.

—— (1969) *The Ritual Process: Structure and Anti-Structure*, Chicago: Aldine Publishing Company.

Van Erven, Eugene (2001) *Community Theater. Global Perspectives*, London and New York: Routledge.

—— (1988) *Radical People's Theater*, Bloomington and Indianapolis: Indiana University Press.

Vidler, Anthony (1994) 'Psychopathology of modern space: Metropolitan fear from agoraphobia to estrangement', in Michael S. Roth (ed.), *Rediscovering History: Culture, Politics and the Psyche*, Stanford: Stanford University Press: 11–29.

Vnuk, Gordana (1998) 'Iconoclastic theater', *Liveartmagazine*, 22: 6–7.

Waldby, Catherine (2000) 'Virtual anatomy: From the body in the text to the body on the screen', *Journal of Medical Humanities*, 21, No. 2: 85–107.

Warr, Tracy (1996) 'Sleeper', *Performance Research*, 1, 2, 1–19.

Watson, Ian (1995) '"Reading" the actor: Performance, presence, and the synaesthetic', *New Theater Quarterly*, 11, 42: 135–145.

Weintraub, Linda with Danto, Arthur and McEvilley, Thomas (1996) *Art on the Edge and Over. Searching for Art's Meaning in Contemporary Society, 1970–1990s*, Litchfield, CT: ArtInsights.

Weiss, Gail (1999) *Body Images: Embodiment as Intercorporeality*, London and New York: Routledge.

Wendell, Susan (1996) *The Rejected Body: Feminist Philosophical Reflections on Disability*, London and New York: Routledge.

Whyte, S.R. (1995) 'Disability between discourse and experience', in B. Ingstad and S.R. Whythe (eds), *Disability and Culture*, Berkeley: University of California Press: 267–291.

Williams, Raymond (1961) *The Long Revolution*, Harmondsworth: Penguin.

Williamson, Aaron (1999) 'Hearing things', *Animated*, Spring: 17–18.

Wilson, James C. and Lewiecki-Wilson, Cynthia (2001) *Embodied Rhetorics: Disability in Language and Culture*, Carbondale and Edwardsville: Southern Illinois University Press.

Wilson, Stephen (2002) *Information Arts: Intersections of Art, Science and Technology*, Cambridge, London: MIT Press.

Wolff, Janet (1997) 'Reinstating corporeality: Feminism and body politics,' in J. Desmond (ed.), *Meaning in Motion*, Durham and London: Duke University Press.

—— (1990) *Feminine Sentences: Essays on Women and Culture*, Cambridge: Polity Press.

Young, Iris Marion (1990) *Justice and the Politics of Difference*, Princeton: Princeton University Press.

—— (1990a) *Throwing Like a Girl and Other Essays in Feminist Philosophy and Social Theory*, Bloomington, Indianapolis: Indiana University Press.

Yuan, David D. (1996) 'The celebrity freak: Michael Jackson's "Grotesque Glory"', in Rosemarie Garland Thomson (ed.), *Freakery: Cultural Spectacles of the Extraordinary Body*, New York and London: New York University Press: 368–384.

Zolberg, Vera and Cherbo, Joni Maya (eds) (1997) *Outsider Art. Contemporary Boundaries in Contemporary Culture*, Cambridge: Cambridge University Press.

Index

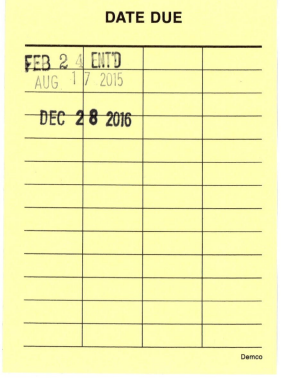